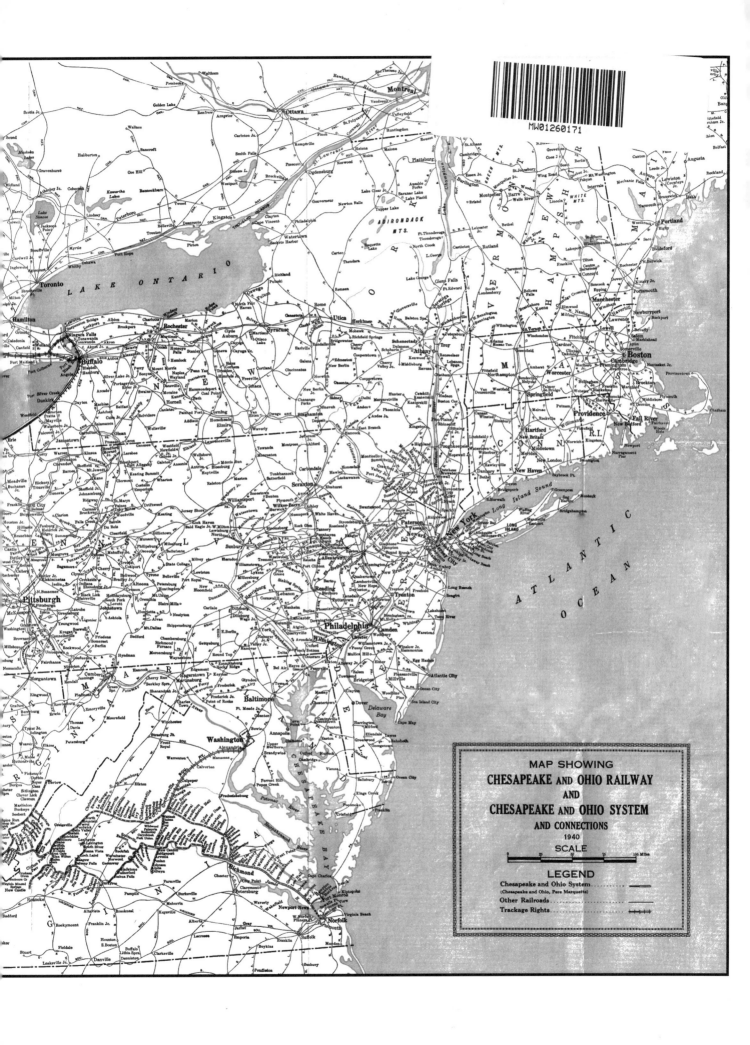

MAP SHOWING

CHESAPEAKE AND OHIO RAILWAY
AND
CHESAPEAKE AND OHIO SYSTEM
AND CONNECTIONS
1940
SCALE

LEGEND

Chesapeake and Ohio System...........
(Chesapeake and Ohio, Pere Marquette)

Other Railroads..................

Trackage Rights..................

The Chesapeake & Ohio Railway
A Concise History and Fact Book
By Thomas W. Dixon, Jr.

The Chesapeake & Ohio Historical Society, Inc. is a non-profit organization dedicated to the collection, preservation and dissemination of information about, and preservation and interpretation of the history of the Chesapeake & Ohio Railway, its predecessors and successors. The Society operates a full-service archives staffed professionally, sells a wide variety of models, books, pamphlets, publishes pamphlets, full length books, and a monthly magazine dealing with all aspects of C&O history.

The Society also operates the C&O Heritage Center in Clifton Forge, a full-service museum dedicated to C&O history with restored and replica buildings, restored passenger and freight equipment, and a ride-on live-steam 7-1/2 inch gauge train for visitors.
The Society may be contacted by writing:

The Chesapeake & Ohio Historical Society, Inc.
312 East Ridgeway Street
Clifton Forge, VA 24422
or calling 1-540-862-2210 (Monday-Saturday 9am-5pm), or by e-mail at: cohs@cohs.com
The Society maintains a history information Internet site at
www.cohs.org, and a full service sales site at www.chessieshop.com.
For information on The C&O Railway Heritage Center visit www.candoheritage.org

This book is made possible by a donation from Mr. Henry Hoffman, C&OHS Member Number 4874, who defrayed the entire cost of printing. This generous gift has allowed us to produce this work in a timely way and use the income for important C&OHS projects.
Mr. Hoffman has contributed to the support of many important C&OHS projects and epitomizes commitment to, and support of the C&OHS mission.

Copy Editors: Mike Oates and Rick Van Horn
Digital Production, Layout and Design: Mac Beard

© 2012

International Standard Book Number 978-0-939487-94-3
Library of Congress Control Number 2012951966

Front Cover: *A colorized version of C&O H-6 No.1479 double-heading a Piney Creek Subdivision mine run in October, 1945. (Original Black and white photograph, C&O Ry. Photo, C&OHS Collection, CSPR 304)*

Table of Contents

Introduction

C&O H-8 No.1645 and K-4 No.2736 in engine terminal circa 1954. (C&OHS Collection, COHS CL304)

The purpose of this book is to provide either the person new to C&O history or the person who has studied C&O history for a long time, with a single-source, quick-reference about the railway.

Included is a short, concise overview history, followed by a tour over the old mainline east-to-west. Following this are chapters and sections about various subjects that may be of interest to modelers, railfans, historians, or others interested in the C&O.

Appropriate emphasis is given to the organization of the railway's line by subdivision and station, including an outline of its facilities and yards. Equipment coverage includes both steam and diesel locomotives, and freight and passenger cars. A special section deals with coal's role on the C&O, and some of the most important leaders of the C&O over time are mentioned. Finally, a short explanation is given about the Romance of the C&O, its lure, its folklore, and all that goes into making its character as a company, as a transportation system, and indeed, as a way of life for many thousands over many decades between the line's conception in Louisa County, Virginia in 1836 until its merger into Chessie System in the 1970s and its disappearance into the CSX of today.

Most chapters have a note at the end that lists the most readily available sources to which the reader may refer for more extensive treatment of the subject of that particular chapter. In this way this book serves as a bibliographic guide for someone wanting more particular information about a subject.

Many of the materials cited have been published by the C&O Historical Society over the years since its inception in 1969, and beyond that, many are still available for purchase from the Society, in which case the catalog number has been cited so that the reader may order it quickly from the Society by calling 800-453-2647, or by consulting the society sales web site at chessieshop.com. The cohs.org web site is about the archives and history and will also be a further reference and guide for anyone wanting more details about the C&O.

It should be understood that this is, in fact, a reference book, so it is arranged as an abbreviated gazetteer and almanac in format, not necessarily to be read from front to back, but to be consulted.

No index is included because it is felt that the subjects arrange themselves in such a way as to make the book itself an index of C&O resources.

It is our hope that this will serve as a guide to C&O related literature, a short explanation of what the C&O was, how it came to be, where it ran, how it was organized, what kinds of equipment and structures it built and used, and how it affected the area that it transversed.

In 1948 a study showed that C&O was the best known railroad name in America. This was largely due to the outstanding work of the company's advertising and publicity operation which conceived "Chessie," "George Washington's Railroad," "The Route to Historyland," "The Coal Bin of America," "C&O for Progress," and so many more early publicity slogans and campaigns. C&O was certainly a leader and forerunner in this regard.

Thomas W. Dixon, Jr.

Lynchburg, Virginia, October 2012

NOTE: Reference is made throughout this book to Catalog Numbers of the C&O Historical Society. To view more information about the referenced publications, go to our website chessieshop.com. Call (540) 862-2210 weekdays 9 a.m. - 3 p.m. to request information or place orders. The Society's Archives are open during these hours Monday-Friday at 312 E. Ridgeway St., Clifton Forge, VA 24422. The Gift shop and Heritage Center (Museum) are open Monday-Saturday 10a.m. to 4pm., Sunday's 1p.m. to 4p.m. at 705 Main Street in Clifton Forge. Visitors are welcome at either site. Also visit www.candoheritage.org for information and historical research.

CHAPTER ONE

Origins of the Chesapeake & Ohio

The C&O used the image of George Washington in its advertising which was an important part of creating the idea of The Great Connection. (C&OHS Collection, CSPR 10883)

This chapter gives a general outline of C&O history. Subsequent chapters will treat various subject areas in more detail.

C&O began calling itself "George Washington's Railroad" in publicity materials in the 1930s. Of course, Washington died almost thirty years before there was any railroad in America and almost forty years before the C&O's first predecessor line was incorporated. So, why did C&O draw this connection? It was for two reasons. First, Washington had been a great proponent for "internal improvements" in Virginia which would link the populous trading region of Tidewater with the great resource-rich interior of the continent. It was his dream of a "Great Connection" that the C&O would finally fulfill, seventy-three years after his death. Secondly, Washington had been one of the incorporators and the "honorary" president of the James River company, which began work in 1785 to connect Tidewater with the "Western Waters" of the Ohio-Mississippi system by means of a canal up the James River, over the Alleghany (spelled with an 'a' in Virginia) summit, and down the rivers leading to the Ohio. Therefore it was a natural publicity advantage for the C&O of the 1930s to connect itself with the Great Man of the nation, making him father of the C&O as well as father of the country.

We can trace two beginnings for the C&O. The first of these was the Louisa Railroad, and the second the James River

& Kanawha Canal, the properties and routes of which would eventually unite under the C&O banner.

The Louisa Railroad was chartered by the Virginia General Assembly in 1836 to build a line from Frederick's Hall to a connection with the new Richmond, Fredericksburg & Potomac Railroad at Taylorsville (now called Doswell) north

A packet boat of the 1830s-1850s era is seen here on the James River & Kanawha Canal. By the 1850s this cheap but slow transportation was supplanted by railroads. Eventually C&O fell heir to the JR&K's route and CSX uses it today. (C&OHS Collection, CSPR 4620)

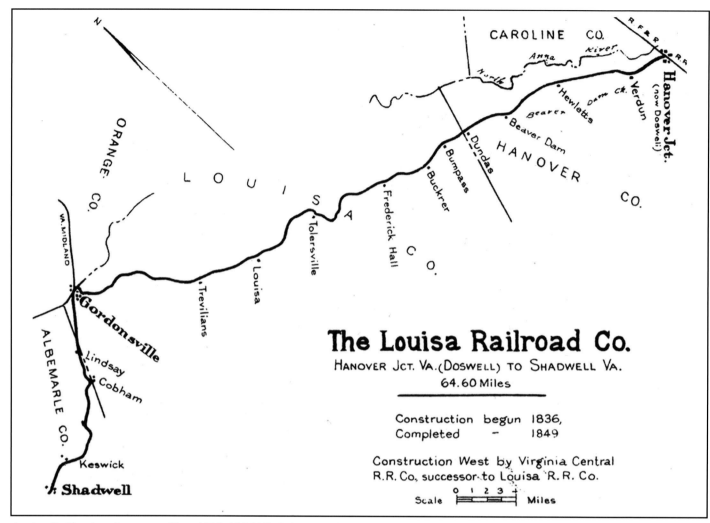

Louisa Railroad system map. Circa 1860. (C&OHS Collection, CSPR 4119)

of Richmond, a distance of about 22 miles,. It was opened in December 1837 and built on to Louisa (an addition just over 11 miles) in 1838. The incorporators were planters of the region wanting to use the new railroad technology to get their crops to market, headed by Frederick Harris of Frederick's Hall as the first president.

Until 1847 the Louisa Railroad's line of about 34 miles was operated under contract with the RF&P, but beginning on that date the directors of the Louisa line, headed by President Edmund Fontaine, took over operation of their own road, bought their own equipment, and began a program of expansion that looked far beyond the initial concept for the railroad.

In 1850 the Louisa was renamed the Virginia Central, in recognition of its wider interests, and was built from Doswell on into Richmond (after a court fight, since the RF&P argued it had exclusive rights to enter Richmond from the north), and to Gordonsville and Charlottesville in the west. Nor was this the limit of the new company's ambition. The desire was to lay the rails on across the Blue Ridge, through the Shenandoah Valley, over the Shenandoah range, and

down to the foot of the Alleghanies. The Virginia Central had the resources for most of this construction but the Blue Ridge barrier just to the west of Charlottesville was so great an impediment that the Commonwealth of Virginia chartered the Blue Ridge Railroad as a state entity, which built the line over the mountain, including Blue Ridge Tunnel under Rockfish Gap, one of the longest tunnels in the world at the time. Claudius Crozet, the great Virginia civil engineer was in charge of the Blue Ridge work, and his famous tunnel, replaced with a new bore by C&O in 1942, is now slated to become part of a walking trail and tourist attraction.

Meanwhile, Virginia Central pushed its track westward. By 1857 it had reached Jackson's River Station, near the present-day Clifton Forge, at the foot of the Alleghany grade. After the Blue Ridge Railroad was completed it was leased to the Virginia. Central and eventually it was sold to the company. While Louisa and Virginia Central had been building, so had the James River & Kanawha Canal, and it had reached Buchanan by 1860. A stagecoach road was built by the canal company to connect from its terminal to the Ohio River. This is the route occupied today by U.S. Rt. 60, and Inter-

The Chesapeake & Ohio Railway - A Concise History and Fact Book

The owners of the road soon had it back in service (July 23, 1865), but they had no capital for further expansion. Finally, in 1868, the company was renamed Chesapeake & Ohio Railroad Company and incorporated both in Virginia and the new state of West Virginia, taking over the old Covington & Ohio route and works. Money for the westward expansion was provided by the new C&O president, Collis P. Huntington of New York, who had just completed the Central Pacific side of the great Transcontinental Railroad in the West.

C&O was pressed westward through the wild, almost inaccessible, mountains and gorges of southern West Virginia, finally reaching the Ohio near the mouth of the Big Sandy River where it established the new city of Huntington, West Virginia. The ceremonial first train over the line carried a barrel of James River water which was dumped into the Ohio and returned with a barrel of Ohio water which was dumped into the James, thus symbolizing the completion of Washington's Great Connection of Tidewater with the Western Waters. . .not by canal but by rail. Although the full extent of the richness of coal underlying the land over which C&O was built was not imagined, it is symbolic that the first regular through train to Richmond carried a car of West

This artist's concept shows a Virginia Central train stopped at Jackson's River Station (now Clifton Forge) in the late 1850s, as people transfer to a stage coach to carry them over a turnpikes to one of the major spring resorts (Hot and White Sulphur Springs being the two most popular). (From cover of July 1922 C&O Magazine, *C&OHS Collection)*

state 64 highways (often called the "Midland Trail," from Indian days). Recognizing the fact that railroad technology had supplanted canal technology, the Commonwealth of Virginia chartered the Covington & Ohio Railroad to build a line from Covington to the Ohio roughly along the route the canal would have used. A good deal of work was done on grading and tunneling for this line by 1860. In this plan, the Virginia Central was to build the additional nine miles from Jackson's River to Covington and connect with the Covington & Ohio. The state would have probably leased and then sold the Covington & Ohio to the Virginia Central as it had the Blue Ridge Railroad, had the plan been carried out.

Then, in 1861, the War Between the States intervened. All work on the Covington & Ohio stopped. The Virginia Central hadn't built anything since its arrival at Jackson's River in 1857. The Virginia Central became a very important lifeline for the Confederacy, transporting troops and supplies between the rich Shenandoah Valley and the capital at Richmond, and by the end of the war was essentially wrecked and out of service because of war-time destruction.

This artist's sketch, which appeared as a wood-cut illustration in the 1881-82 C&O Industrial and Shippers Guide *is the earliest known illustration showing C&O operations in the town of Williamson's, (now Clifton Forge) which is today roughly in the area around the Town Hall and the C&OHS-owned ex-C&O freight station and yard. The bridge crossing the Jackson river at left carried the new Richmond & Alleghany line to its C&O connection. The two-story building at right seems to be the depot with a passenger train beside it, and the structure across from it is probably the telegraph office situated on top of a water tank. Another large building is on the riverbank at left is likely the new McCurdy Hotel (built 1881), to which C&O later moved its passenger station. (C&OHS Collection, COHS 35784)*

A typical wartime railroad scene. Bridges and railroads were the primary targets of raids. Note the number of guards posted at this bridge. At the end of the war, most of the Virginia Central had been destroyed and had to be rebuilt. (C&OHS Collection, CSPR 2795)

Virginia coal from Cannelton (today's Montgomery). It was the first of what would become a torrent in the first half of the 20th Century.

Just as C&O was completed in 1873, the United States was seized by a financial panic followed by an economic depression. Many railroads hastily built following the war went into bankruptcy, as did the C&O. Without the funds to upgrade or rebuild its roughly built roadway, the C&O struggled along with its local business, connecting with a line of steamers at Huntington, which carried freight and passengers between that point at and Cincinnati.

Finally, in 1878, the line emerged from bankruptcy and became part of a link that Huntington was putting together which gave him control of railroads reaching from Sacramento, California, to Newport News, Virginia (C&O built its line from Richmond to Newport News in 1881). When the C&O was reorganized in 1878 it changed its name from "Railroad" to "Railway," so the official name of the company was the Chesapeake & Ohio Railway Company until its merger into CSXT on August 31, 1987.

However, it was not until 1888-89 that the C&O began to move forward vigorously, as Huntington lost control to Morgan and Vanderbilt interests and Melville E. Ingalls became president of the C&O. In 1889 the Huntington-Cincinnati line was completed, giving C&O connections to western lines through the Big Four Railroad (later NYC) at Cincinnati. Ingalls was also president of the Big Four.

Meanwhile in the east, the old James River & Kanawha Canal had finally given up its outdated plans for westward construction in 1878 and was supplanted by a railroad built along its tow-path called the Richmond & Alleghany. This line connected with the C&O at Richmond in the east and Williamson's (Clifton Forge) in the west, in 1881, but was soon in receivership. Ingalls recognized the fact that the R&A was built on a "water level" route along the James with a gently descending grade to Richmond. As coal headed for coastal shipping at Newport News had begun to become an important C&O commodity, he purchased the R&A in 1890 and it became C&O's James River Line. Over this line C&O would ship its huge flow of eastward coal right up to the present day under CSX. It is also this acquisition that let

The Chesapeake & Ohio Railway - A Concise History and Fact Book

Symbolic of C&O's early iron-industry connection is this woodcut view of the Low Moor, Va. iron furnace, which was a big C&O customer for several decades beginning in the 1870s. (C&OHS Collection, COHS 35785)

C&O claim its direct descent from Washington and his Great Connection dream, which it used in its publicity so well in the 1930s-40s. (The C&O followed the R&A, which had followed the JR&K Canal, which was Washington's company.)

It was also in 1889 that the C&O was completely reorganized operationally. A large shop facility and yard was built at Clifton Forge, Virginia, the yard and small shop at Hinton, W. Va. was enlarged, a new yard and roundhouse/shop was placed at Handley, W.Va., and the terminal yard at Huntington was moved to Russell, Ky. Huntington remained as the major locomotive repair shop on the system. East of Clifton Forge, Charlottesville remained the division point for the Mountain (to Clifton Forge), Piedmont (to Richmond) and Washington (to Washington) Subdivisions. C&O didn't have a line to Washington, but in 1891 negotiated an agreement with the Virginia Midland Railroad (later Southern, now Norfolk Southern) for trackage rights from Orange (end of C&O track) to the capital city. This was a key connection for future passenger traffic.

Also east of Clifton Forge along the James River line, a new yard and engine terminal was built at Gladstone, Virginia, about 28 miles east of Lynchburg, the principal city on the line. At the same time a massive improvement was begun at Newport News to accommodate increasing coal traffic and also a concerted effort was made to expand overseas traffic. A partially-C&O owned steamship line operating between Newport News and Liverpool, England, put several ships on the Atlantic shipping lanes.

In the 1870s and 1880s C&O's heaviest traffic was agricultural products and products of mines. The latter category was made up of coal, coke, and iron ore, as well as finished pig iron, which resulted from a happy combination of iron ore deposits in western Virginia and coking coal in West Virginia.

Typical of the Virginia Central and early C&O locomotives is Westward Ho, built by Rogers Locomotive Works in 1857. It served well during the war and its evocative name suited the new C&O afterward. Photographed here in the early 1870s. (C&OHS Collection, CSPR 2798)

From a woodcut illustration of 1884, a typical small coal mine in C&O's Kanawha, W. Va. coal field.
(C&OHS Collection, COHS 35786)

The West Virginia coal came from along the mainline in the Kanawha and New River regions. Coal business along the Kanawha had been a going concern even before the arrival of the railroad, using the river for transportation.

Huntington had never allocated very much money for C&O improvements, thus in 1889 it was little improved from its original 1870s construction. During the 1890s, Ingalls oversaw the complete rebuilding of the C&O. This included heavier steel rails replacing light iron previously laid, ballasting of roadbeds, enlarging and brick-lining major tunnels, replacing wooden trestles with earthen fills or new steel bridges, replacing light iron bridges with heavier steel ones, as well as hundreds of new station buildings, towers, and ancillary structures. After 1900 much of the mainline was given a second track.

By the end of the 1890s, C&O was expanding with branches away from the main line, to tap coal lands in West Virginia. The coal business eastward to Newport News had become the company's heaviest traffic. It was at this time that a consortium of eastern railroad magnates including owners of the Pennsylvania and Reading gained control of the C&O. They also took control of Norfolk & Western, which was tapping West Virginia coal just to the south of the C&O and also transporting it to Hampton Roads. The Pennsylvania Railroad

and Reading Railroad were concerned that C&O bituminous coal shipped to New York City from Newport News was edging out their market for Pennsylvania anthracite coal.

The new owners installed George W. Stevens as president of the C&O. He had been the general manager of C&O under Ingalls. Stevens had supervised the rebuilding of the line and its expansion in the 1890s decade.

During the era when Stevens was president from 1900 until 1920, C&O experienced its greatest expansion, with over 100 branch lines being built to reach the rich coal lands of southern West Virginia and eastern Kentucky. During this era coal business not only increased eastbound to Newport News, but began to flow in ever greater quantities westward to the Midwestern industrial region. Because of this, C&O needed better western connections. In 1910 it purchased the Chicago, Cincinnati & Louisville Railroad and thus gained a line across Indiana between Cincinnati and Chicago, giving it many more connections for its traffic. At the same time, it acquired control of the Hocking Valley Railway of Ohio, which possessed not only coal fields lines southeast of Columbus, but also a fast straight line from Columbus to Toledo and thus access to Great Lakes shipping. C&O used a connection with Norfolk & Western to forward coal to Columbus and thence over the HV to Toledo. Then, in 1917 C&O built a massive bridge across the Ohio River at Limeville, Kentucky, just west of its big coal classification yard at Russell and reached the N&W at Waverly, Ohio, many miles closer to Columbus, thus reducing the length of haul over the competing N&W line. Finally, in 1927, just as westbound coal was growing to about three times the volume of eastbound traffic, the last link from Waverly to Columbus was made and C&O had its own line through Ohio. The whole HV line was merged into C&O in 1930.

By the end of George Stevens' presidency (he died in 1920), the modern C&O was in place; most branches had been built, the patterns of coal and other traffic were set, and the line was constantly and consistently plowing much of its net income into improvements.

In the early 1920s C&O fell into the financial orbit of the Van Sweringen brothers of Cleveland. These two men put together a huge railroad empire based on the new concept of holding companies. C&O, Nickel Plate Road (New York, Chicago & St. Louis Railroad), Hocking Valley, Pere Marquette Railway of Michigan and Ontario, and the old Erie Railroad were closely allied during this period, often sharing officials, and also sharing joint committees involved in mechanical and maintenance of way operations for all lines.

The Van Sweringen lost their grip on the railroads in the Great Depression, but C&O, with its consistent coal income, even in bad times, weathered the storm and kept control of the Nickel Plate and Pere Marquette, while merging the Hocking Valley into C&O.

The Chesapeake & Ohio Railway - A Concise History and Fact Book

With the environment of the early 1920s, it was difficult to get ICC permission to combine railroads or even to combine their management by allowing directors of one line to sit on the boards of other lines, or to allow combined or consolidated operations, even when such would result in better service. However, World War I had demonstrated some of the inherent inefficiency of the American railroad system to the point that the government assumed control of the railroads during the war emergency and immediately thereafter using the United States Railroad Administration. When the companies were given back to their owners in 1920, Congress, still interested in meddling, initiated a study that proposed various groupings of railroads, and it held hearings over almost a decade during which the many interests involved fought over how the systems would be constructed. Finally, the coming of the Depression ended this bureaucratically mired project entirely.

While all this was going on, O. P. and M. J. Van Sweringen of Cleveland, Ohio, had begun to buy into railroad stocks. Their influence on the C&O from the early 1920s onward became large as they used the power of its purse to build one of the largest railroad empires up to that time.

The eastern portal of Blue Ridge Tunnel was never provided with a rock, concrete, or brick portal, but retained this natural rock appearance until it was bypassed by the new bore in 1942. (C&OHS Collection, COHS 9565)

In the early days of railroading, most large systems were created by constant merging of smaller lines into large more efficient systems, but after the Federal Government began regulation of the railroads by using the Interstate Commerce Commission (ICC), and especially so beginning in the administration of Theodore Roosevelt, the ability of railroads to merge and combine was restricted because the government (through the ICC) wanted railroads to remain competitive within regions. It was thought that this would keep rates low by allowing for broad competition. Since railroads as a group were a monopoly in ground transportation of people and goods, it was believed that they needed to be controlled for the public good, as the idea of government intervention into the free market began to gain ground. What this regulation also allowed was the overbuilt railroad system to preserve inherently inefficient services far longer than the marketplace would have allowed. This heavy regulatory hand was evident throughout the 20th Century up to the 1980s when regulation was rationalized and the ICC disestablished.

One of the most scenic spots in the New River Gorge is Hawks Nest, where a great rock outcrop hangs above the gorge below. (C&OHS Collection, COHS 32006)

C&O's history following the 1920s was largely influenced by decisions made during the 1920s-early 1930s era of Van Sweringen control.

Under the Vans the C&O was put into what they called the "Greater Nickel Plate System," which was based on their first acquisition, the NYC&St. L. (Nickel Plate Road). However, it was the C&O and its huge income and profit from coal hauling that really became the bedrock of their empire, which soon included the Pere Marquette Railway of Michigan and Ontario, the Erie, and of course the Hocking Valley of Ohio, which came with the C&O because of C&O's ownership. Eventually other lines were added as well as part interest in others. However, each railroad remained an independent operation with only its finances coordinated.

Some important standardizations were made including locomotive and car research, development and design, and roadway standards. At various time directorates interlocked and one person was often president of several of the lines .

During the good years of the 1920s, C&O put a huge amount of money into rebuilding and improving its roadway, tunnels, bridges and other infrastructure. Then, when the Depression hit, it was able not only to weather the storm (since coal was still needed and though diminished in volume proved to continue making money for the line throughout lean years), but enough cash was available for C&O to continue its massive Improvement program which resulted in a dozen enlarged or new tunnels and cuts, improve rail and ballast, strengthened bridges, new yards an terminals, shops, and all kinds of facilities, so that by the time World War Two was on the horizon, the line was superbly equipped to handle the unprecedented traffic.

In the 1930s, at the dawn of the Great Depression, The C&O made a great publicity splash with its new *Sportsman* train, running from the Virginia coast past the springs resorts of the Virginias to the vacation areas of western Michigan on an all new scheduling with luxury coaches and sleepers. Then, at the very height of the Depression it inaugurated the *George Washington* as its premier overnight Washington-Cincinnati train (with usual eastern and western connections) as an all-air-conditioned train (the second in America by a week - B&O was first with *The Capitol Limited* the week before.)

By the time World War Two was being fought C&O had become the nation's number 1 originator of bituminous coal and would soon be the world's largest. It has a passenger service that had a high reputation and was widely known through its great publicity efforts, even though it accounted for only about 5% of its revenue, and its fast freight service was very good.

When the war came its terminal at Newport News became part of the government-controlled Hampton Roads Port of Embarkation, which included the C&O coal and merchandise piers at Newport News , those of N&W and Virginian at Norfolk, across the Roads. As one of the principal ports through men and materiel flowed to the European theatre o operations, C&O became a prime carrier of war goods and people. The money put into its lines in the 1920s and 1930s prove its worth during the war.

Following the war, C&O embarked on another massive program of modernization and improvement that included large-scale line straightening and realigning, new tunnels, replaced bridges, new signal systems, and much more. Under visionary Chairman Robert R. Young the line adopted the motto "C&O for Progress," and did much to try and bring

HUNTINGTON, ON THE OHIO RIVER.

The C&O was opened through to the Ohio River in 1873 and the new city of Huntington was laid out. This allowed C&O to connect with river traffic which even today is an important means of transporting large quantities of material.
(C&OHS Collection, Routes, Resorts, and Resources, of the Chesapeake & Ohio Railway, 1879)

The Chesapeake & Ohio Railway - A Concise History and Fact Book

the generally ultra-conservative railroad industry into the post-war age when competition from airlines and highway truckers, not to mention barges, was beginning to be felt.

Young's passion was passenger service and though C&O was a very small player in the passenger game his ideas rocked the industry. His idea of "Train-X" with a low-center-of-gravity, ultra lightweight car that could travel at high speeds on existing roadways was well ahead of its time. His idea of maximum comfort, luxury, and service embodied in the never-run Chessie train of 1946-48, and many other invocations, made C&O an industry leader.

As the 1950s wore on and the competition from other modes began to erode railroad profits, C&O began looking for a merger partner, and in 1958 began talks with B&O. This was a natural combination as the lines were basically end-to-end and didn't duplicate service very much. B&O needed a savior as it was in bad financial condition. By 1963 when C&O finally gained control, the situation was so bad that C&O had to transfer over 50,000 freight cars and several hundred locomotives to the B&O to get its operations back in condition.

Together the C&O and B&O, calling themselves C&O/B&O Railroads, confronted the deepening crisis of the 1960s. Their "affiliation" was almost a merger but not quite. More and more things were combined, mechanical, engineering, motive power dispatching, purchasing, and executive, so that by 1970 they were merged all but in dame.

In 1972 a holding company called Chessie System was created to further combine the operations, and in 1975 Western Maryland was brought into it since B&O controlled WM. The new system did only fairly well thanks to the continued strength of coal, especially in the export market, until the deregulation era. By the merger of railroads had become endemic and Chessie System and Seaboard System became a part of yet another holding company, CSX Corporation in 1987. Seaboard System was a combination of former Class I railroads of the southeast including Atlantic Coast Line, Seaboard Air Line, Clinchfield, Louisville & Nashville, Georgia, and Central of Georgia railroads. This formed Norfolk and Western and Southern into a major merger, thus leaving the two large systems as masters of railroading east o the Mississippi. In 1997 CSX and NS carved up Conrail, which was a government entity that had been operating bankrupt northeastern railroads for over a decade (including principally the old Pennsylvania and New York Central Systems.) With this, NS and CSX became almost the only lines in the region, and left them as major competitors in almost all markets. This is the situation that persists today, as this is written (2012).

The C&O in Clifton Forge, Virginia, circa 1900. (C&OHS Collection, COHS 5678

C&O and the Railroad YMCA.

In the 1880s C&O was plagued by the fact that many of its employees had no good place to stay when they were away from home at a distant terminal waiting for a train assignment back. Many of them would go to bars or brothels and spend their time in dissipation, and report for unable to work. The general condition of the work force was poor, so when the YMCA approached President Ingalls with a proposition that they put one of their newly conceived railroad Y's in one of C&O's worst locations, Ingalls is said to have told them that if they could make it work at Hinton, he would give them buildings and establish the YMCA system over all his railroads, C&O and Big Four.

The YMCA people installed their facility at Hinton, right beside the depot, and it was an instant success in giving the men good, wholesome, Christian atmosphere, food, reading, and bunking rooms. Ingalls was true to his word and built YMCA buildings at every C&O terminal, which remained in operation into the 1970s. The two largest YMCAs were built at Clifton Forge, Virginia, and Russell, Kentucky in 1893. In recognition of C&O's prominence in promoting the Railroad YMCA department, the organization held its national convention at Clifton Forge in 1896.

Woodcut of Hawk's Nest, West Virginia. Taken from Routes, Resorts, and Resources, of the Chesapeake & Ohio Railway, 1879. (C&OHS Collection)

Woodcut of Jerry's Run, Virginia. Taken from Routes, Resorts, and Resources, of the Chesapeake & Ohio Railway, 1879. (C&OHS Collection)

Additional Sources of Information for The Origins of the Chesapeake & Ohio

- *Story of the Railroad "Y"* by John F. Moore, Association Press, NY 1930, 309 pages.

- *Virginia Central and C&O Railway Annual Reports* 1850 through 1986 (C&OHS Archives).

- *Chessie's Road,* by Charles W. Turner, updated by Thomas W. Dixon, Jr. and Eugene L. Huddleston (Richmond 1956, Clifton Forge 1986 and 1993), publishing in final expanded form by C&O Historical Society, Clifton Forge, Va. 323 pages. Reprint available from C&O Historical Society (Catalog No. BK-10-539) -The first part of this book, which is the 1956 book, gives a good corporate history of the C&O.

- *The History of the The Chesapeake and Ohio Railway,* by James Poyntz Nelson, C&O Railway, 1927, Richmond Virginia, 191 pages.

- *The Chesapeake and Ohio Railway - George Washington's Railroad,* by Patrick Dorin, Superior Publishing Co. 232 pages.

- *West Virginia Railroads: Volume 2 Chesapeake & Ohio,* TLC Publishing, 144 pages. (Catalog number BK-10-509)

- *Virginia Railroads: Volume 2 Chesapeake & Ohio,* TLC Publishing, 128 pages. (Catalog number BK-11-605)

- *The Virginia Central Railroad at War, 1861-1865,* Charles W. Turner, Southern Historical Association.

- *Sons of Martha,* by Dixon, Lanier, Merritt, Mason and Hanger company, inc., 1928. The life and times of C.R. Mason.

- *Recollections,* by Harry Frazier, Chesapeake and Ohio Railway Company, Public relations dept., 1938. (DS-03-284)

- *The Chesapeake & Ohio in Thurmond, West Virginia,* Chesapeake & Ohio Historical Society (Catalog number BK-04-381)

- *The Chesapeake & Ohio in Clifton Forge, Virginia,* Chesapeake & Ohio Historical Society (Catalog number BK-06-432)

CHAPTER TWO

A C&O Primer

A Guide to the C&O From East-to-West

In reading the history or studying the operations of the C&O, it is helpful to understand where the railway is geographically placed, to be able to picture various locations on the map, and to understand how operations were affected by the terrain. The purpose of this chapter is to help the reader locate places and understand the geography, operations, and background of the C&O. A map is shown that should be referred to in reading this narrative and the basic historical part of the book. We will look at the C&O, beginning at its eastern terminal on Hampton Roads, and travel west to Cincinnati and Chicago, with side trips as necessary along the way.

The C&O's eastern terminal is located on Hampton Roads, one of the world's best ice-free natural harbors. On the south side of the roads, Norfolk, Portsmouth, and Chesapeake are close to each other, along with the resort and residential city of Virginia Beach. The Norfolk & Western, Virginian, Pennsylvania (New York, Philadelphia, & Norfolk), Norfolk & Portsmouth Belt Line, and the Norfolk Southern (old) all served these cities, with the N&W dominating, especially after its 1959 merger with the Virginian. The C&O also served Norfolk by car float. These tug-powered, barge-like car floats left the C&O's large terminal at Newport News, on the north (Peninsula) side of the harbor, and brought freight to a small C&O-owned yard in downtown Norfolk at Brooke Avenue, as well as the Norfolk & Portsmouth Belt Line's terminal at Sewell's Point. Connections were made at Brooke Avenue with the NYP&N (PRR). In the steam era a small 0-6-0 was usually the power for the Brooke Avenue Yard, and in diesel years an equally tiny 55-ton center cab unit did the work.

When association with the Seaboard System came with the CSX merger in 1980, access to Norfolk was available by former Seaboard Air Line trackage and N&P Belt Line, so the Brooke Avenue terminal was abandoned. It was from the depot at Brooke Avenue that the passenger ferries departed, taking people from the south Hampton Roads cities to Newport News to board C&O trains for the west, in direct competition with the N&W (at least for through traffic). The ferry was abandoned in 1950 and the 1902-era steamer Virginia was retired. Buses thereafter took passengers to the trains at Newport News until Amtrak discontinued the Norfolk service altogether in 1971.

In Newport News the C&O had its major eastern facility, located on a large tract of land laid out in 1881 when the Peninsula subdivision was extended down from Richmond. The large yard there grew as the coal trade expanded, adding more and more modern piers as needed. Coal dumping there was first to fill ships in the coastal trade. Later, especially after World War Two, most coal dumping was for export to Europe and Japan, and more recently China. In recent years

To get from its huge yard and piers at Newport News across Hampton Roads to its small Brooke Avenue Yard in Norfolk, C&O used car floats such as this one, which happens to be loaded with coal cars and is about ready to leave Newport News. Although the car floats had power for steering, they also required the help of tugboats to get across the Roads. A C&O tug is seen at left, as well as one of the company's house barges, in 1953. (C&O Ry. Photo, C&OHS Collection, CSPR 3188)

private coal terminals have been built on former C&O land, and much of the business of the terminal has been taken out of the railroad's hands.

A line completed in 1882 leaves the main yard area at the engine terminal at a point called Old Point Junction, or XA Cabin, and traveled 11.3 miles through Hampton and Phoebus, terminating at the Army's Fort Monroe on Old Point Comfort. Milepost 0 for the C&O's distance measurements was located at Fort Monroe depot, which served not only the Army post but also the large resort hotels that was located there as long as the railroad. The earliest was the Hygeia Hotel and later it was joined by the Chamberlin. The Chamberlin is now used for apartments.. Before 1940 C&O passenger trains began and ended their runs at Ft. Monroe, but the line was abandoned in 1939. They then terminated a mile west, at Phoebus, until the mid-1950s, when passenger service on the Hampton branch was completely eliminated and the mainline trains were started at the Newport News passenger depot/pier. When the trains originated at Phoebus, they had to be backed the 1.3 miles from Old Point Junction to the station/pier to pick up Newport News passengers and those who came in by ferry. After 1956 the passengers from Phoebus, Old Point Comfort, and Hampton were bused to a new station called Hampton Roads Transfer. In 1982 Amtrak abandoned the old C&O station/pier and built a new station at Hampton Roads Transfer.

C&O Coal piers 14 & 15 at Newport News with coal ships being loaded in the early 1950s. (C&O Ry. Photo, C&OHS Collection, CSPR 2806)

So important was the Newport News terminal and so extensive its operations, which included a large group of warehouses that stored merchandise awaiting transfer to ships for transport around the world, that it was created as a separate division known as the Newport News & Norfolk Terminal Division. It was integrated into the Virginia Division in 1984.

Outside the Newport News Yard limit, the Peninsula subdivision begins. This line, originally built in 1881, runs on a good grade up to the Virginia capital at Richmond (75 miles from Newport News). Its major traffic has always been coal for dumping into ships, but merchandise traffic has also been important, and during the great days of passenger service, each main-line train had a section which separated at Charlottesville and traveled to Richmond and Newport News. The resorts of the seashore attracted tourist passenger traffic in addition to the normal commerce of the cities and the ports involved. Williamsburg, 22 miles up the line from Newport News, became a major tourist attraction after its Colonial restoration in the 1930s. The C&O's Georgian-style station there has hosted many a tourist. The major operational feature of the line was a grade of 0.2 percent against eastbound movements at Norge, which required doubling of heavy trains or double heading in the latter steam days. To accommodate the heavy traffic, the line was double-tracked soon after 1900 (it went back to single track with long sidings in the early 1970s as an economy measure). The western end of the Peninsula subdivision was Fulton Yard, on the southeast side of Richmond. This became the largest C&O yard in Richmond after the Peninsula subdivision was completed. The 17th Street Yard was the main C&O operation previously and remained active until the 1970s, interchanging with the nearby SAL Brown Street Yard, and handling traffic on the C&O's Piedmont subdivision.

West of Fulton Yard the trains move out onto the long James River Viaduct, built in 1901 to better connect the Piedmont and James River lines and the Peninsula Subdivision, and to accommodate the new Main Street Station. The viaduct is laid in the bed of the river for a considerable distance and has been one of the C&O's major engineering concerns. At Rivanna Junction, on the viaduct, the line splits, with the Rivanna Subdivision of the James River Line continuing directly west following the river past the now now gone 2nd Street Yard, which was the terminal facility of the old Richmond & Alleghany Railroad when it was built along the James in 1881. The Rivanna subdivision then follows the James to Gladstone, while the other line goes northward to

One of the most famous railroad fixtures of Richmond was the triple crossing, which was world famous and was featured on countless postcards over the years. This ca. 1910 view shows a C&O local passenger train on the Rivanna Subdivision (James River Line) on the top, a Seaboard Air Line train in the center, headed south, and a Southern Railway train on the bottom, headed for West Point, Virginia. (C&OHS Collection, COHS 29001)

The Chesapeake & Ohio Railway - A Concise History and Fact Book

C&O's mile-and-a-half long James River Viaduct allowed a direct connection for coal coming down the James River Line from Clifton Forge to bypass the built up area of the city and go directly to Fulton Yard. Here a switcher has a cut of cars on the viaduct with waters of the old canal in the foreground, in 1945. (C&O Ry. Photo, C&OHS Collection, CSPR 57.204)

Richmond's Main Street Station, built by the C&O and SAL as a Union Station in 1901-03. It has an imposing French Renaissance headhouse and a large steel train shed, the tracks being elevated above street level. This building is the C&O's principal contribution to large station architecture in America. It accommodated the SAL and C&O trains until the SAL moved to Richmond's other Union Station, Broad Street, which already handled Richmond, Fredericksburg, & Potomac, Atlantic Coast Line, and N&W trains. C&O continued using Main Street Station along with Amtrak until 1975. It was sold to developers as Amtrak consolidated all its trains in a new suburban station, but Main Street has been revived as a station for Amtrak trains coming to and from the C&O's Peninsula Subdivision and to and from the North .

On leaving Main Street Station, trains descended to ground level into 17th Street Yard, and passed a C&O passenger car repair facility (eliminated in 1952) and the former Richmond Locomotive Works (ALCO) plant that produced so many of the C&O's steam locomotives until its closing in 1926. In the 1870s, when the C&O needed an outlet to the Richmond docks, long before the viaduct was built, a tunnel was bored under Church Hill to connect 17th Street Yard with the Richmond docks. It was taken out of service when the viaduct was built, but was reactivated in 1925. During construction work that year the tunnel collapsed on a work train, killing many of the crew. The train remains buried in the abandoned tunnel.

Westward out of the 17th Street Yard, the Piedmont Subdivision takes the C&O to Gordonsville, through Louisa and Frederick's Hall, and over the original Louisa Railroad of 1837. The line has generated rural agricultural traffic and was mainly a passenger road after the coal for Richmond and Newport News began coming via the James River Line in the 1890s. It crosses the RF&P at Doswell, known in the early days as Hanover Junction. A branch once ran from Mineral (originally called Tolersville) to the sulphur mines nearby. At

Gordonsville the Piedmont Subdivision intersects the Washington Subdivision that originates at Orange, Virginia, nine miles north. Orange is the junction at which C&O trains began their trackage rights operation over the former Southern Railway's main line into Alexandria, the RF&P's Potomac Yard, and Washington Union Station. This line and trackage rights were used for all the C&O trains that terminated in Washington, and for several merchandise trains to Potomac Yard for interchange. Little coal was sent by this line (except during World War Two); most coal for the Northeast went by ship or barge from Newport News. At Gordonsville the Washington Subdivision terminated, joining the Piedmont Subdivision that carried the main line westward to Jefferson's city of Charlottesville. At Lindsay, five miles west of Gordonsville, the Virginia Air Line Subdivision (now abandoned) connected it with the Rivanna subdivision on the James River Line. The VAL was built as a short line in 1906 and was soon taken over by the C&O. It was used at various times to ship northbound coal from the James River Line's low level gradient and for high-wide loads which couldn't be sent via the Mountain Subdivision.

In Charlottesville the C&O maintained a sizable yard, shop, roundhouse, and station. The large colonial style red brick depot on Main Street was built in 1901 and was an important feature in the road's passenger service, because at its platform the name trains had their consists shifted, sending cars eastward to Washington and to Richmond and Newport News, and consolidating sections from both these locations westward. About a mile west of the C&O depot, the main line crosses the Southern Railway (now NS) main line and passes Charlottesville Union Station, where C&O trains made a second stop during most of their years of service to accommodate University of Virginia students. The C&O station was sold and is occupied by private offices. Amtrak uses Union Station for its C&O-route trains.

K-2 Mikado No. 1189 is switching the Rivanna Subdivision eastbound local freight beside the C&O depot at Bremo, Virginia, November 3, 1950. The station is typical of those built by the Richmond & Alleghany RR before it merged into C&O in 1890. K-2s were standard on almost all trains on this line, local and through. (J. D. Welsh Photo, C&OHS Collection, CSPR 1233)

Gladstone was the division point and yard mid-way between Clifton Forge and Richmond on the James River Line, dividing the Rivanna and James River Subdivisions. Here an 0-8-0 switcher occupies the three-stall engine house on April 25, 1953. (D. Wallace Johnson Photo, C&OHS Collection, COHS 26665)

The Piedmont, Washington, and Mountain Subdivisions are now (2012) leased by CSX to the Buckingham Branch Railroad, which operates its own trains and hosts CSX trains operating by trackage agreement.

The Mountain Subdivision runs west from Charlottesville to Clifton Forge. It passes through mainly rural countryside and crosses the Blue Ridge at Afton, over the line built by Claudius Crozet in the 1850s. Blue Ridge Tunnel carries the C&O under the ridge. An engineering marvel in its day, the old tunnel was replaced by a new bore in 1942. Descending on the main line west, one reaches the city of Waynesboro. The C&O-owned Waynesboro Union Station accommodated C&O trains on its upper level and N&W's Shenandoah Valley Line trains on the lower. This station was originally called Basic by the C&O, with the main station for Waynesboro about a mile west. The Basic station was used exclusively for Waynesboro traffic beginning in the 1920s, even though the towns of Basic and Waynesboro were not merged until the 1940s. A small yard and facilities served N&W interchange traffic here. Westward from Waynesboro the C&O crosses the famous Shenandoah Valley, arriving at Staunton on the western side of the valley before climbing the Shenandoah range. Staunton, an old commercial town, had a large masonry station built in 1906 to replace the equally impressive structure dating from the 1870s. Staunton was once a major C&O terminal and the point at which the line was divided into two divisions in the years before the 1873 expansion. It was eliminated as a division point when Clifton Forge was established in 1889-90. The line leaves Staunton on a sharp 1.48 percent grade, making this one of the most difficult locations to start a westbound passenger train in the steam era. The line then climbs out of the valley and crosses Little North Mountain at Buffalo Gap, the highest point on the main line at 2,082 feet. Rugged terrain is followed from there for the 43 miles to Clifton Forge, through a series of tunnels and fills that challenged the engineers of the 1850s when the line was built. The steep grades on both sides of North Mountain and the Blue Ridge that gave the subdivision its name also made it an operating nightmare that impelled the C&O to obtain a low-grade line through Virginia when its coal business began rapid expansion.

Clifton Forge lies in a high valley between the Shenandoah and the Alleghany ranges. The C&O established it as a major operational division point in 1889-90. The Virginia Central reached this point in 1857 and called it Jackson's River Station. It became steadily more important after the Richmond & Alleghany Railroad (R&A) was completed to this point in 1881, following the line of the old James River & Kanawha Canal from Richmond.

Going back to Richmond, we can trace the C&O's second main line through Virginia, beginning at Rivanna Junction on the James River Viaduct in downtown Richmond. This is the James River Line, originally the R&A Railroad, taken over by the C&O in 1890 after a shaky nine-year existence, mainly in receivership. It is split into two subdivisions. The first, the Rivanna, begins at the junction and once used 2nd Street Yard in Richmond (which was the R&A's main facility, now gone). The line follows the towpath of the James River & Kanawha Canal and still uses many of its viaducts. The Rivanna subdivision goes as far as the little railroad town of Gladstone, through rural countryside. At Bremo, the Buckingham Branch connects its 16-mile railroad from Dillwyn. The line was sold to the Buckingham Branch short line in the 1980s and is currently (2012) operated by that company. Its terminal as well as that of the southern end of the Virginia Air Line subdivision was at Strathmore, about a mile west of Bremo station. Gladstone's sole reason to exist was to be the C&O's division point halfway down the James River Line. It had a medium-sized yard used to classify coal, a small engine terminal (discontinued in 1985), and a large old frame station still standing (2012). Gladstone Yard was used to stage coal trains when the Newport News Yard was over capacity. West of Gladstone the James River Subdivision carries the C&O west through Lynchburg, the major city on the line, one of the earliest industrial cities of the South. Here C&O crossed N&W and Southern Railways. Buchanan was where the JR&K Canal had its western end. From there through the gorge of the James to Balcony Falls (Glasgow) the line connected with the now-abandoned, 21-mile-long Lexington branch, which had a small yard at this point. The Craig Valley Branch connected with the main line at Eagle Rock, seven miles east of Clifton Forge, and served 26 miles of line south of there. It was abandoned in 1961 and today a state road uses much of its old right-of-way, including some ancient ex-C&O bridges.

Clifton Forge Yard was built in 1889-1890 and was steadily expanded through the mid-1920s, by which time the huge facility was in place. Clifton Forge was an important locomotive repair facility, second only to Huntington, W. Va. shops for locomotive repair. It was converted to diesel repair in 1955, and finally closed in 1992. This location was well suited to handle the locomotive and consist shifts between the Mountain and James River lines to the east and the Alleghany Subdivision to the west. After having served as the railroad YMCA since the mid-1920s, its huge depot/hotel building dating from 1896 was a distinguishing feature

The Chesapeake & Ohio Railway - A Concise History and Fact Book

until it was razed in 1975. Clifton Forge was headquarters for the Clifton Forge Division which generally controlled the Mountain, James River and Alleghany mainline subdivisions and their branches.

West from Clifton Forge the Alleghany Subdivision runs 78 miles to Hinton, West Virginia. [A note about the spelling of Alleghany is appropriate here. In old Virginia it was spelled with an "a" but in Pennsylvania and other northern regions it was spelled with an "e." When the C&O motive power people named their 2-6-6-6 locomotives in 1941, they intended to name them for the grade they were to conquer, but all being Midwesterners in Cleveland, they spelled it with an e. Therefore the C&O's Allegheny type locomotives traverse the Alleghany grade!] Ten miles west of Clifton Forge, Covington, Virginia, has a medium yard which once served the Hot Springs and the Potts Creek branches and now is mainly for the West Virginia Pulp & Paper Company's (Mead-Westvaco) giant mill. The Hot Springs branch, built in 1891 to take passengers to the Homestead Hotel 25 miles north at Hot Springs, was abandoned in 1972 after the end of passenger service. For most of those intervening 80 years, the main-line trains dropped sleepers from New York and Washington at Covington or Clifton Forge, where they were picked up by mixed trains for the trip up the branch.

The Potts Creek Branch was built in 1906 and abandoned in 1934, when it was realized that the iron industry was moribund in Virginia. It had been built mainly to tap iron ore deposits for the Low Moor Iron Company's furnace near Clifton Forge. Immediately west of Covington the line begins a sharp rise to the crest of Alleghany Mountain, passing through Mud, Lake's, Kelly's, Moore's, and Lewis tunnels to reach the summit at Alleghany at 2,072 feet. Because of its strategic position at the top of the grade, Alleghany station was an important operational point on the line until the end of steam. A turntable was located here to turn pushers helping the coal trains from the west.

Leaving Alleghany, the twin bores of Alleghany Tunnel carry the main line under the crest of the mountains and onto the Alleghany plateau of West Virginia (the state line is in the middle of the tunnel). The first important West Virginia station is White Sulphur Springs, site of the great mineral spring resort, famous since colonial days. Always a big passenger stop, here is where the C&O built a fine Colonial-style brick depot in 1929 and equipped it with park tracks to accommodate a whole special train of sleepers, as well as a pocket track so that trains could pull through and simply drop a sleeping car to be switched later. In the 1930s-1950s pushers returning to Hinton often stopped to switch passenger cars. The Resort Specials, all-Pullman trains, ran between the White Sulphur Springs and Washington/New York during the summer seasons up until 1968. The C&O bought the Greenbrier Hotel in 1910 and upgraded it steadily over the years. CSX recently sold the hotel to a local man and it is now operating under private ownership. In the later years

of C&O passenger service, its mainline trains were largely coordinated and operated for the "springs trade," consisting of people coming to The Homestead and The Greenbrier mainly from the northeastern cities.

West from White Sulphur Springs, the C&O main line crosses the Greenbrier River at Whitcomb, for the first of three times. Whitcomb was also the junction point of the now abandoned Greenbrier Branch. The branch, built in 1899-1904, served the rich lumber country of Greenbrier and Pocahontas counties and was 101 miles long. As the forest production declined, so did the branch. Gas-electric motor cars replaced steam powered trains in passenger service beginning in 1930 and until discontinuance in 1957. It was reduced to a daily, then a weekly, local freight out of Ronceverte, its old terminal, then a weekly local out of Hinton, and finally in 1978, abandonment. In the 1920s the line was an important fast freight route connecting with the Western Maryland at Durbin. The WM's line is now also abandoned and the Greenbrier branch is now a hiking trail except for a few miles out of Durbin, used as a tourist railroad.. Ronceverte is just a few miles west of Whitcomb and had a small yard. Once the Greenbrier Branch's division point, it had a small engine terminal and also was once the place where pushers coupled on to the eastbound coal drags. It was a very important location in the 1880s and had a large lumber mill using logs floated down the Greenbrier. Its large 1915-era brick passenger station and train shed attest to its importance as a passenger stop serving Lewisburg, Greenbrier County's seat, four miles distant. The pusher service returned in the 1980s.

Class J-3 4-8-4 No. 600 bursts out of Brookville Tunnel as it ascends the Blue Ridge out of Charlottesville westbound in July 1948. Brookville was one of the tunnels on the east slope of the grade, and is now gone, having been daylighted when Interstate 64 was built. (J. I. Kelly Photo, C&OHS Collection, COHS 222)

A long Train No. 4, the eastbound Sportsman, *passing the tiny station at Afton in June 1961 with E8 4022 in the lead. It has just emerged from Blue Ridge Tunnel at the top of the grade, and is now going downhill toward Charlottesville.*
(W. E. Warden Photo, C&OHS Collection, COHS 26668)

The main line passes through Second Creek Tunnel just west of Ronceverte, crosses the Greenbrier again, and immediately plunges into Fort Spring tunnel, built in 1947 to eliminate a long curve following the river. After passing through Fort Spring the line goes through the short Mann's Tunnel, and emerges at Snow Flake, the location of a limestone quarry since before the turn of the century. Nearby the C&O operated a quarry from which it obtained most of its rock ballast for many years. The line then follows a shelf along the south bank of the Greenbrier as it passes through a short gorge, and emerges at Alderson, once an important station for forest and agricultural products and site of the Women's Federal Prison built in 1928. Leaving Alderson the rails continue to follow the river, but on a wider plain, reaching Pence Springs, known in the nineteenth century on the railroad as "Stockyards" because of the rest stop stock pens maintained here in the early days. It was another of the mineral springs of the Virginias and had a large hotel which was made into the state women's prison in the 1930s, and more recently has been used again as a hotel.

From Pence Springs, the line reaches Lowell, where it makes its final crossing of the Greenbrier, and at Talcott (named for R. H. Talcott, one of the resident engineers of the C&O) passes through Big Bend Tunnel, the longest bore on the line. This was supposedly the location of John Henry's legendary contest with the steam drill during its construction in 1871-72. The old tunnel is out of service, with the now single tracked main line passing through the new (1932) bore. The tunnel saves 13 miles of track that would have been necessary had the river been followed. West of Big Bend the line passed through a smaller tunnel, called Little Bend (eliminated in 1970), and then hugs the mountainside on the north side of the river until it reaches Hinton's Avis Yard near the junction of the Greenbrier and New rivers. Hinton became a division point when the C&O reached it in 1872. Hinton is the end of the Alleghany and beginning

of the New River Subdivision, and, as the transition point between the mountains to the east and the water level line to the west, was host to a wide variety of motive power in the steam season. From the 1920s through the 1950s, it was the point from which pushers helped the coal trains east as far as Alleghany. Hinton has always been a railroad community, with no other industry. It is the seat of Summers County, created in 1871 with the coming of the railway. Its yard is set on a narrow area between the hills and the river, and the city itself is backed up against the steep mountainside with little room to spare. The once bustling yard, roundhouse, coaling station all are now largely removed.

The C&O follows New River out of Hinton along a fairly open valley for several miles. At Meadow Creek, 12 miles west of Hinton, the Nicholas, Fayette, and Greenbrier Railroad joined the main line. This railroad was a coal hauler from the Greenbrier coalfield and was once important in logging the huge hardwood forests nearby through a massive mill at Rainelle. The NF&G was created in 1926 with some new construction and consolidation of some existing short lines, and was jointly owned and operated by the New York Central and the C&O (it connected with the NYC's Kanawha & Michigan lines at Swiss Junction, West Virginia). CSX and NS now operate the line. The original line used several switchbacks to descend to the New River valley, but these were eliminated and long grade-climbing loops were installed in 1948.

West of Meadow Creek the New River Gorge crowds the C&O onto a narrow shelf for the next 46 miles to Gauley. This was a rugged, remote, and almost unexplored and unsettled area before 1870. The C&O's locating engineers had to lower themselves from the cliffs above by ropes to survey the route. Soon after the C&O line was built through the gorge with great difficulty, coal was found along its walls in abundance, and the New River coalfields became the road's most important in the nineteenth and well into the twentieth century. As coal near the main line in the gorge began to play out, more mines opened on the various creeks and rivers intersecting the valley and were served by branches from the main line. At Quinnimont (Latin for five-mountains) 11 miles west of Meadow Creek, the C&O had a small yard and terminal. From this location Joseph Beury, the first New River coal operator, shipped the first car load of New River coal over the C&O in 1873. Also at this point the Low Moor Iron Company, which had a furnace near Clifton Forge, established an iron blast furnace. It was a large operation well into the 1890s. Quinnimont was the terminal for the Laurel Creek Branch that ran six miles to Layland and had several productive mines.

Quinnimont was also the terminal for the Piney Creek Branch, which left the main line at Prince, a mile west. This important coal branch ran 27 miles up a steep gorge replete with mines and 13 miles from Prince had its major terminal/yard at Raleigh, near Beckley. Raleigh had a large engine facility and coal-gathering yard, from which mine runs operated on a number of branches. Two short spurs-the 1.5-mile Terry subdivision and the 2.0-mile Glade Creek & Raleigh subdivision-branch off from the Piney Creek line before it reaches Raleigh, the former just after it crosses New River at Prince. The 16-mile-long Blue Jay subdivision connected with the Glade Creek & Raleigh as well. From Raleigh's Yard the Raleigh and Southwestern subdivision served mines on a 10-mile stretch of road that was an independent line incorporated in 1903 and built 1906-9.

From the Raleigh & Southwestern subdivision another branch, the Winding Gulf, joined at Forest and ran 16 miles to Stone Coal Junction. This branch taped the smokeless coal region, and was always both an operating headache with steep grades and a rich source of revenue. It crossed and joined the Virginian Railway (now NS) at a number of locations and served some mines jointly. The Piney River and Paint Creek subdivision, also originally an independent road, runs from near Raleigh through the large town of Beckley to Cranberry, a total of six miles. Finally, the Stone Coal subdivision, which began at the end of the Winding Gulf, ran 10 miles to Princewick and was jointly operated by the C&O and the Virginian. With all these lines feeding coal into Raleigh, it became a major marshalling yard, sending 100-car trains to Quinnimont, where they were sent mainly east to Hinton for classification. A few mines are still in service but the Raleigh Yard is gone.

Leaving the Raleigh coalfields and returning to the main line, we find Prince, one mile west of Quinnimont. A small town of never more than 50 people, it had a large C&O station and tremendous passenger revenues, because it was the station for Beckley. Local passenger trains carried Beckley people down to the main-line trains at Prince, and after the coming of good roads they drove or took a taxi, making Prince one of the three or four largest passenger boarding stations on the C&O. In 1946 the old wooden Prince depot building was replaced by a modern Art Deco style station, the only one of many that C&O planned in the postwar era. It is still used by AMTRAK.

Just west of Prince station the Piney Creek branch begins, while the main line plunges into Stretcher's Neck Tunnel, the first tunnel west of Hinton. The next major station is Thurmond, 10 miles beyond Prince. Thurmond is a location of much lore and legend, being the very epitome of the rough mining boomtown. It was the main-line terminal and marshalling area for another maze of coal branches. The principal connector to these coalfield operations was the Loup Creek branch, which ran 11.5 miles to MacDonald and had several branches connecting, including Glen Jean subdivision, Sugar Creek branch, South Side subdivision, Rend subdivision, Rock Lick subdivision, White Oak subdivision, Price Hill subdivision, and the White Oak Railway (a joint C&O and Virginian operation). The south main line, which ran from Sewell to Hawks Nest, and the Keeney's Creek

branch west of Sewell were both operated out of Thurmond as well. All these branches brought in huge amounts of coal, which was sent both east and west and made Thurmond the largest revenue-producing station on the C&O. Thurmond was a classic boomtown from the turn of the century until the 1920s. It was populated with coal barons and operators, making its banks the richest in the state. Because of its lawlessness it was known as the "Dodge City of the East," with some justification. Even today, as the town lies largely in ruins, the old flavor of adventure seems to hang yet heavy in the air. The National Park Service has refurbished the station to its 1920 appearance as a museum and now owns the whole town as part of the New River Gorge National River park.. A mile-long yard extended east of the town. A steel bridge carried the Loup Creek line across New River and connects with the coal branches.

Beyond Thurmond in the days of the New River coal boom were several important mining towns, all of which have disappeared and are now marked by a stone foundation or two largely overgrown with weeds. The New River Gorge today has reverted somewhat to an unpopulated region, as it was when the railroad came in 1873, a sharp contrast to the many mines, coke ovens, towns, tipples, and commerce that dotted its banks in the 1880-1930 period. Sewell, seven miles west of Thurmond, was once an important town with 600 people, a yard, depot, coke ovens, tipple, etc., but now cannot be distinguished from the undergrowth. The Keeney's Creek branch left the main line three miles beyond Sewell and ran 10 miles to Lookout, West Virginia. Its mines are played out and its rails long gone. It had one of the steepest grades on any C&O line at 4.6 percent.

Hawks Nest is located eight miles west of Keeney's Creek and was the site of a junction of the Hawks Nest Subdivision, a three-mile line to Ansted that handled a mine and the local business of that town. At Hawks Nest, the old main line crosses New-River and joins with the South Main Line. When a second track was needed in the area soon

C&O yards at Clifton Forge looking west from Smith Creek yard, showing the LCL freight station to the right, with the depot/YMCA and other facilities in background. The major portion of the yard was around the bend out of the photo. The C&O Historical Society now has its heritage center where the freight house is in this photo. (C&O Ry. Photo, C&OHS Collection, COHS 2332)

C&O J-1 No. 541 with passenger train at White Sulphur Springs, West Virginia station June 1943. (C&OHS Collection, COHS 252)

after the turn of the century, the C&O found it was easier to build on the south side of the river. The south main line left the old line just west of Sewell and rejoined it at Hawks Nest. Hawks Nest overlook and state park are located on the canyon rim overlooking the C&O bridge. The overlook is a popular tourist stop on U.S. Highway 60, and the C&O is a major attraction as trains can be watched in the gorge below. Cotton Hill is the next major station, about two miles beyond Hawks Nest. It was the station for the town of Fayetteville, located three miles south.

The C&O emerges from the New River Gorge at Gauley (five miles from Cotton Hill), where the New River joins the Gauley to form the Kanawha River. The C&O follows the south side of the Kanawha for 38 miles to Charleston, West Virginia's capital. At Gauley a branch crossed the river to Gauley Bridge, where it served coal mines to the north and joined with the old Kanawha & Michigan (later NYC). From Gauley, the main line passes Kanawha Falls, once an important station with a hotel of wide repute, and Coalburg, an early mining town even before the arrival of the railroad. At Deepwater the Virginian Railway had its western terminal and junction with the C&O. Virginian passenger trains once joined the C&O here and ran to Charleston, until the VGN built a bridge across the Kanawha and began using the Kanawha & Michigan line to Charleston. One mile west is Mount Carbon, where the short five-mile Powellton branch served mines south of the C&O main line. Four miles further is Montgomery, the first western terminal of the James River & Kanawha Turnpike that ran across the mountains from the end of the JR&K Canal at Buchanan, Virginia. It became a sizable town and the site of West Virginia Institute of Technology, supplying college student travellers to C&O trains. A mile west is Handley, the division point between the New River and Kanawha subdivisions.

This yard served as marshalling point for coal from nearby mines and for trains from the Cabin Creek and Paint Creek branches to the west, and is now abandoned and removed.

From Handley, the Kanawha Subdivision follows its namesake river two miles to Pratt, where the coal-rich 20-mile-long Paint Creek branch followed the meandering of that creek through the deep hollows populated once with mine tipples and coal camps. It had a prodigious production of high-grade coal for the C&O. Seven miles west of Pratt, the Cabin Creek subdivision wandered 15 miles through the rich Kanawha coalfield, with a maze of other short subdivisions branching off from its main stem, including the 19-mile-long Seng Creek subdivision and the shorter Leewood and Republic Subdivisions. Leewood had one branch of its own while Seng Creek had two, and one of these had two more. Most of these lines were built during the C&O's great coal boom in the period from about 1895 to about 1915. A moderately sized engine terminal and yard was located at Cane Fork, about half-way up the Cabin Creek Line. It serviced mine runs working the maze of lines just mentioned. In the steam era the territory was known as the Cabin Creek "District," encompassing all the short branches. To the west 15.5 miles is Charleston.

Although the C&O serves Charleston, it does so from the south side of the river, while most of the city is on the north side. The large passenger depot was built here in 1906 at the foot of a highway bridge linking the north and south sides of the city with one of the largest depot buildings the C&O ever constructed. The station is privately used now, though the platform is used by AMTRAK passengers. Charleston developed a large chemical industry after World War I, and this traffic has been an important revenue producer for the C&O in this region.

St. Albans is the next important station on the main line, 12 miles west of Charleston, where the Coal River branch connects and still supplies CSX with large quantities of coal. As the river's name indicates, it was an area of early coal exploitation. Cannel and splint coal was mined and shipped by water long before the C&O arrived. The Coal River Branch was built about the turn of the century by a private company and was taken over by the C&O in 1909. The Coal River "District," as it was called in the boom days of Kanawha coal business, had a long main stem of 61 miles, with six branches from it, many of which also had branches themselves. A major yard and terminal were located at Danville, 35 miles up the branch from St. Albans. Big Coal subdivision was a major branch, running 20 miles from Sproul to Whitesville, with a large mine run terminal at Elk Run Junction near its end. Twelve other branches constituted the rest of the "District," ranging from 1 to 23 miles long. Coal River's production, like that of Cabin and Paint Creek, went in both directions, so one could and can see loaded and empty coal trains going both east and west in this area, whereas loads east and empties west is the rule east of Handley, and vice versa west of Russell.

The Chesapeake & Ohio Railway - A Concise History and Fact Book

St. Albans was also the engine terminal in the steam era for pushers helping trains over Scary Hill grade, a 0.3 percent rise running for nine miles west beyond St. Albans. The Kanawha River runs to Point Pleasant, West Virginia, to join the Ohio, but the C&O diverges at St. Albans. Beyond Scary the C&O follows the ancient Teays Valley, whose river disappeared in prehistoric times. The railway passes several small stations, including Milton, where high quality West Virginia glass has been blown for a long time. When the line reaches Barboursville, it joins with the Logan Branch, another massive coal producer built between 1900 and 1905 to serve the fabulously rich Logan fields. Barboursville is also the long-time site of the C&O reclamation plant, where it shiped its scrap and used parts, equipment, etc., for refurbishment or salvage.

The Logan Branch began as the Guyandotte Railroad, a dummy C&O company. It was merged with the C&O shortly after completion. Its 92-mile main line runs south to the town of West Gilbert and had its main terminal at Peach Creek, near the city of Logan. It too had a maze of branches reaching up the many hollows to find the coal seams. Several of these short lines were built by coal companies and later taken over by the C&O. Peach Creek, as it is called on the C&O, was a large engine facility and yard in West Logan. It was alive with 2-6-6-2 Mallets in the days of steam. In later years (after 1930) passenger service from Huntington to Logan was handled by gas-electric motor cars, until it was abandoned in 1960, one of the last users of the "Doodle-bug" cars on the C&O. Once the coal trains were assembled at Peach Creek, they were sent to the main line at Barboursville, thence to Russell Yard. Eastbound loads were then back hauled to Handley. CSX coal still originates on this line.

Leaving Barboursville, it is a scant eight miles to the C&O's large shop town of Huntington, West Virginia, on the banks of the Ohio River. Huntington was the C&O's western terminal from 1873 until it made connections with the Elizabethtown, Lexington, and Big Sandy Railroad in 1881 and finally built its own line to Cincinnati in 1888. Started as a C&O town, Huntington attracted industry and commerce and grew into West Virginia's largest city. The C&O completed its major shops at Huntington in 1872, and they grew in importance over the years. The shops went through several expansions and modernizations in the nineteenth century and were extensively enlarged in 1911-13 and again in 1929, when a great deal of new construction was done. Finally, in 1954, a major renovation converted the shops from steam to diesel-electric locomotive repair. In 1960, most of the mechanical department moved there from Richmond, and after the C&O/B&O/WM merger the activities of the latter two roads' mechanical departments were consolidated there. Under the Chessie System, Huntington shop was the principal location for heavy locomotive repair. Huntington's extensive yards were not used for through traffic, which was handled at Russell. In addition to the locomotive shops, Huntington had one of two main passenger car repair shops

on the C&O until 1952 when Richmond's 17th Street facility was closed and all passenger work transferred to Huntington. CSX maintains the shops today (2012) as a major locomotive repair facility.

Seven miles west of Huntington, the C&O crosses the N&W main line at Kenova, West Virginia. A two-level union passenger station handled the C&O trains on its lower level and the N&W above during most of this century and up to the end of passenger service on the N&W in 1971. Kenova was also a junction with the B&O's Ohio River Division, which had a line running along the river from Parkersburg, West Virginia, to Huntington and Kenova. The line was built in 1892 by the Ohio River Railroad and later absorbed by the B&O. At the turn of the century, the B&O planned to expand from Kenova up the coal-rich Big Sandy River valley, but was beaten out by the C&O. After the creation of C&O/B&O and Chessie System, the B&O Line has been abandoned between Huntington and Kenova.

Leaving Kenova, the C&O crosses the Big Sandy River near its mouth on the Ohio, and enters the town of Catlettsburg, Kentucky. Here the Big Sandy Subdivision diverges into the coalfields of eastern Kentucky. Five miles beyond Catlettsburg, the main line reaches Ashland, where a passenger line ran through the center of the city, while a yard and freight line was located near the river just outside the town's flood wall. A large two story stone passenger station was built on the passenger line, and was replaced in 1925 with a brick depot of high design that became the busiest strictly C&O passenger depot. The new station was an imposing red brick structure of three floors housing the station, division offices, dispatchers, and other C&O offices, including the dining car department and commissary in its later days. It had a large coach yard and platforms covered with umbrella sheds. It was here that trains coming in from the east were broken up and sections sent to Cincinnati, Detroit, and Lou-

As part of a general upgrade of its mainline, C&O bored Fort Spring Tunnel in 1947. K-3 Mikado No. 1229 is see here in November 1947, with a local freight train coming through the new bore. The other track has just been laid and is not yet ballasted. (C&O Ry. Photo, C&OHS Collection, CSPR 1313)

isville and eastbound trains from these points were consolidated for their eastward trek to Charlottesville. Branch-line trains from the Big Sandy and locals added to the traffic the station had to handle. The Lexington Subdivision branched off from the main line near the coach yard, which was at the west end of the platforms. Amtrak used the Ashland station until 1975, when a small facility was built in Catlettsburg. The impressive depot building became the home of the Third National Bank in 1982, using a railroad motif, and thus is practically preserved by adaptive use. AMTRAK now (2012) uses an excellently restored ex-C&O freight station at Ashland. Four miles west of Ashland the Kanawha Subdivision ends at Russell Yard.

The Big Sandy Subdivision was built in the period 1902-06, during which time several railroads, including the Clinchfield and the B&O, were competing to build lines to the rich eastern Kentucky coalfields. The C&O's line was completed for 129 miles to a junction with the Clinchfield at Elkhorn City, Kentucky, in 1906. In addition to several coal operations along the Big Sandy's main line, other areas were served by its shorter branches, ranging in length from 1.5 to 30 miles. Some of these branches started life as independent short lines, as was often the case in coal country. But two, the Sandy Valley & Elkhorn and the Elkhorn and Beaver Valley Railroads, were B&O subsidiaries built in the hope that their line could be extended up Big Sandy from Kenova; however, the scheme fell apart, and the isolated branches had to turn their coal over to the C&O. Ultimately the B&O sold these bothersome lines to the C&O, where they became fruitful sources of revenue.

Diverging from the main line at Ashland, the Lexington Subdivision ran 124 miles to Lexington, Kentucky. Here trackage rights on the Louisville & Nashville carried the C&O trains the additional 84 miles to Louisville, serving Kentucky's rural capital at Frankfort en route. This line was built by the Elizabethtown, Lexington & Big Sandy Railroad

This overhead view shows the giant Huntington shops from the air. C&O performed all heavy work on steam at this site. Today the buildings (erected 1925), are used by CSX as one of its major diesel shops. (C&O Ry. Photo, C&OHS Collection, CSPR 57.335)

in 1881 as part of C. P. Huntington's railroad empire. It was acquired by the C&O and the L&N on the breakup of the Newport News & Mississippi Valley Company after 1889.. The line had no coal deposits and was largely a rural branch-like operation, always important for passenger connections and through merchandise freight. Its major operational feature was Corey Hill, which had a 2.6 percent grade in both directions, necessitating helpers in the steam era. In later days the Lexington subdivision waned after the CSX merger and was mostly abandoned in 1985.

At Russell, where the Kanawha Subdivision ended, the C&O established a major yard in 1889 to handle traffic on the newly completed Cincinnati Division running along the Kentucky side of the Ohio River. Russell grew in importance as time passed, becoming a terminal for coal trains from the Big Sandy, Coal River, and Logan branches, and freights from the Lexington line. After construction of the Northern subdivision in 1917 and the increased volume of westbound coal, Russell was the major coal marshalling yard for the west. In the 1930s and 1940s Russell became the C&O's largest yard and at one time was the largest facility in the world owned by a single railroad. Just west of the main yard, at Raceland, the C&O established a large car shop which has built most of the road's coal-carrying hopper cars from about 1930 to the 1980s. In the 1930s, Russell Terminal

The C&O main lines in the New River Gorge at Hawks Nest, W.Va. as seen from Lovers' Leap in 1944. (C&OHS Collection, CSPR 181)

The Chesapeake & Ohio Railway - A Concise History and Fact Book

This previously unpublished photo was taken of the Thurmond depot area by famous railroad executive John W. Barringer, III from the rear of a C&O special train about 1935. Photo from T. W. Dixon. (C&OHS Collection, COHS 20655)

was made into a separate five-mile-long subdivision with its own management in the same way as the Newport News & Norfolk Terminal. Russell has dispatched more trains than any other C&O terminal since the 1930s and is today an active CSX hub.

With Russell as its terminal, the Cincinnati division began at Riverton, Kentucky, 532 miles west of Fort Monroe. The line follows the Ohio River to Covington, Kentucky, where an impressive bridge built in 1888 (replaced in 1929) carries it across to the "Queen City of the West" – Cincinnati. The line had no coal or other remarkable resources and has always served as a connection for through coal, fast freight, and passenger traffic. At Limeville Junction, 19 miles west of Russell, the Northern subdivision branches off to the north on a high embankment leading to the monumental Limeville Bridge (also known as the Sciotoville bridge after the community at its Ohio end). This bridge and the new line as far as Waverly, Ohio (27 miles from Limeville), were begun in 1914 and opened in 1917 to supply the C&O with a direct outlet for its westbound coal, headed for the Great Lakes at Toledo. With the final link to the HV in Columbus completed in 1927, the C&O had its own line to send coal to the Midwest and Great Lakes. Being a new line built for through business, it skirted cities and towns along its route and never had any amount of local business. The only passenger service on this line was the *Sportsman*, which had no stops between Ashland and Columbus. The line was well built and was populated with 2-6-6-2 Mallets, then by H-7 2-8-8-2s. For the 1930-50 period the huge 2-10-4s were kings of the road, following by a brief period of 2-6-6-6 use before the coming of the diesels.

South Portsmouth, nine miles beyond Limeville Junction on the Cincinnati Division mainline, served the city of Portsmouth, Ohio, first by railroad-owned ferry and later by highway bridge. The only branch line on the Cincinnati Division was the Kinniconnick & Freestone. It was built as a narrow gauge short line in 1890-91 and leased to the C&O in the latter year (it was merged in 1906). It ran 20 miles from Garrison to Carter, Kentucky. The K&F was operated as a narrow gauge road by the C&O for a while, and then it was standard gauged, and was finally abandoned in 1941. Several other Ohio towns on the north side of the river were served by ferries, the largest being Manchester.

Handley was the division point separating the New River and Kanawha Subdivisions and had a sizable yard, roundhouse and engine terminal facility. This photo is looking west toward the roundhouse, coaling, and water stations in May 1948. (C&O Ry. Photo, C&OHS Collection, CSPR 1460)

The C&O's first Super Power locomotive, the T-1 2-10-4 Texas type, is shown here eastbound crossing the famous Limeville Bridge heading toward Russell with empties from Toledo. The T-1s were used exclusively on the Russell-Toledo route until the last year of their life. Photo by Gene Huddleston (C&OHS Collection, COHS 1210)

Maysville, 60 miles from Cincinnati, was the line's principal city, with a small yard and in latter years a fine Colonial-style red brick passenger station. Because it owned no land and had few facilities available in Cincinnati proper, C&O placed a large yard in 1911-12, at Stevens, Kentucky, also known as Silver Grove, which is 12 miles east of Cincinnati. Stevens Yard was named for George W. Stevens, who started as the C&O's general manager in 1890 and was its president from 1900 to 1920. Transfer runs carried cars between Stevens and Covington, Kentucky, (which also had a C&O yard that was largely phased out as Stevens was built up) and to various terminals in Cincinnati, as well as to the C&O's Chicago Division Yard at Cheviot, Ohio. Stevens disappeared when the C&O consolidated with B&O facilities in Cincinnati to create Queensgate Yard.

The C&O built a large depot at Covington, which it shared with the L&N. The L&N also had trackage rights over the C&O bridge into Cincinnati. Little terminal space was available when the C&O arrived in Cincinnati in 1888. It operated on several large viaducts and terminated its local passenger trains and freights at a somewhat makeshift terminal and station on 4th Street. A former residential structure served as the station building. Name trains used Central Union Depot until 1933, when Cincinnati Union Terminal was built. The C&O operated its trackage in the city as the Cincinnati Inter-Terminal Railroad. It operated its bridge as the Covington & Cincinnati Bridge and Elevated Railroad and Transfer Company. It was known as "The Bridge Co." and at the turn of the century had its own 0-6-0 switchers.

Cincinnati was the western terminal of the C&O from 1888 until 1910. In the 1890s it made principal connections with the Big Four (Cleveland, Cincinnati, Chicago, & St. Louis) since it shared its president with that company. Through cars operated on both roads to and from St. Louis and Chicago. Although the New York Central (which owned the Big Four) ownership of the C&O stopped in 1899, the Big Four Lines continued to carry C&O's through sleeping cars and coach transfer passengers to St. Louis and Chicago almost to the end of passenger service.

The Cincinnati division ended at Cheviot, Ohio, about seven miles west of Cincinnati on the line toward Chicago. The road west of Cincinnati was acquired in 1910 when the C&O purchased the Chicago, Cincinnati, and Louisville Railroad at foreclosure sale. The CC&L had been built diagonally across Indiana from 1902 to 1907. It passed through no large cities, was a latecomer to an area already overpopulated with railroads, and was unable to get enough business to survive. The C&O took it over as a separate subsidiary called the Chesapeake & Ohio Railway of Indiana, which was finally merged into the main company in 1933 as the Chicago Division. Leaving Cincinnati proper, the line climbed a steep grade out of Mill Creek Valley, using a number of spectacular bridges. Cheviot, at the top of the grade, was a small yard and engine facility (now gone). At Cheviot the Miami subdivision began (named for the river in the vicinity), running through a largely rural territory and crossing the

B&O at Cottage Grove, Ohio, 41 miles west of Cheviot. The line's first major town is Richmond, Indiana, 58 miles from Cheviot, where the Pennsylvania Railroad crossed. Forty miles west of Richmond is Muncie where the PRR, NKP, and Big Four all crossed. The Miami Subdivision ended at Peru, 28 miles farther, a total of 162 miles from Cincinnati. Peru had a medium-sized yard, engine terminal, and shops inherited from the CC&L. It remained an important station on the C&O until the 1970s. The NKP was the other big railroad in Peru, and for a time both roads shared a joint engine terminal, since both were constituents of the Van Sweringen System.

The Wabash subdivision began at Peru and ran 121 miles to near Chicago. Populated by many rural stations, most with agents, the line had no large towns and crossed several other railroads. At LaCrosse, 62 miles west of Peru, the road intersected the east-west line of the PRR and the Pere Marquette's branch running down from New Buffalo, Michigan. The C&O's line actually ended at Hammond, Indiana. There it connected with Erie, which it used on trackage rights to the IC and other railroads to enter Chicago. The Chicago Division was abandoned in the 1980s, since Chessie System and then CSX had other routes available.

This completes a review of the C&O's original line as it existed up to 1930, which is the thrust of the basic text of this essay. In that year the 349-mile Hocking Valley Railway, which had been owned since 1910, was merged, and in 1947 the 1,950-mile Pere Marquette Railway was absorbed into the C&O. This was the height of C&O's route mileage. In 1961 C&O began a process to control the Baltimore & Ohio. After 1963 when ownership was secured, the two railroads operated as C&O/B&O in an "affiliated" status that gradually resulted in complete integration of the two systems. In 1972 they were renamed Chessie System when that holding company was established. The Western Maryland was incorporated into Chessie System a few years later. Ultimately, in 1982 Chessie System and Seaboard System were merged to form what is still CSX. The Seaboard System consisted of the old Atlantic Coast Line, Seaboard Air Line, Louisville & Nashville, Clinchfield, Georgia, and other railroads. C&O's corporate existence ended in 1987, and its former lines now form only a part of CSX's system.

In the steam era, C&O was widely known for its large, powerful locomotives, use to haul heavy coal trains both east and west from its coal area. In the earlier period C&O used small 4-4-0 American types and 4-6-0 Ten-Wheeler types, then in the 1880s it started using 2-8-0 Consolidation types for freight. It was just after the turn of the 20th Century that C&O started it big locomotive development. First for passenger service it got 4-4-2 Atlantic types and pioneered the 4-6-2 Pacific and 4-8-2 Mountain types. For freight service it expanded the 2-8-0 into 2-8-2 Mikados, and in 1911 acquired its first 2-6-6-2 compound articulated types of which

it acquired hundreds for heavy coal trains. In 1922-25 period new 2-8-8-2 simple articulateds took over the heaviest coal trains over Alleghany and 2-6-6-2s went to work on secondary trains and in the coal fields on mine runs. For passenger trains over the mountains between Charlottesville and Hinton, C&O acquired 4-8-4 Greenbrier types in 1935, 1942 and 1948. In 1942 the 2-6-6-6 simple articulated Allegheny types arrived and by 1948 C&O had 60 of these most powerful of all steam locomotives handling its heaviest mainline traffic. Also during World War Two the 2-8-4 Kanawha types arrived in numbers (C&O had 90 by 1948) which could handle coal trains, mine run, fast freights, locals, and even passenger trains, as needed. The 4-6-4 types was added for fast passenger trains on the lower-grade lines.

C&O was reluctant to dieselize because of its close association with coal and bought new steam up through 1949. In fact some 2-6-6-2s for C&O were the last commercially built steam in America. But, the inevitable happened starting in 1949 when C&O dieselized its switching operations, and then in 1950, when the Chicago Division was dieselized. After that, the pace of diesel purchases increased, and by 1954 over 80% of opera tons were diesel. The last steam runs occurred in the August 1956. In the diesel era C&O bought diesels from most of the major early builders, but soon settled of General Motors' Electro-Motive Division as its preferred builder.

C&O's passenger business initially was mainly local, but once the line reached Cincinnati, it began to carry through traffic from east of Washington and west of Cincinnati through its connections, and inaugurated its first and some would say most famous train, the *Fast Flying Virginian*, on May 11, 1889. It was the most modern and technologically advanced train of its area and made a great reputation for C&O in the passenger business even though C&O was a

Maysville was one of the major stops for passenger trains on the Cincinnati Division. Here a C&O train pauses 60 miles out of its origin point at Cincinnati.
(C&O Ry. Photo, C&OHS Collection, CSPR 4069)

Along the Cincinnati Division, C&O follows the Ohio River closely. Here the Fast Flying Virginian, *No. 3 flies west with a heavy consist in July 1945, with F-19 Pacific No. 493 for power. (C&O Ry. Photo, C&OHS Collection, CSPR 57.83)*

In the east a train would meet connections from New York at Washington and travel to Charlottesville, Virginia. At this point it would be joined with cars that came up C&O's line from Newport News (a ferry brought passengers from Norfolk to Newport News). The combined train would then go west to Ashland, Kentucky, where it was again broken up, with one section going to Cincinnati and another going over C&O's, line to Lexington, and the via trackage rights on the L&N to Louisville. The *Sportsman* was an exception. It's sections were broken at Ashland with one to Cincinnati and the other to Detroit via C&O's Hocking Valley line through Columbus. This pattern continued until the last C&O passenger operations on May 1, 1971 when AMTRAK took over.

In freight operations, most of C&O's concentration, certainly after about 1890, was on coal, which grew in quantity through World War Two. It was this coal business that made C&O one of the best run, best built, best equipped, and best financed railroads in the country and the commodity on which its reputation was founded. C&O did operate a considerable merchandise freight business including fast freights operated over the entire system with important connections at Washington in the east and Cincinnati, Chicago, Louisville, and Columbus in the west. C&O reached its height of operations in the era 1945-1965. It suffered from the same decline that other lines experience after that, but because of its coal business survived well, and was able to combine with B&O, WM, and later the southeastern roads of Seaboard System to form CSX.

very minor player in that arena. The company gave great attention to passenger operations, steadily improved its equipment, installed trains on all its branches, and by the 1920s operated a large and well run system. After 1932 three sets of mainline name trains were operated: the *George Washington*, the *Fast Flying Virginian* (*FFV*), and the *Sportsman*.

In about 1947 C&O K-2 No. 1169 under coaling station at Peru, Indiana, the center of the Chicago Division. The terminal was shared with the Nickel Plate since both lines were under unified financial control until 1947. (C&OHS Collection, COHS 7319)

The Chesapeake & Ohio Railway - A Concise History and Fact Book

CHAPTER THREE

C&O's Routes, Stations, Divisions, Yards, and Terminals

Following is a list of stations, by subdivision, as they existed in 1948. The year 1948 was chosen because we could use a C&O publication called *Agents, Officers, Stations, Etc. No. 82, August 1948*. This publication was issued periodically. No. 82 shows all the former Pere Marquette Railway stations as well as the old C&O lines. It was also issued before wholesale abandonments and discontinuances that began in the early 1950s. Therefore, this booklet's lists are the most complete for the "modern" C&O.

C&O began calling its subdivisions by that title in the 1930s. Before they were called various things, most often "districts." The subdivision names and composition never (with minor exceptions) changed right up to the end of C&O and are still almost all used by CSX today. This is not the case for divisions. These larger components of the railway's operational composition had different subdivisions under their control at various times. Again, using 1948 as the benchmark of our study, the divisions were:

Chesapeake District (Former C&O Lines Proper):

- Newport News & Norfolk Terminal Division: Composed of the yards and terminal facilities at these two Hampton Roads cities.

- Richmond Division: Composed of Peninsula, Piedmont, Washington, and Rivanna Subdivisions and branches.

- Clifton Forge Division: Composed of Mountain, James River, and Alleghany Subdivisions and branches.

- Hinton Division: Composed of the New River Subdivision and many branches.

- Huntington Division: Composed of the Kanawha Subdivision and many branches.

- Ashland Division: Composed of Big Sandy Subdivision, Lexington Subdivision, and many branches.

- Russell Division: Composed of the giant yard and terminal at Russell, Ky.

- Cincinnati Division: Composed of the mainline from Russell to Cincinnati and a single branch. [Cincinnati and Russell Divisions were administered as a single unit.]

- Chicago Division: Composed of the Wabash and
- Miami Subdivisions.

Pere Marquette District (Former PM Lines):

- Grand Rapids Division
- Saginaw Division
- Canadian Division

Operator H.A. Sampson looks over the new interlocking plant just installed at NI Cabin, Prince, West Virginia in 1920. (C&OHS Collection, COHS 22810)

In 1947, C&O merged with the Pere Marquette Railway. The PM consisted of a maze of lines in Michigan and Ontario (with a single line in Northern Indiana to Chicago), which it had controlled since 1928 (under the Van Sweringen arrangement). When this merger occurred the two former railways were administered as separate, fairly autonomous districts. The old C&O proper lines being called the "Chesapeake District," and the former PM lines called the "Pere Marquette District." This arrangement continued until 1955 when the PM District was renamed the "Northern Region," and the Chesapeake District the "Southern Region." This continued until about 1960, by which time all operations and functions were totally integrated.

Beginning in the 1960s, the C&O and B&O "affiliation" took effect, and executive and operating offices were combined, but the two lines continued to operate fairly autonomously, along with Western Maryland. In 1972 a holding company called Chessie System Railroads was created which effectively totally merged the operations. This essentially had occurred by that time anyway.

Shops

Initially C&O had shops located at Richmond when it was building west, but when it reached Huntington, a major shop facility was erected there to handle equipment on the western end of the road. In 1889-92, when C&O was completely rebuilt under M. E. Ingalls, Huntington shop was improved and a new large shop was built at Clifton Forge, Va. and other smaller repair facilities remained at Richmond (17th Street). This shop was used mainly for passenger car repair until the early 1950s when that work was moved to Huntington. 17th Street was slowly downgraded and closed by 1970. Both Huntington and Clifton Forge were rebuilt as diesel shops.

With the Hocking Valley merger in 1930 the HV shops at Mound Street in Columbus and at Logan, Ohio, were used by C&O for a time, and eventually downgraded to running repair work before being closed. Logan built many of the latter HV and C&O wooden cabooses.

With the PM merger in 1947, that line's massive shops at Wyoming Yard in Grand Rapids, Mich. came to C&O and were operated as a full service diesel shop until modern times, taking care of locomotives and cars on the Michigan lines.

Major Yards (East-to-West)

Newport News: Second largest in track mileage. Used to store and stage coal for dumping at coal piers and for merchandise bound to and from merchandise and ore piers. Included in the complex were coal, ore, and merchandise piers, large warehouse areas (for staging merchandise, mainly tobacco), and a small engine terminal with one-stall engine house.

Richmond: Fulton Yard to the east of the city was used for staging coal bound for Newport News and west-bound empty cars, with a large roundhouse and many tracks. Important feature was that it was built on a 0.57% eastbound grade, which required use of pushers to start heavy coal trains east.

Richmond: 17th Street: Oldest of the C&O yards, it was near where the original Virginia Central facilities were located. It included several tracks and the shops, near Main Street Station.

Richmond: 2nd Street: Originally at the end of the Richmond & Alleghany, used by trains on the Rivanna Subdivision after the 1901 construction of the James River Viaduct, and for local trains. Very small with only a few short tracks.

Two other small yards were used for inbound and outbound LCL freight for the city.

Charlottesville: It had a medium-sized yard for the use of Piedmont, Washington, and Mountain Subdivisions that converged here. Since little coal was involved, it was mainly for passenger cars (coach yard) and merchandise freight. It had a medium-sized roundhouse and engine terminal.

Strathmore: (Rivanna Subdivision - James River Line). Small yard with large coaling station, water station, bunkhouse, and depot, but no engine house. It survived as the terminal for Buckingham Branch and VAL branches.

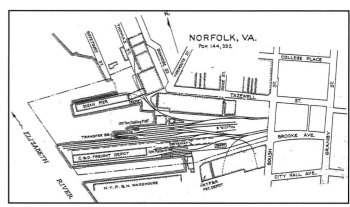

Norfolk, Virginia

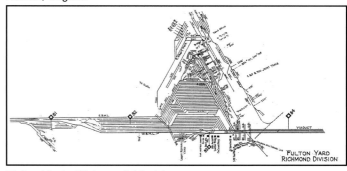

Fulton Yard - Richmond, Virginia

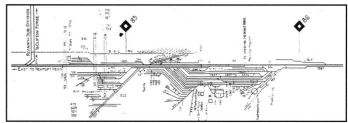

17th Street Yard Richmond, Virginia

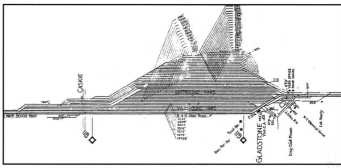

Gladstone, Virginia

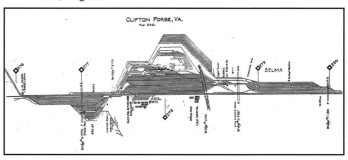

Clifton Forge, Virginia

Gladstone: Medium-large yard for staging coal between Clifton Forge and Richmond. Mainly used to store coal waiting space/ships at Newport News.

Lynchburg: Sandy Hook Yard, small in size for use in switching city traffic and connections with SR and N&W at this point.

Clifton Forge: Second largest shop facility, with yards stretching over four miles and a major classification and staging yard for all eastbound coal. it once had a large engine terminal with two roundhouses.

Ronceverte: Small yard served as terminal for Greenbrier Branch and staging for trains using Alleghany Subdivision.

Hinton: Large yard complex for staging eastbound coal for transport to Clifton Forge. It collected coal from New River Subdivision branches. It had a large roundhouse and engine terminal for transition of motive power between easy and heavy grade lines.

Quinnimont: Small yard for collecting coal from Laurel Creek Branch and Piney Creek Subdivision and its branches, with a small engine terminal and no engine house.

Handley: Installed in 1889-92 as the terminal between New River and Kanawha Subdivisions. It had a large engine house and engine terminal, medium sized yard for collecting/marshalling coal from several W. Va. Branches.

Charleston: Elk Yard here was for switching traffic to and from the city industries.

Huntington: Very large yard complex for all types of traffic and incoming coal from branches, assembly and rearrangement of freight trains, engine changes, etc. It had a large engine terminal and roundhouse, as well as the site of C&O's largest locomotive and car shops.

Ashland, Ky.: Small yard, mainly for industrial traffic.

Russell: C&O's largest facility and at one time the largest yard operated by a single railroad in the world. Consisted of merchandise, hump, and coal yards. It had a large engine terminal, roundhouse and adjacent shop. Busiest yard on C&O. Raceland Car Shops was located at the west end.

Stevens: At Silver Grove, Ky., about 14 miles east of Cincinnati, with a large roundhouse, engine terminal, and large yard. Used for staging of trains and west end of Cincinnati Division for interchange at Cincinnati and forwarding to Chicago Division, west of Cincinnati,.

Covington, Ky.: Small yard just across river from Cincinnati. First used for freight service for the city before building of Stevens Yard in 1913.

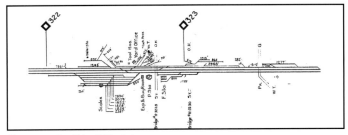
Ronceverte, West Virginia

Hinton, West Virginia

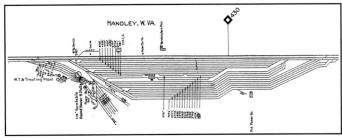
Handley, West Virginia

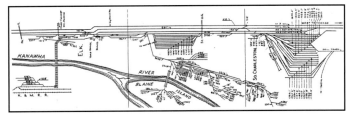
South Charleston, West Virginia

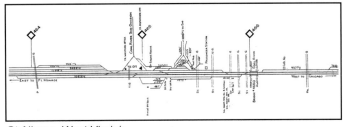
St Albans, West Virginia

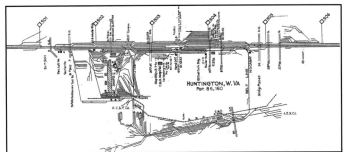
Huntington, West Virginia

Cincinnati: C&O was a latecomer to Cincinnati and there was little room for yards, thus it used Stevens and Cheviot. Within the city, it connected with B&O, PRR, Southern, L&N, and NYC. It has a few tracks called Liberty Street Yard. - In the 1980s a giant C&O/B&O yard was built, called "Queensgate Yard", which is today's CSX terminal.

Cheviot: Large engine terminal, roundhouse and yard for east end of the Chicago Division through Indiana.

Peru, Ind.: Largest roundhouse and engine terminal plus large yard serving as division point for Miami and Wabash Subdivisions, comprising the Chicago Division. It was important for throughput and servicing of fast freight to/from Chicago.

Toledo: Huge yard facility for storage and forwarding of coal and empty coal cars to and from Toledo docks at Presque Isle. It included Walbridge Yard, which had an engine house and engine terminal, similar in service to Newport News in the east.

Detroit: C&O inherited massive operations from Pere Marquette. Rougemere was the principal yard, but a boat yard was also available (for carfloats to Windsor, Ont.). A special yard served the Ford Rouge plant. Detroit's Fort Street Union Depot was jointly owned by passenger railroads serving Detroit. C&O ended as its sole owner.

Grand Rapids: Largest yard and engine facility on C&O in Michigan (old PM) with large shops attached, with many tracks. It worked mainly for managing merchandise freight traffic on/off the old PM lines.

Saginaw: Very large yard, engine facility and roundhouse with attendant shop. Many yard tracks were used to serve several subdivisions radiating in several directions.

Ludington: Medium yard used mainly to stage cars to and from the cross-Lake Michigan car ferries.

New Buffalo: Yard was mainly for mainline traffic adjustments and inputs from other lines between Chicago and Grand Rapids.

Holland: Small terminal yard was used for connecting branch to Muskegon and other nearby lines.

This does not include all facilities and no coalfield marshalling yards are in the above list.

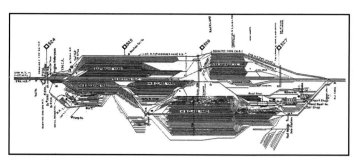
Russell, Kentucky

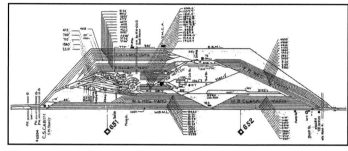
Stevens Yard, Kentucky

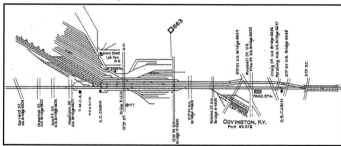
Covington, Kentucky

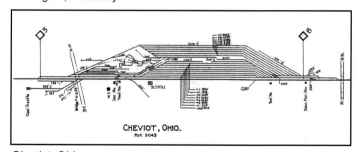
Cheviot, Ohio

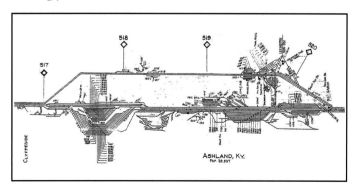
Ashland, Kentucky

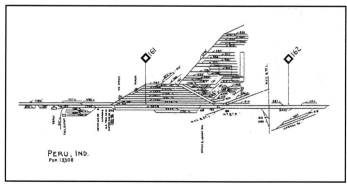
Peru, Indiana

The Chesapeake & Ohio Railway - A Concise History and Fact Book

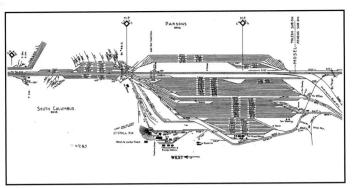

Parsons Yard - Columbus, Ohio

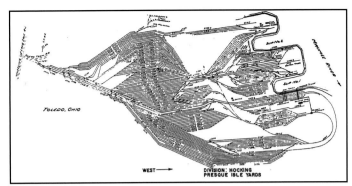

Presque Isle, Ohio

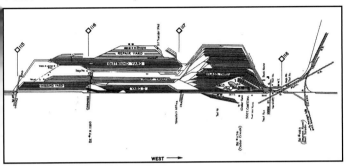

Walbridge, Ohio

Full sized track charts (7x14 inches) such as these are available from C&O Historical Society in two groups: Mainline (Cat. No. DS-08-69), and Branch Lines (Cat No. DS-08-70). Individual subdivisions may also be purchased. Side track charts are also available by subdivision. These are 8½ x 11 plats that show each side track, both C&O owned and privately owned. Consult chessie-shop.com for full availability in both categories.

Newport News Yards - Newport News and Norfolk Terminal Divisions

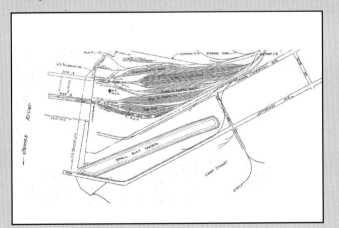

Newport News Yards Drawing 2-A

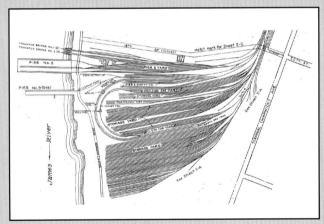

Newport News Yards Drawing 2-B

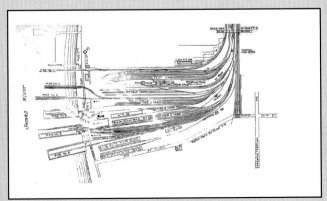

Newport News Yards Drawing 2-C

These three maps are printed here so small that the hundreds of tracks blur together, but they are intended to show the immensity of the yards at the Newport News terminal where often as many as 5,000 coal cars sat waiting for ships to take their cargo.
(C&OHS Collection, taken from DS-03-277)

The following four aerial photos (this page and next) show typical C&O yards in the mid-20th Century era. Part of the Newport News Yard complex is this incoming storage yard to the west of the pier yards. The warehouses center left near the yard were for storage of tobacco awaiting export. But, of course, coal was the primary export commodity. (C&O Ry Photo, C&OHS Collection, CSPR 3577)

Clifton Forge with its sprawling 4-1/2 mile facility was second only to Huntington in mechanical operations (except for Grand Rapids on the Northern Region). This 1956 photo is looking west at the entrance of the yard, showing the former coaling station and engine terminal in the foreground and the large shops at left. The new diesel; shop has just been completed at the center left. (C&O Ry. Photo, C&OHS Collection, CSPR 10469.407)

The Chesapeake & Ohio Railway - A Concise History and Fact Book

Russell, Kentucky was the largest yard facility in the world owned by a single railroad when this photo was taken in 1948. The round-house and shop (third in size on the old C&O lines) are at center, with the coaling station and ready tracks to left foreground, At right is the large water tank, and in the left background is the new YMCA under construction at this date. The yards that comprise the facility stretched outward to the west (bottom) of this scene. (C&O Ry. Photo, C&OHS Collection, CSPR 57.338)

Parsons Yard, on the south side of Columbus, was the principal Hocking Valley (later C&O Hocking Division) yard after 1930. This photo shows the large roundhouse, one of two coaling stations, car repair track and office far left, as well as a portion of the yard track-age. (C&O Ry. Photo, C&OHS Collection, CSPR 57.346)

C&O Stations by Mile Post and Division/Sub-Division, Arranged East-to-West. Taken from the 1948 edition of C&O *Officers, Agents, Stations, Etc. No. 82, August 1948.*

Legend:

*-Day and Night Telegraph Office.

1-Junction with connecting line.

2-Junction of Sub-division shown elsewhere.

3-Within switching limits of Newport News; carload freight should be waybilled to Newport News, Va.

4-Coupon Stations.

6-Established for operating purposes only-not a station for passengers or freight business.

†-No Siding.

‡-Private Siding only.

NEWPORT NEWS AND NORFOLK TERMINAL DIVISION

Dist. from Ft. Monroe	Tel. Calls	Station No.	Code No.	STATIONS
0.0			0001	①④Norfolk_____Va
			0010	City Tkt. Office
				214 Granby St.
				(Monticello Hotel)
			0011	Wharf Tkt. Office___
			0012	
			0002	①④Portsmouth____Va
10.0	NS	10	0016	Newport News__Va
			0017	④Newport News, Va., Ticket Office_____
11.3	*XA	11		Old Point Jct____Va
1.0			0006	Phoebus_____Va
0.5			0004	{Fort Monroe_____Va
			0005	U. S. Govt. TrackVa
2.9	HM	3	0009	①④Hampton____Va
3.25				Langley Field Connection___Va
11.3	*XA	11		Old Point Jct____Va
13.7		14		N. Y. Cabin_____Va

Richmond Division — PENINSULA SUB-DIVISION

Dist. from Ft. Monroe	Tel. Calls	Station No.	Code No.	STATIONS
14.3		14		No. Newport News__Va
14.6		14½	0025	③Hilton Village__Va
16.5	MN	16	0028	Morrison_____Va
20.3		20	0032	Oyster Point_____Va
22.7		23	0036	Oriana_____Va
				Camp Patrick Henry___Va
25.6		26	0040	†Reservoir____Va
			0042	④Ft. Eustis_____Va
27.6	JM	28	0043	④Lee Hall____Va
32.3		32	0050	†Grove_____Va
34.9		35		Penniman_____Va
36.9	WM	37	0064	④Williamsburg__Va
40.1	CB	40	0068	Magruder (Camp Peary)_____Va
40.8		41	0069	Ewell_____Va
42.7		43	0072	Lightfoot____Va
44.6	*UG	45	0075	Norge_____Va
47.0	AN	47	0077	Toano_____Va
51.1		51	0083	Diascund_____Va
53.4		53	0086	†Lanexa_____Va
55.4		55	0089	Walker_____Va
58.0		58	0092	Windsor Shades_Va
61.2	FG	61	0095	Providence Forge Va
64.3		64	0099	Mountcastle____Va
66.3		66	0102	Nance_____Va
66.9	RX	67	0103	Roxbury_____Va
71.3		72	0109	Elko_____Va
74.9		75	0112	Poplar Springs___Va
78.4		78	0115	Fort Lee_____Va
80.3		81	0118	†East Richmond__Va
80.9		81¼	0119	Twohy_____Va
81.5		81½		East End Fulton Yard_____Va
				James River_____Va
82.7			0121	①Fulton_____Va
83.2	*R	83		R. Cabin_____Va
84.4		84		②Rivanna Jct._____Va
84.7		85	0128	④Main St. Station Va
				①(Richmond)

PIEDMONT SUB-DIVISION

Dist. from Ft. Monroe	Tel. Calls	Station No.	Code No.	STATIONS
83.2		83	0125	①②④Richmond___Va
				R. Cabin_____
84.7	*JN	85		J. N. Cabin_____
84.7	*DO	85		Dispatcher's Office____
84.7		85	0128	Main St. Station____
			0130	Baggage_____
				{Broad St. Station____
				9th St. Station_____
			0129	④City Tkt. Office, 706 E. Grace St...
			0127	Salvage Ware-house_____Va
85.4				Richmond Shops_Va
85.7				A. R. Cabin____Va
87.9		88	0130	Highland Park___Va
88.6		89	0132	Atlantic Rural Exposition Depot____Va
90.1		90	0134	†Chickahominy___Va
91.3		91	0136	Ellerson_____Va
94.5		93	1040	Atlee_____Va
97.0		97	0146	†Ashcake_____Va
99.2		99	0149	Peake_____Va
101.1		101	0151	†Cady_____Va
102.7	HA	103	0154	Hanover_____Va
105.4		105	0158	†Wickham_____Va
107.3		107	0161	††South Anna___Va
111.8	*HN	112	0168	①Doswell_____Va
114.7		115	0172	Verdon_____Va
115.9		116	0173	†North Anna___Va
117.6		118	0178	††Noel_____Va
119.7		120	0181	Hewlett_____Va
121.6		122	0184	†Holliday_____Va
122.8		123	0186	Teman_____Va
124.4	BD	124	0188	Beaver Dam____Va
127.2		127	0191	Tyler_____Va
129.4		129	0193	Bumpass_____Va
131.3		131	0195	Buckner_____Va
134.6	FH	135	0198	Frederick Hall___Va
139.4		139	0201	Pendleton_____Va
140.7	SV	141	0204	④Mineral_____Va
146.5	CU	147	0215	④Louisa_____Va
147.2		148	0216	Bibb_____Va
151.0	ON	151	0219	Trevilian_____Va
154.2		154	0222	Green Spring____Va
157.1		157	0225	Melton_____Va
160.4	*G	160	0228	②④Gordonsville__Va
165.2	*DA	165	0250	②Lindsay_____Va
167.4		167	0285	④Cobham_____Va
170.3		170	0288	Campbell_____Va
172.0		172	0290	†Rugby_____Va
174.1	K	174	0292	④Keswick_____Va
176.3		176	0295	Shadwell_____Va
181.4	*MO	181	0301	①④Charlottesville_Va

WASHINGTON SUB-DIVISION

Dist. from Ft. Monroe	Tel. Calls	Station No.	Code No.	STATIONS
160.4	*G	160	0228	④Gordonsville_____Va
165.3		VM89	0233	††Madison Run___Va
169.0		VM86	0235	So. Orange____Va
169.4	*OH	VM85	0238	①④Orange_____Va
			0239	Orange Ticket Office____Va
		VM79		Rapidan_____Va
		VM67		Culpeper_____Va
		VM46		Calverton_____Va
		VM33		Manassas_____Va
		VM23		Fairfax_____Va

WASHINGTON SUB-DIVISION Continued

Dist. from Ft. Monroe	Tel. Calls	Station No.	Code No.	STATIONS
	*Z	VM 7	0245	Alexandria_____Va
	*YD			①Potomac Yard__Va
254.1	*H	VM 0	0246	④Washington_____D C
			0247	④Union Station_____
			0248	Baggage_____
			0249	④City Ticket Office,
	PA			714 14th St., N. W.
			0242	④Arlington_____Va

RIVANNA SUB-DIVISION

Dist. from Ft. Monroe	Tel. Calls	Station No.	Code No.	STATIONS
84.4		84		†Rivanna Jct._____Va
84.7	*JN	85	0125	①Richmond_____Va
	*DO			J. N. Cabin_____
				Dispatcher's Office___
			0128	④Main St. Station___
			0130	Baggage_____
88.9	*VA	A4	0307	‡Korah_____Va
91.9		A7	0309	Westham_____Va
93.9		A10	0312	‡Bosher_____Va
95.6		A11	0315	†Mooreland_____Va
96.6		A12	0317	Lorraine_____Va
				†Saunders CrossingVa
98.2		A13	0319	†Tuckahoe_____Va
100.1		A15	0320	Vinita_____Va
101.5		A17	0322	†Manakin_____Va
102.8		A18	0324	‡Harris Siding____Va
103.3		A19	0326	†Boscobel_____Va
105.9	*D	A20	0328	Sabot_____Va
106.4		A21	0329	‡Boice Siding_____Va
109.2		A24	0332	Lee_____Va
111.6		A27	0334	State Farm_____Va
112.9		A28	0336	‡Thorncliff_____Va
113.3		A29	0338	‡Mt. Bernard_____Va
115.3	J	A30	0340	Maidens_____Va
117.4		A33	0342	‡Cedar Point_____Va
118.3		A34	0344	Irwin_____Va
122.6		A37	0348	†Ben Lomond____Va
124.9	*RC	A40	0351	Rock Castle_____Va
127.0		A42	0353	West View_____Va
129.1		A44	0355	‡Stokes_____Va
131.3		A45	0357	Selden_____Va
131.9	A	A47	0360	Pemberton_____Va
136.4	*KI	A52	0362	Elk Hill_____Va
138.6		A54	0364	Island_____Va
141.3	C	A57	0366	Columbia_____Va
144.0		A60	0370	†Rivanna_____Va
147.2		A62	0372	Stearnes_____Va
151.2	B	A66	0375	②Bremo_____Va
152.8	*SM	A68	0409	②Strathmore_____Va
155.0		A70	0412	Shores_____Va
157.4		A73	0416	Hardware_____Va
159.8		A75	0418	†Paynes_____Va
161.8		A77	0420	††Nicholas_____Va
164.1	S	A79	0422	Scottsville_____Va
167.5		A83	0424	Hatton_____Va
170.2	RN	A85	0428	②Warren_____Va
175.8	HN	A91	0441	Howardsville_____Va
178.6		A94	0443	Highland_____Va
180.8		A96	0445	Manteo_____Va
183.9	*WR	A99	0448	Warminster_____Va
186.7		A102	0451	Midway_____Va
188.7	H	A104	0453	Wingina_____Va
193.4	W	A109	0455	Norwood_____Va
195.6		A111	0457	Buffalo Station__Va
198.8		A114	0461	Greenway_____Va
202.8		A118	0463	Caskie_____Va
203.8	*GS	A119	0465	Gladstone_____Va

BUCKINGHAM SUB-DIVISION

Dist. from Ft. Monroe	Tel. Calls	Station No.	Code No.	STATIONS
151.2	B	A66	0375	Bremo____Va
151.8		C1	0376	New Canton____Va
153.6		C2	0379	Bridgeport____Va
153.9		C3	0380	‡Dutch Gap____Va
155.2	Booth	C4	0382	Arvonia____Va
155.5		C4½	0383	Lesuers____Va
157.2	Booth	C6	0387	Penlan____Va
160.7	Booth	C10	0393	Johnson____Va
163.5		C12	0397	Alpha____Va
166.1		C14	0400	Newton____Va
167.6	Booth	C16	0401	Dillwyn____Va

ALBERENE SUB-DIVISION

Dist. from Ft. Monroe	Tel. Calls	Station No.	Code No.	STATIONS
170.2	RN	A85	0428	Warren____Va
172.3		J2	0430	Boiling Spring___Va
174.2		J4	0432	Dawson Mill____Va
176.3		J6	0435	(1)Esmont____Va

Clifton Forge Division
MOUNTAIN SUB-DIVISION

Dist. from Ft. Monroe	Tel. Calls	Station No.	Code No.	STATIONS
181.4	*MO	181	0301	(1)Charlottesville___Va
182.3	*JC	182	0302	(4)Union Station___Va
			0300	Baggage____
			0303	University of Virginia____
185.7		186	0503	Farmington____Va
188.9	VY	189	0505	Ivy____Va
190.8		191	0506	†Oakland____Va
191.9		192	0507	Mechum's River__Va
194.8	*ZX	195	0509	(4)Crozet____Va
197.8		198	0510	Jarman Gap___Va
199.5	DG	199	0512	(4)Greenwood____Va
203.9	AF	204	0515	Afton____Va
207.8	*BS	208	0518	(1)(4)Waynesboro Union Station__Va
208.2		209	0519	Waynesboro____Va
213.5	FR	214	0521	Fishersville____Va
217.5		218	0523	††Brand____Va
218.7		219	0524	‡Peyton____Va
220.9	*HD	221	0525	(1)(4)Staunton____Va
			0526	Staunton Tkt. Office
224.3		224	0528	La Grange____Va
225.2		225	0529	†Snyder____Va
228.8	WO	229	0531	Swoope____Va
230.8	CF	231	0533	Christian____Va
234.0		234	0537	North Mountain_Va
234.9		235	0539	Chapin____Va
237.8		238	0543	Ferrol____Va
239.6		240	0545	Augusta Springs__Va
242.9		243	0548	Fordwick____Va
243.9	*CI	244	0550	Craigsville____Va
248.9		249	0553	Bell's Valley____Va
252.9	GO	253	0556	Goshen____Va
259.9	MB	260	0563	(4)Milboro____Va
266.2		266	0565	Crane____Va
268.1		268	0567	‡Copeland____Va
270.2		270	0569	Griffith____Va
274.1		274	0571	Longdale____Va
276.1	*JD			J. D. Cabin____Va
277.1	*F	277	0577	(2)(4)Clifton Forge__Va
			0578	Ticket Office____
	*F			Sup't Office____
	*DE			Dispatcher's Office_

JAMES RIVER SUB-DIVISION

Dist. from Ft. Monroe	Tel. Calls	Station No.	Code No.	STATIONS
203.8	*GS	A119	0465	Gladstone____Va
205.1		A120	0579	Allen Creek____Va
207.8		A123	0581	Riverville____Va
211.0		A126	0583	Walkerford____Va
215.6		A131	0585	Stapleton____Va
218.1		A133	0587	Galt's Mill____Va
221.1		A136	0589	††Joshua Falls____Va
224.2		A139	0591	‡Deacon____Va
225.0		A140	0593	‡Six Mile____Va
225.8		A141	0594	Kelly____Va
228.3		A144	0596	Tyree____Va
231.0		A146	0598	(1)Lynchburg(F.D.)Va
231.3	*ND		0593	(4) " Union Station____
232.2		A147		" So. R'y Crossing_
			0595	City Tkt. Office____

JAMES RIVER SUB-DIVISION
Continued

Dist. from Ft. Monroe	Tel. Calls	Station No.	Code No.	STATIONS
235.1	RM	A150	0602	Reusens____Va
235.5		A151	0604	‡Judith Dam____Va
239.0		A154		††G. W. Cabin____Va
239.4		A155	0606	Abert____Va
243.0	RK	A158	0608	Holcomb Rock___Va
244.1		A159	0610	Pearch____Va
245.5		A161	0612	Coleman____Va
245.8		A161½	0613	Logan____Va
248.6		A164	0615	Waugh____Va
250.2	BD	A165	0617	Big Island____Va
251.7	M	A167	0619	Major____Va
255.4		A171	0622	Snowden____Va
260.2	*K	A175	0626	(2)Balcony Falls___Va
261.1		A176	0640	‡Locher____Va
262.1		A177	0642	†Virginia Manor__Va
262.8	VM	A178	0643	(4)Natural Bridge_Va
265.9		A181	0647	Gilmore Mills____Va
269.8	AP	A185	0649	Alpine____Va
270.8		A186	0651	‡Rocky Point____Va
273.6		A192	0653	Indian Rock____Va
276.5		A192	0655	††Dillon____Va
280.1	*BN	A195	0657	(4)Buchanan____Va
284.2		A199	0662	Springwood____Va
283.5		A198½		†J. N. Cabin____Va
287.9		A203	0664	Lyle____Va
290.0		A205	0666	†Saltpetre____Va
291.9		A207	0669	†All____Va
293.0		A208	0671	†Salisbury____Va
294.8		A210	0673	††Dunn____Va
297.2	*RA	A212	0675	(2)Eagle Rock____Va
301.4		A217	0712	Gala____Va
304.0		A219	0714	Haden____Va
305.7		A221	0716	†Baldwin____Va
308.2		A223	0718	Glen Wilton____Va
310.9		A226	0720	‡Lick Run____Va
313.0		A228	0722	Iron Gate____Va
314.2	*JD	A229		J. D. Cabin____Va
277.5	*F	277	0577	(4)Clifton Forge____Va

LEXINGTON SUB-DIVISION

Dist. from Ft. Monroe	Tel. Calls	Station No.	Code No.	STATIONS
260.2	*K	A175	0626	Balcony Falls____Va
261.3		B0	0627	Montridge____Va
			0628	(1)Glasgow____Va
			0629	Emil____Va
			0630	†Agnor____Va
			0631	Buffalo Forge___Va
			0641	†Thompson____Va
270.4		B10	0632	Loch Laird____Va
271.3	QN	B11	0633	(1)(4)Buena Vista___Va
275.1		B16	0635	South River____Va
278.7	AX	B20	0637	East Lexington___Va
281.0	XN	B21	0638	(4)Lexington____Va

CRAIG VALLEY SUB-DIVISION

Dist. from Ft. Monroe	Tel. Calls	Station No.	Code No.	STATIONS
297.2	*RA	A212	0675	Eagle Rock____Va
298.5		D1	0676	†Whitten____Va
301.3		D4	0680	Stull____Va
304.5		D6	0682	†Horton____Va
304.8		D7	0684	Parr____Va
305.9		D8	0686	†Hipes____Va
308.3		D10	0688	Lemon____Va
309.4		D12	0690	†Surber____Va
311.8		D13	0692	†Ruble____Va
312.8		D15	0695	Oriskany____Va
316.0		D18	0698	†Charlton____Va
317.3		D20	0700	†Given____Va
319.1		D21	0702	Barbour's Creek_Va
320.7		D23	0704	†Marshalltown____Va
321.3		D24	0706	†Virginia Mineral Springs____Va
322.3		D25	0708	†Pine Top____Va
324.1	CY	D26	0710	New Castle____Va

ALLEGHANY SUB-DIVISION

Dist. from Ft. Monroe	Tel. Calls	Station No.	Code No.	STATIONS
277.5	*F	277	0577	(4)Clifton Forge____Va
278.1		278		†H. Y. Cabin____Va
281.2		281	0730	Low Moor____Va
286.6		287	0734	†Mallow____Va
289.7	CD	290	0738	(2)(4)Covington____Va
291.2	*BS	291		††B. S. Cabin____Va
292.1		292	0782	Boys Home____Va
293.4		293	0784	McDowell____Va
295.3		295	0786	Callaghan____Va
297.7		298	0788	Moss Run____Va

ALLEGHANY SUB-DIVISION
Continued

Dist. from Ft. Monroe	Tel. Calls	Station No.	Code No.	STATIONS
300.2		300	0790	Backbone____Va
304.2		304	0792	Jerry's Run____Va
306.4	*A	306	0797	(4)Alleghany____Va
308.0		308	1000	Tuckahoe____W Va
311.9	*WS	312	1002	(4)White Sulphur Springs____W Va
			1003	" Hotel____
315.5		315	1008	Hart's Run____W Va
317.3		317	1010	Caldwell____W Va
319.8		320	1012	(2)†Whitcomb___W Va
322.8	*RV	323	1014	(4)Ronceverte____W Va
326.5		326	1018	†Rockland____W Va
329.0		329	1022	(4)Fort Spring____W Va
330.1		330	1024	Snow Flake____W Va
330.8		331	1026	‡Frazier____W Va
335.8		336	1030	(4)Alderson____W Va
336.4	*AD	336½		††A. D. Cabin____W Va
337.4		337	1032	†Glenray____W Va
339.4		339	1034	Wolf Creek____W Va
341.5		341	1036	†Riffe____W Va
343.4		343	1038	Pence Spring____W Va
345.3		345	1040	Lowell____W Va
347.2		347	1042	Talcott____W Va
349.5	*MW	350	1046	Hildale____W Va
352.6		353	1049	Wiggins____W Va
355.3	*MX	355		M. X. Cabin____W Va

POTTS CREEK SUB-DIVISION

Dist. from Ft. Monroe	Tel. Calls	Station No.	Code No.	STATIONS
289.7	CD	290	0738	Covington____Va
292.9				End of Line____Va

HOT SPRINGS SUB-DIVISION

Dist. from Ft. Monroe	Tel. Calls	Station No.	Code No.	STATIONS
289.7	CD	290	0738	(4)Covington____Va
292.5		E3	0757	†Intervale____Va
294.4		E4	0758	†Clearwater Park_Va
295.2		E5	0760	†Harrington____Va
300.6		E11	0764	Falling Spring____Va
301.6		E12	0765	†Camp Appalachia_Va
302.0		E13	0766	Natural Well____Va
304.7		E15	0768	††Jenkins Ford____Va
305.4		E16	0771	Kincaid____Va
308.7		E19	0772	Callison____Va
311.7		E22	0774	Bacova Jct.____Va
312.9		E23	0776	New Siding____Va
314.4	QA	E25	0778	(4)Hot Springs____Va

GREENBRIER SUB-DIVISION

Dist. from Ft. Monroe	Tel. Calls	Station No.	Code No.	STATIONS
319.8		320	1012	†Whitcomb____W Va
321.6		R2	1060	North Caldwell_W Va
323.3		R4	1061	†Camp Alleghany___W Va
325.3		R6	1062	†Hopper____W Va
328.5		R8	1065	†Loopemount___W Va
330.8		R11	1068	Keister____W Va
333.9		R15	1070	Anthony____W Va
336.0		R17	1072	†Woodman____W Va
341.4		R22	1076	Spring Creek___W Va
344.6	RN	R25	1078	(4)Renick____W Va
347.9		R27	1080	†Golden____W Va
349.4		R30	1082	†Horrock____W Va
350.4		R31	1084	Rorer____W Va
351.8		R33	1086	†Droop Mountain____W Va
355.7		R37	1090	†Spice Run____W Va
357.0		R38	1092	†Locust____W Va
358.3		R39	1094	Beard____W Va
359.1		R40	1096	‡Den Mar____W Va
361.5		R42	1100	†Burnsides____W Va
362.4		R43	1102	†Kennison____W Va
365.6	SB	R46	1104	Seebert____W Va
367.9		R49	1106	†Watoga____W Va
369.1		R50	1108	†Violet____W Va
372.0		R53	1110	†Buckeye____W Va
374.7		R56	1111	†Stillwell____W Va
375.9	MO	R57	1114	(4)Marlinton____W Va
380.8		R62	1119	Thorny Creek_W Va
382.1		R63	1121	††Clawson____W Va
384.4		R65	1123	†Harter____W Va
386.4		R67	1125	Big Run____W Va
390.9		R72	1129	Clover Lick____W Va
394.2		R75	1131	Stony Bottom_W Va
396.7		R77	1133	†Sitlington____W Va
398.7		R79	1135	†Raywood____W Va
400.5	CS	R81	1139	(4)Cass____W Va

C&O Stations by Mile Post and Division/Sub-Division, Arranged East-to-West.

Taken from the 1948 edition of *C&O Officers, Agents, Stations, Etc. No. 82, August 1948.* Continued

Legend:

4-Coupon Stations.

*-Day and Night Telegraph Office.

1-Junction with connecting line.

2-Junction of Sub-division shown elsewhere.

6-Established for operating purposes only-not a station for passengers or freight business.

3-Within switching limits of Newport News; carload freight should be waybilled to Newport News, Va.

†-No Siding.

‡-Private Siding only.

GREENBRIER SUB-DIVISION Continued

Dist. from Ft. Monroe	Tel. Calls	Station No.	Code No.	STATIONS
404.5		R84	1142	Wanless W Va
407.9		R89	1146	Hosterman W Va
411.8		R93	1148	†Boyer W Va
412.5		R94	1150	†Whiting W Va
415.4	DR	R96	1152	①④Durbin W Va
416.4		R97	1154	Frank W Va
417.9		R98	1156	Bartow W Va

Hinton Division
NEW RIVER SUB-DIVISION

Dist. from Ft. Monroe	Tel. Calls	Station No.	Code No.	STATIONS
354.6	*MX	355		M. X. Cabin W Va
356.5		356½	1054	Avis W Va
357.0	*HX	357	1165	④**Hinton** W Va
	*H			" Dispatcher's Off.
358.0	*CW	358		C. W. Cabin W Va
360.0		360	1168	Barksdale W Va
361.3		361	1170	Brooks W Va
362.0	RK	362		††R. K. Cabin W Va
366.3		366	1175	Sandstone W Va
369.6	*MD	369	1177	②④Meadow Creek W Va
374.3		374	1183	Glade W Va
378.7	*QN	379	1185	②④**Quinnimont** W Va
380.0	*NI	380	1200	②④†**Prince** W Va
383.2		383	1372	McKendree W Va
385.3		385	1373	‡Thayer W Va
386.1		386	1374	‡Dunfee W Va
387.9		387	1376	Claremont W Va
388.6		388	1377	Beechwood Jct. W Va
389.1		389	1378	‡Stone Cliff W Va
389.4	*CS	390		††C. S. Cabin W Va
390.8	*DU	391	1380	②④**Thurmond** W Va
391.9		392	1500	†Dimmock W Va
392.4		392½	1501	†Rush Run W Va
393.8		393	1503	‡Beury W Va
394.4		395	1505	‡Fire Creek W Va
395.2		395½	1506	†Pennbrook W Va
396.4		396	1508	E. Sewell W Va
397.6	*ED	397	1510	④**Sewell** W Va
399.3		399	1526	Caperton W Va
400.4		400	1527	②Keeneys Creek W Va
401.4		401	1524	East Nuttall W Va
401.6		402	1542	Nuttall W Va
404.3		FA	1545	‡④Fayette W Va
405.6		406	1549	‡Ames W Va
408.6		409	1552	②Hawks Nest W Va
408.9	*MA	409½	1558	②Macdougal W Va
410.8		411	1560	Cotton Hill W Va
415.0	*GU	414		G. U. Cabin W Va
415.2		415	1565	①②④Gauley W Va
416.1		416	1610	†Old Gauley W Va
417.9		418	1614	Kanawha Falls W Va
421.3	*VN	422	1616	①Deepwater W Va
422.1		423	1621	①†West Deepwater W Va
423.7		424	1618	②Mt. Carbon W Va
425.3		425½	1641	†Eagle W Va
427.5	CN	428	1645	④**Montgomery** W Va
428.2		428½	1647	②Morris Creek Jct W Va

NICHOLAS, FAYETTE & GREENBRIER RAILROAD COMPANY

(Operated Jointly by C. & O. and N. Y. C. R. R. Co., Lessees.)
Sewell Valley Sub-division (of N. F. & G. R. R. Co

Dist. from Ft. Monroe	Tel. Calls	Station No.	Code No.	STATIONS
369.6	*MD	369	1177	Meadow Creek W Va
371.9		RG2	3004	†Dondale W Va
373.8		RG4	3008	†Claypool W Va
377.9	*IL	RG8	3016	Meadow Bridge W Va
378.2		RG8½	3017	②Hawley W Va
380.5		RG11	3021	Top Siding W Va
381.2	25*	RG11½	3023	Springdale W Va
384.6		RG15	3031	‡Bellwood W Va
385.1		RG15½	3032	Griffith Siding W Va
386.9		RG17	3037	Simms W Va
389.2		RG19	3041	Rainelle W Va
390.0		RG20	3044	②†Rainelle Junction W Va
390.2		RG20½	3046	②G. & E. Junction W Va
391.4		RG21	3160	†Dwyer W Va
392.4		RG22	3163	‡Green Siding W Va
394.3		RG24	3165	†Surbaugh W Va
397.3		RG27	3172	†Cruickshanks W Va
400.2		RG30	3176	Burdettes Creek W Va
401.9		RG32	3178	†Camp 20 W Va
404.1		RG34	3180	†Dry Creek W Va
406.5		RG37	3184	Russellville W Va
409.0		RG39	3189	Nallen W Va
415.1		RG46	3193	††Deegans W Va
422.5		RG53	3195	††Carnifex W Va
431.8		RG61	3198	Koontz W Va
437.1		RG68	3200	①Swiss Jct. W Va

HAWLEY SUB-DIVISION

(Of N. F. & G. R. R. Co.)

Dist. from Ft. Monroe	Tel. Calls	Station No.	Code No.	STATIONS
378.2		RG8½	3017	Hawley W Va
380.3				End of Track W Va

RUPERT SUB-DIVISION

(Of N. F. & G. R. R. Co.)

Dist. from Ft. Monroe	Tel. Calls	Station No.	Code No.	STATIONS
390.0		RG20	3044	†Rainelle Junction W Va
391.0		RB1	3100	‡McRoss W Va
391.7		RB2	3102	‡Reese W Va
392.9		RB3	3104	‡Midland Mine W Va
394.3		RB4	3105	†MillCreekRoad W Va
397.1		RB7	3112	②Rupert W Va
397.2	2L1S	RB8	3113	②Rupert Jct W Va
399.3		RB9	3114	Shawvers Crossing W Va
401.1		RB11	3117	‡Jeter W Va

BIG CLEAR CREEK SUB-DIVISION

(Of N. F. & G. R. R. Co.)

Dist. from Ft. Monroe	Tel. Calls	Station No.	Code No.	STATIONS
397.2		RB8	3112	Rupert Jct. W Va
400.6	Booth	ARB4	3144	††Gumm W Va
403.1	Booth	ARB7	3147	†Anjean W Va
407.2		ARB10	3151	‡Duo W Va
407.6		ARB11½	3152	‡Wade W Va
408.6		ARB12	3153	Cobb W Va
410.3	Booth	ARB14	3154	‡Clearco W Va
410.5				End of Track W Va

GREENBRIER AND EASTERN SUB-DIVISION

Dist. from Ft. Monroe	Tel. Calls	Station No.	Code No.	STATIONS
390.2	Booth	RG20½	3046	G. & E. Jct. W Va
392.4		GE2½	3052	†Foothill W Va
393.2	Booth	GE3	3053	‡Evelyn W Va
394.9	Booth	GE5	3056	Russellville Road W Va
396.6		GE6½	3059	†Bryant W Va
397.7	Booth	GE7½	3062	‡Bellburn W Va
398.5	Booth	GE8½	3065	‡Leslie W Va
399.2	Booth	GE9	3068	‡Crichton W Va
399.3		GE9½		⑥②Hominy Creek Jct W Va
400.0	1L1S1L	GE10	3070	Quinwood W Va
400.8		GE10½	3073	Marfrance W Va
401.3	Booth	GE11½	3077	†Johnstown W Va

HOMINY CREEK SUB-DIVISION

(Of N. F. & G. R. R. Co.)

Dist. from Ft. Monroe	Tel. Calls	Station No.	Code No.	STATIONS
399.3		GE9¼		⑥Hominy Creek Jct W Va
403.5		GEH4		⑥Peaser Jct W Va
404.5		GEH8	3071	‡Lee W Va
405.0		GER1½		⑥Brushy Jct W Va
407.2		GER4	3081	‡Watts W Va
409.8				⑥Leivasy Jct W Va
410.3		GEBL1	3091	‡Leivasy W Va
410.4		GEB5	3089	Petersen W Va

LAUREL CREEK SUB-DIVISION

Dist. from Ft. Monroe	Tel. Calls	Station No.	Code No.	STATIONS
378.7	*QN	379	1185	④**Quinnimont** W Va
381.8		T3	1188	‡Export W Va
382.5		T4	1190	‡Laurel W Va
383.5		T4½	1193	†Big Q W Va
383.7		T5	1195	‡Brownwood W Va
384.0		T5½	1197	‡Hemlock Hollow W Va
384.4		T6	1198	Layland W Va

PINEY CREEK SUB-DIVISION

Dist. from Ft. Monroe	Tel. Calls	Station No.	Code No.	STATIONS
380.0	*NI	380	1200	④**Prince** W Va
380.5		W½	1201	‡Royal W Va
381.4		W1	1202	††②Terry Jct W Va
381.7		W2	1206	†McCreery W Va
382.9		W3	1208	Norvell W Va
383.4		W4	1209	‡Wright W Va
384.6				††Stonewall W Va
385.1		W5	1211	‡Jonancy W Va
385.5		W5½	1212	‡Lanark W Va
385.7		W5¾	1210	‡Penman W Va
386.0		W6	1213	‡Stanaford W Va
386.3		W6½	1214	††Dorsey W Va
388.0		W8	1216	†White Stick W Va
389.3		W9	1218	‡Pinepoca W Va
389.8		W10	1220	††Rodes W Va
392.7		W11	1222	‡Raleigh No. 7 W Va
393.2		W11½	1224	†McQuaid W Va
393.3		W12	1226	②Blue Jay Jct W Va
393.6	*RA	W13	1228	②Raleigh W Va
394.2		W14	1230	‡West Raleigh W Va
396.1	BJ	W15	1232	②Beckley Jct W Va
396.4		W16	1234	Mabscott W Va
396.6		W16½	1235	‡Mabscott Mine W Va

PINEY CREEK SUB-DIVISION
Continued

Dist. from Ft. Monroe	Tel. Calls	Station No.	Code No.	STATIONS
396.9		W17	1236	Bickell W Va
397.4		W17½	1237	†Westwood W Va
398.4		W18	1239	Cabell W Va
399.0		W19	1241	††Burks W Va
401.5		W21	1243	①Admiralty W Va
402.1		W21½	------	⑥Eccles Jct W Va
402.8		W22	1244	†Metalton W Va
403.1		W23	1245	†Glen White Jct WVa
403.7		W24	1248	Baylor W Va
404.7		W24½	------	⑥Marsh Fork Jct W Va
405.4	VO	W25	1250	Surveyor W Va
406.2		W26	1252	†Tolleys W Va
407.1		W26½	1253	†Hoo Hoo W Va
407.6		W27	1255	Lester W Va

TERRY SUB-DIVISION

Dist. from Ft. Monroe	Tel. Calls	Station No.	Code No.	STATIONS
381.4		W1	1202	†Terry Jct W Va
383.1		W1½	1204	‡Terry W Va

GLADE CREEK & RALEIGH SUB-DIVISION

Dist. from Ft. Monroe	Tel. Calls	Station No.	Code No.	STATIONS
393.3		W12	1226	Blue Jay Jct W Va
394.4		BJ1	1258	†Glen Jct W Va
394.5		BJ2	1259	Glen Morgan W Va

RALEIGH SOUTHWESTERN SUB-DIVISION

Dist. from Ft. Monroe	Tel. Calls	Station No.	Code No.	STATIONS
393.6	*RA	W13	1228	Raleigh W Va
394.6		WA1	1261	‡Raleigh No. 6 W Va
395.9		WA3	1263	Fitzpatrick W Va
396.8		WA4	1267	‡Crab Orchard W Va
397.2		WA5¼	1265	†Spangler's Mill W Va
398.2		Wa5½	1268	†Viacova W Va
398.8		WA7	1269	②Forest W Va

WINDING GULF SUB-DIVISION

Dist. from Ft. Monroe	Tel. Calls	Station No.	Code No.	STATIONS
398.8		WA7	1269	Forest W Va
399.1	ON	WB1	1287	①Pemberton W Va
400.2		WB2	1289	‡Affinity W Va
401.5		WB3	1290	†Diehl W Va
402.4		WB4	1292	‡Wigul W Va
402.6	GS	WB5	1294	†Gulf Switch W Va
404.2		WB6	1295	†Hotcoal W Va
404.7		WB7	1296	†Big Stick W Va
406.3		WB9	1300	‡MacAlpin W Va
407.0		WB10	1301	‡Stotesbury W Va
408.7		WB11	1303	‡Tams W Va
409.5	U	WB12	1304	††Ury W Va
410.6		WB13	1305	‡Helen W Va
413.6		WB16	1306	①②Stone Coal Jct W Va

PINEY RIVER & PAINT CREEK SUB-DIVISION

Dist. from Ft. Monroe	Tel. Calls	Station No.	Code No.	STATIONS
396.1	BJ	W15	1232	Beckley Jct W Va
397.3		PR1	1277	④Beckley W Va
398.3	RG	PR3	1279	Sprague W Va
400.6		PR5	1281	Skelton W Va
402.1		PR6	1282	‡Cranberry W Va

STONE COAL SUB-DIVISION
(Operated Jointly by The C. & O. and Virginian R'Y)

Dist. from Ft. Monroe	Tel. Calls	Station No.	Code No.	STATIONS
413.6		WB16	1306	①Stone Coal Jct W Va
414.0		SC½	1311	Tommy Creek W Va
414.3		SC1	1307	Rhodell W Va
415.0		SC2	1308	Francis W Va
416.9		SC3	1309	East Gulf W Va
417.9		SC3½	1317	‡Winding Gulf No. 4 W Va
418.0		SC4	1310	Killarney W Va
419.7		SC5	1312	Mead W Va

STONE COAL SUB-DIVISION
Continued

Dist. from Ft. Monroe	Tel. Calls	Station No.	Code No.	STATIONS
420.4		SC6	1313	Besoco W Va
420.7		SC6½	1316	Laurel Siding W Va
421.3		SC7	1314	Lego W Va
421.7		SC8	1315	Pickshin W Va
422.0		SC9	1318	Lillybrook W Va

LOUP CREEK SUB-DIVISION

Dist. from Ft. Monroe	Tel. Calls	Station No.	Code No.	STATIONS
390.8	*DU	391	1380	④**Thurmond** W Va
391.1		M½	1381	②South Side Jct W Va
391.7		M1	1382	†Dun Glen W Va
391.9		M2	1383	†Newlyn W Va
392.6		M2½	1384	†Cadle Ridge W Va
393.4		M3	1385	Meadow Fork W Va
395.1		M4½	1387	†De Witt W Va
395.9	Booth	M5	1388	‡Harvey W Va
396.0		M5½	1389	‡Prudence W Va
396.7		M6	1390	‡Red Star W Va
397.2	GJ	M7	1392	Glen Jean W Va
397.7	Booth	M7½	1394	②White Oak Jct W Va
398.2		M8	1395	†Sun W Va
398.9		M8½	1396	Derryhale W Va
400.0		M9½	1399	†Turkey Knob W Va
400.5		M10½	1401	②Price Hill Jct W Va
400.7		M11	1402	†②Kilsyth Jct W Va
401.0		M11½	1400	Macdonald W Va

GLEN JEAN SUB-DIVISION

Dist. from Ft. Monroe	Tel. Calls	Station No.	Code No.	STATIONS
400.7		M11	1402	①⑥Kilsyth Jct W Va
400.8				⑥Mill Creek Jct W Va
401.1		KT¼	1438	Mount Hope W Va
401.8		KT1	1444	Kilsyth W Va
403.1		KT2	1443	Cepece W Va
403.9		KT3¼	1442	‡Oswald W Va
400.8		KGO	1445	②⑥Sugar Creek Jct W Va

MILL CREEK SUB-DIVISION

Dist. from Ft. Monroe	Tel. Calls	Station No.	Code No.	STATIONS
400.8				⑥Mill Creek Jct W Va
404.0		MA3	1460	‡Cleve W Va
405.3		MA5	1463	‡Garden Ground W Va

SUGAR CREEK JUNCTION TO PAX

Dist. from Ft. Monroe	Tel. Calls	Station No.	Code No.	STATIONS
400.5		KG0	1445	Sugar Creek Jct W Va
401.7		KP1¼	1446	‡Siltix W Va
403.3		KP2¾	1456	Tunnel W Va
404.7		KP4¼	1457	Veasey W Va
405.6		KP5¼	1458	Millers Camp W Va
406.6		KP6¼	1447	Pax W Va

SOUTH SIDE SUB-DIVISION

Dist. from Ft. Monroe	Tel. Calls	Station No.	Code No.	STATIONS
391.1		M½	1381	South Side Jct W Va
391.5		Q1	1407	‡Weewin W Va
391.6		Q1½	1408	Concho W Va
392.1		Q2	1409	‡Erskine W Va
393.3		Q3	1411	‡South Rush Run W Va
393.9		Q4	1412	Red Ash W Va
396.5		Q5	1414	‡Brooklyn W Va
397.8		Q6	1415	‡Cunard W Va
393.8			1416	†②Bridge Jct W Va

REND SUB-DIVISION

Dist. from Ft. Monroe	Tel. Calls	Station No.	Code No.	STATIONS
391.1		M½	1381	South Side Jct W Va
391.9		QA1	1417	†Boyd W Va
394.5		QA3½	1419	Rock Lick Jct W Va
394.8		QA5	1421	Minden W Va
395.2		QA6	1423	Minden Nos. 3 and 4 W Va
395.6		QA7		End of Line W Va

WHITE OAK SUB-DIVISION

Dist. from Ft. Monroe	Tel. Calls	Station No.	Code No.	STATIONS
397.7	Booth	M7½	1394	White Oak Jct W Va
398.0			1428	†McKell W Va
400.2		Z2½	1431	Scarbro W Va
401.1		Z4	1433	①②Carlisle W Va
401.6		Z5	1437	‡Oakwood W Va

WHITE OAK RAILROAD
(Operated Jointly by The C. & O. and Virginian)

Dist. from Ft. Monroe	Tel. Calls	Station No.	Code No.	STATIONS
401.1		Z4	1433	①Carlisle W Va
403.3		H419	1434	Oak Hill W Va
406.7		H422	1435	Summerlee W Va
407.4		H423	1436	Lochgelly W Va

PRINCE HILL SUB-DIVISION

Dist. from Ft. Monroe	Tel. Calls	Station No.	Code No.	STATIONS
400.5		M10½	1401	Price Hill Jct W Va
401.0		PH½	1438	④Mount Hope W Va

SOUTH MAIN LINE

Dist. from Ft. Monroe	Tel. Calls	Station No.	Code No.	STATIONS
398.8			1416	†Bridge Jct W Va
399.0		Q7	1514	‡South Caperton W Va
399.8		Q8	1515	‡Elverton W Va
401.6		Q9	1517	‡South Nuttall W Va
402.3		Q10	1518	Kaymoor W Va
404.8		Q11	1520	④South Fayette W Va
408.9	*MA	409½	1558	Macdougal W Va

KEENY'S CREEK SUB-DIVISION

Dist. from Ft. Monroe	Tel. Calls	Station No.	Code No.	STATIONS
400.4		400	1527	Keeneys Creek W Va
401.1		P1	1528	†Hollands Crossing W Va
402.9		P2	1529	‡Lynch W Va
404.4		P4	1530	†Dearien W Va
405.1		P5	1531	‡Boone W Va
406.1		P6	1533	Ballanger W Va
406.5		P7	1535	Masters W Va
406.9		P8	1536	‡Rothwell W Va
407.7		P9	1539	‡Blume W Va
408.2		P10	1541	Lookout W Va

HAWK'S NEST SUB_DIVISION

Dist. from Ft. Monroe	Tel. Calls	Station No.	Code No.	STATIONS
408.6		409	1552	Hawks Nest W Va
409.1		G2	1555	‡Mill Creek Mine W Va
410.7	AV	G3	1553	Ansted W Va
412.1				End of Track W Va

GAULEY SUB-DIVISION

Dist. from Ft. Monroe	Tel. Calls	Station No.	Code No.	STATIONS
415.2		415	1565	①Gauley W Va
				K. & M. Jct W Va
417.5		N2	1568	Vanetta W Va
419.1		N4	1569	‡Gamoca W Va
421.2		N6½	1571	Wyndal W Va
421.9		N6¾	1572	②Rick Creek Jct W Va
422.3		N7	1573	①Belva W Va
422.8		N7½	1574	②†Open Fork Jct W Va
427.8		N13	1579	Vaughan W Va
429.1		N15	1581	Greendale W Va
429.3				End of Track W Va

GAULEY AND RICH CREEK SUB-DIVISION

Dist. from Ft. Monroe	Tel. Calls	Station No.	Code No.	STATIONS
408.6		409	1552	Hawks Nest W Va
409.1		G2	1555	‡Mill Creek Mine W Va
410.7	AV	G3	1553	Ansted W Va
412.1				End of Track W Va

OPEN FORK SUB-DIVISION

Dist. from Ft. Monroe	Tel. Calls	Station No.	Code No.	STATIONS
408.6		409	1552	Hawks Nest W Va
409.1		G2	1555	‡Mill Creek Mine W Va
410.7	AV	G3	1553	Ansted W Va
412.1				End of Track W Va

POWELLTON SUB-DIVISION

Dist. from Ft. Monroe	Tel. Calls	Station No.	Code No.	STATIONS
423.7		424	1618	Mt. Carbon W Va
426.2		02½	1620	‡Columbia W Va
427.3		O3½	1622	†Ridenour W Va
427.9		O4	1623	†②Elkridge Jct W Va
428.6		O5	1625	Powellton W Va

C&O Stations by Mile Post and Division/Sub-Division, Arranged East-to-West.

Taken from the 1948 edition of *Officers, Agents, Stations, Etc. No. 82, August 1948.* Continued

Legend:

4-Coupon Stations.

*-Day and Night Telegraph Office.

1-Junction with connecting line.

2-Junction of Sub-division shown elsewhere.

6-Established for operating purposes only-not a station for passengers or freight business.

3-Within switching limits of Newport News; carload freight should be waybilled to Newport News, Va.

†-No Siding.

‡-Private Siding only.

Dist. from Ft. Monroe	Tel. Calls	Station No.	Code No.	STATIONS
				ELKRIDGE SUB-DIVISION
427.9		04	1623	②Elkridge Jct._W Va
430.2		OA3	1629	Elkridge_____W Va
430.5				End of Track__W Va
				Huntington Division
				KANAWHA SUB-DIVISION
428.2		428½	1647	②Morris Creek Junction_____W Va
429.6	*RO	430	1670	Handley_____W Va
431.8	P	431	1672	②Pratt_____W Va
432.8		432	1720	Hansford_____W Va
433.5		434	1721	Crown Hill___W Va
435.0		435½	1723	‡Black Cat____W Va
435.6		436	1725	East Bank____W Va
437.5		437	1726	‡Coalburg_____W Va
438.1	*CA	438	1730	②④Cabin Creek Junction____W Va
438.5		439	1900	†Chelyan_____W Va
440.6		441	1902	Winifrede Jct._W Va
441.6		442	1904	†Chesapeake___W Va
444.5		444	1905	Marmet_____W Va
448.2		448	1908	South Malden_W Va
449.8		450	1910	Owens_____W Va
451.8	*KO	452	1912	South Ruffner_W Va
453.6		454	1915	①④Charleston__W Va
			1916	" Depot
			1917	" City
455.2		455	1916	Elk_____W Va
457.3		457	1918	④South Charles-ton_____W Va
458.9	XY	459	1920	Spring Hill___W Va
465.5	*VF	465	1925	②④St Albans___W Va
466.9		467	2500	Dock_____W Va
469.6		469	2502	Scary_____W Va
473.2	*SC	473	2505	Scott_____W Va
475.1		475	2507	Teays_____W Va
479.2	*KX	479	2510	Hurricane_____W Va
481.5		481	2513	Culloden_____W Va
485.8	*MI	486	2515	Milton_____W Va
487.8		488	2517	Yates_____W Va
490.3		490	2519	Ona_____W Va
491.9		492	2521	†Blue Sulphur_W Va
494.7	*BR	495	2525	②Barboursville W Va
498.2		498	2980	†Wilson_____W Va
499.8		500	2981	‡East Hunting-ton_____W Va
501.0		501	2982	Guyandotte___W Va
501.2	*DK	501½		††D. K. Cabin__W Va
502.4		502	2984	Huntington Shops_____W Va
			2987	Coal Acct._____
504.0	*HU	504	2986	①④Huntington_W Va
			2985	" Tkt Office_____
	*UN			" Disprs' Office_____

Dist. from Ft. Monroe	Tel. Calls	Station No.	Code No.	STATIONS
				KANAWHA SUB-DIVISION Continued
504.6	*HO	505		H. O. Cabin___W Va
506.1		506	2988	W. Huntington W Va
507.6		508	2990	Westmoreland_W Va
508.2		509	2991	‡Kellog_____W Va
510.2		510	2995	Ceredo_____W Va
511.2	*KV	511		††K. V. Cabin__W Va
511.3		512	2999	①④Kenova____W Va
			3000	" Tkt Office_____
513.3	*BS	513	4000	②Big Sandy Jct._Ky
514.0		514	4500	④Catlettsburg___Ky
516.0		517	4505	Normal_____Ky
516.6	*SX	517½	4506	Clyffeside_____Ky
519.2	*AU	520	4509	②④Ashland____Ky
			4510	" Tkt Office_____
519.5	*AX	521	4510	Ashland Jct.___Ky
520.4	*NC	521½		N. C. Cabin___Ky
521.1		522	4701	Bellefonte_____Ky
523.9	*RU	524	4705	④Russell_____Ky
				MORRIS CREEK SUB-DIVISION
428.2		428½	1647	Morris Creek Junction_____W Va
428.6		Y1	1646	†Mt. Morris____W Va
430.0		Y3	1649	‡Eureka_____W Va
430.7		Y4	1650	‡Morris Creek_W Va
				PAINT CREEK SUB-DIVISION
431.8	Booth	431	1672	Pratt_____W Va
433.0		U1½	1673	†Holly Grove___W Va
433.6		U2	1674	Scale Yard____W Va
434.8		U3	1676	Gallagher_____W Va
436.0		U4	1677	†Livingston____W Va
436.9		U6	1679	†Standard_____W Va
437.0		U7	1680	††Bedford_____W Va
439.2		U8	1681	†Glen Huddy___W Va
441.3		U10	1684	†Nuckolls_____W Va
442.3		U11	1685	†Whitaker_____W Va
443.6		U12	1686	†Green Castle__W Va
444.1		U12½	1688	②†Imperial Jct.__W Va
446.0		U14	1689	††Collinsdale___W Va
446.6		U15	1690	†Mahan_____W Va
448.2		U15½	1692	†Coalfield_____W Va
448.6		U16	1693	†Milburn_____W Va
451.1		U20	1695	†Westerly_____W Va
452.8		U21	1697	†Mossy_____W Va
453.4		U22	1699	†Kingston_____W Va
				IMPERIAL SUB-DIVISION
428.2		428½	1647	Morris Creek Junction_____W Va
428.6		Y1	1646	‡Mt. Morris____W Va
430.0		Y3	1649	‡Eureka_____W Va
430.7		Y4	1650	‡Morris Creek_W Va

Dist. from Ft. Monroe	Tel. Calls	Station No.	Code No.	STATIONS
				CABIN CREEK SUB-DIVISION
438.1	*CA	438	1730	④Cabin Creek Junction_____W Va
440.0		F2	1732	Dry Branch___W Va
441.7		F3	1734	†Ronda_____W Va
442.3		F4	1736	Sharon_____W Va
442.9		F5	1738	†Miami_____W Va
443.5		F6½	1741	Dawes_____W Va
444.0		F7	1742	†Giles_____W Va
445.5		F8	1745	‡Coal_____W Va
446.7		F9	1747	†Ohley_____W Va
447.4	*CJ	F10	1748	Cane Fork____W Va
448.5	1L1S1L	F10½	1750	Eskdale_____W Va
449.4		F12	1752	②Leewood____W Va
449.7		F13	1754	Cherokee_____W Va
450.6		F13½	1756	②†Red Warrior Junction_____W Va
450.7		F13½	1757	†Red Warrior_W Va
451.2		F14	1758	‡Empire_____W Va
451.9		F15	1760	‡Acme_____W Va
453.1		F15	1761	‡Rosecoal____W Va
453.6		F18	1762	Kayford_____W Va
454.1		F18½		End of Line___W Va
				LEEWOOD SUB-DIVISION
449.4		F12	1752	Leewood_____W Va
450.3		FA1	1775	†Holly_____W Va
451.6		FA1	1777	†Quarrier_____W Va
452.1		FA2	1778	†Wake Forest__W Va
452.4		FA2½	1779	‡Laing_____W Va
453.5		FA3½	1781	‡Nabob_____W Va
454.0		FA4	1782	②Decota_____W Va
455.0		FA5	1784	W. Va. No. 1__W Va
456.0		FA6	1785	United_____W Va
456.5		FA7	1787	W. Va. No. 2__W Va
457.3		FA8	1790	W. Va. No. 4__W Va
				REPUBLIC SUB-DIVISION
454.0		FA4	1782	Decota_____W Va
454.7		FB1	1795	South Carbon_W Va
456.6		FB3	1797	Republic No. 2W Va
				SENG CREEK SUB-DIVISION
450.6	_____	F13½	1756	†Red Warrior Jct._____W Va
454.0	1S2L2S	FC3	1800	††Tunnel SidingW Va
455.5	1L4S	FC5	1802	‡High Coal____W Va
457.2	4S2L	FC7	1805	†Ferndale_____W Va
460.9	2L2S	FC9	1808	Whitesville___W Va
451.6	3S	FC11	1810	②Jarrolds Valley_____W Va
462.1		FC11½	1811	‡Leevale_____W Va
463.7		FC13	1812	†Rock House___W Va
465.6	3L1S	FC15	1813	Dorothy_____W Va
466.2		FC15½	1814	Sarita_____W Va
468.2	1L1S	FC17	1816	Colcord_____W Va
469.2		FC18	1817	‡Ameagle_____W Va

MARSH FORK SUB-DIVISION

Dist. from Ft. Monroe	Tel. Calls	Station No.	Code No.	STATIONS
461.6	3S	FC11	1810	Jarrolds Valley_____W Va
462.6	S31L	FD1	1830	②Pettus_____W Va
463.6		FD2	1833	Eunice_____W Va
464.6		FD3	1832	†Birchton_____W Va
466.6	2S3L1S	FD5	1835	†Montcoal____W Va
467.4		FD6	1836	†Stickney_____W Va
468.0		FD7	1834	†Jarro_____W Va
469.1	3S	FD8	1837	②Edwight_____W Va

LITTLE MARSH FORK SUB-DIVISION

Dist. from Ft. Monroe	Tel. Calls	Station No.	Code No.	STATIONS
462.6	3S1L	FD1	1830	Pettus_____W Va
464.5		FDA2	1831	†Marfork_____W Va

HAZY CREEK SUB-DIVISION

Dist. from Ft. Monroe	Tel. Calls	Station No.	Code No.	STATIONS
469.1		FD8	1837	Edwight_____W Va
471.1		FDB2	1838	†Hazy Creek____W Va

COAL RIVER SUB-DIVISION

Dist. from Ft. Monroe	Tel. Calls	Station No.	Code No.	STATIONS
465.5	*1L4S	465	1925	④St. Albans_____W Va
467.5		CR2	1927	Indian_____W Va
468.2		CR3	1928	††Calvert_____W Va
470.6	*2S	CR5	1930	†Ferrell_____W Va
471.7	1L3S1L	CR6	1931	†Upper Falls ___W Va
473.8		CR8	1933	†Lincoln_____W Va
475.9		CR10	1935	†Fuqua_____W Va
477.7	1L2S	CR12	1937	Alum Creek____W Va
478.8		CR13	1940	†Forks of Coal__W Va
480.9	*1L	CR15	1942	②Sproul_____W Va
482.1		CR16	1944	Bluetom_____W Va
485.1		CR20	1946	†Dunlapville____W Va
487.6	4S	CR22	1948	MacCorkle____W Va
488.6		CR23	1949	†Dice_____W Va
489.7		CR24	1951	†Irene_____W Va
491.7		CR26	1952	††Adams_____W Va
492.0	2L	CR27	1953	Altman_____W Va
492.5		CR27½	1954	②†Horse Creek Junction_____W Va
493.1		CR28	1955	Julian_____W Va
495.3		CR30	1957	†Lory_____W Va
498.3		CR33	1959	Rock Creek____W Va
499.4		CR34	1960	†Hopkins_____W Va
500.7	*2S1L	CR35	1961	Danville____W Va
502.6	1L3S	CR37	1962	Madison_____W Va
503.0		CR38	2035	②Pond Jct.____W Va
505.5		CR40	1963	Haddleton____W Va
506.1		CR41	1964	†Low Gap_____W Va
507.8		CR42	1965	†Powell Creek__W Va
509.7		CR44	1966	Greenview____W Va
510.7		CR45	1968	†Ramage_____W Va
511.8		CR46	1969	†Secoal_____W Va
513.0		CR48	1970	Jeffrey_____W Va
513.5		CR49	1971	Ottawa_____W Va
514.6	4L	CR50	1973	Clothier_____W Va
515.7		CR51	1975	†Mifflin_____W Va
516.3		CR52	1976	†Dobra_____W Va
517.4	1S1L2S	CR53	1977	②†Sharples____W Va
519.2		CR55	2063	†Five Block____W Va
523.0		CR58	2064	†Spruce Valley_W Va
523.8	1L2S1L	CR59	1982	Blair_____W Va

BIG COAL SUB-DIVISION

Dist. from Ft. Monroe	Tel. Calls	Station No.	Code No.	STATIONS
480.9	*1L	CR15	1942	Sproul_____W Va
482.9	1S2L	BC2	2200	①††Brounland__W Va
483.4		BC3	2201	Hollyhurst____W Va
486.0		BC5	2202	†Emmons_____W Va
487.1		BC6	2203	†Grippe_____W Va
488.3		BC8	2205	Dartmont____W Va
489.8	2L1S	BC9	2206	Ashford_____W Va
491.1		BC10	2208	②Brushton____W Va
492.7		BC12	2209	†Johns_____W Va
494.7	1L1S1L	BC14	2210	Peytona_____W Va
496.1		BC15	2213	†Myrtle_____W Va
496.5		BC16	2214	Racine_____W Va
498.3		BC17	2216	†Toney's Branch_W Va
499.0		BC18	2217	†Sharlow_____W Va
499.7		BC19	2218	†Maxine_____W Va
500.4		BC20	2220	Joe Creek____W Va

BIG COAL SUB-DIVISION
Continued

Dist. from Ft. Monroe	Tel. Calls	Station No.	Code No.	STATIONS
501.8	*3L1S	BC21	2222	②Seth_____W Va
502.8		BC22	2223	†Kirbyton_____W Va
505.2		BC25	2224	Fred_____W Va
507.2		BC26	2225	†Unique_____W Va
508.9		BC27	2226	†Orgas_____W Va
509.2		BC28	2228	†Darby_____W Va
510.2		BC29	2229	†Keith_____W Va
514.4	*1S1L1S	BC33	2232	②Elk Run Jct.__W Va
460.9	2L2S	FC9	1808	Whitesville____W Va (1.4 miles from Elk Run Jct.)

BRUSH CREEK SUB-DIVISION

Dist. from Ft. Monroe	Tel. Calls	Station No.	Code No.	STATIONS
491.1		BC10	2208	Brushton_____W Va
493.1		BCB2	2305	†Easley_____W Va
493.6		BCB3	2302	†Nellis_____W Va
495.1		BCB4	2304	†Ridgeview____W Va

SETH SUB-DIVISION

Dist. from Ft. Monroe	Tel. Calls	Station No.	Code No.	STATIONS
501.8	*3S1L	BC21	2222	Seth_____W Va
504.8		SL3	2234	†Hopkins Fork_W Va
505.7		SL4	2235	†Nelson_____W Va
509.0		SL7	2239	Cabot_____W Va
511.1		SL9	2243	†Prenter_____W Va

ELK RUN SUB-DIVISION

Dist. from Ft. Monroe	Tel. Calls	Station No.	Code No.	STATIONS
514.4	1S1L1S	BC33	2232	Elk Run Jct.___W Va
515.4		ER1	2370	†Janie_____W Va
517.5		ER3	2371	†Blue Pennant__W Va

HORSE CREEK SUB-DIVISION

Dist. from Ft. Monroe	Tel. Calls	Station No.	Code No.	STATIONS
492.5	2L1S	CR27½	1954	†Horse Creek Jct_W Va
492.9		HC1	2020	†Craft_____W Va
494.4		HC2	2022	Woodville____W Va
494.8		HC3	2023	Fork Jct._____W Va
497.4		HC5	2025	†Breece_____W Va
498.0		HC6	2026	†Morrisvale____W Va
499.0		HC7	2027	†Dodson Jct.___W Va
500.4		HC8	2030	†Cameo_____W Va

POND FORK SUB-DIVISION

Dist. from Ft. Monroe	Tel. Calls	Station No.	Code No.	STATIONS
503.0		CR38	2035	Pond Jct._____W Va
504.9		PF2	2036	†Foch_____W Va
506.9		PF4	2037	†Uneeda_____W Va
507.9		PF5	2038	†Quinland____W Va
508.9		PF6	2039	†Reston_____W Va
511.4		PF8	2040	†Lanta_____W Va
512.9		PF10	2041	†Bigson_____W Va
514.5	2S1L3S	PF12	2042	②West Jct.____W Va
515.4		PF13	2068	†Fennimore____W Va
516.4		PF14	2070	†Bob White____W Va
518.1		PF15	2072	Kohlsaat_____W Va
518.8		PF16	2073	†Jackson_____W Va
520.8		PF18	2077	†Bim_____W Va
521.9		PF19	2079	†Wharton_____W Va
522.5		PF20	2080	†Pondco_____W Va
523.4	2L1S1S	PF21	2082	Barrett_____W Va

WEST FORK SUB-DIVISION

Dist. from Ft. Monroe	Tel. Calls	Station No.	Code No.	STATIONS
514.5	2S1L3S	PF12	2042	West Jct._____W Va
514.8		WPF0	2043	Van_____W Va
514.9		WPF½	2046	Essex_____W Va
515.3		WPF1	2044	Van Jct._____W Va
518.6		WPF4	2049	Marnie_____W Va
523.9		WPF8	2047	Robinhood____W Va
524.3				End of line____W Va

WHITES BRANCH SUB-DIVISION

Dist. from Ft. Monroe	Tel. Calls	Station No.	Code No.	STATIONS
515.3		WPF1	2045	†Van Jct._____W Va
515.8		WPW1	2044	†Gordon_____W Va
517.7				End of Line____W Va

BEECH CREEK SUB-DIVISION

Dist. from Ft. Monroe	Tel. Calls	Station No.	Code No.	STATIONS
517.4	1S1L2S	CR53	1977	†Sharples_____W Va
518.4		CB2	2060	†Monclo_____W Va

LOGAN SUB-DIVISION RAILROAD

Dist. from Ft. Monroe	Tel. Calls	Station No.	Code No.	STATIONS
494.7	*BR	495	2525	Barboursville _W Va
500.1		X5	2531	Martha_____W Va
504.6		X10	2535	Inez_____W Va
505.8		X13	2536	Roach_____W Va
508.8		X14	2538	Salt Rock____W Va
511.9	WA	X17	2540	West Hamlin__W Va
514.0	*WH	X19		†W. H. Cabin__W Va
515.6		X21	2542	Sheridan____W Va
517.2	BN	X22	2545	Branchland__W Va
518.7		X24	2546	†Hubball____W Va
521.1	MF	X26	2548	Midkiff_____W Va
523.1		X28	2549	†Brady_____W Va
524.7		X30		†N. G. Cabin__W Va
526.0	*RG	X31	2551	Ranger_____W Va
529.6		X35	2553	Lattin_____W Va
531.1	GI	X36	2554	Gill_____W Va
534.8		X40	2557	Sand Creek___W Va
537.1		X42	2559	†Atenville____W Va
538.8		X44	2561	Harts_____W Va
540.0		X46	2562	Ferrellsburg___W Va
541.3		X47	2565	†Fry_____W Va
543.3		X49	2565	†Toney_____W Va
544.4			2564	†Baber_____W Va
544.9	*BC	X50	2566	Big Creek____W Va
546.1		X51	2567	†Stone Branch_W Va
546.5	SA	X51½	2568	Kitchen_____W Va
549.1		X54	2570	Chapmanville_ W Va
550.7		X56	2571	†Phico_____W Va
551.9		X57	2572	†Godby_____W Va
553.4		X58	2575	Pecks Mill____W Va
556.3		X62	2578	②Henlawson__W Va
558.1	*OB	X64	2579	Peach Creek__W Va
559.8	*FD			F. D. Cabin___W Va
560.1		X65	2581	②④**Logan**____W Va
561.9		X67	2583	②†Stollings____W Va
562.7		X68	2584	†McConnell____W Va
563.6	*SW			S. W. Cabin___W Va
565.5	1L1S1L	X70	2586	②††Rum Jct.___W Va
566.9		X72	2588	†Lyburn_____W Va
568.0		X73	2590	†Neibert_____W Va
569.4		X74	2592	†Wilber_____W Va
570.0		X75	2593	†Manbar_____W Va
570.2	3S	X76	2594	†Earling_____W Va
571.8	1L3S1L	X77	2595	Taplin_____W Va
573.3	4S	X79	2597	②Man_____W Va
576.7		RH-3	2596	Garnette_____W Va
573.9	2S1L	X80	2598	②†Huff Jct.____W Va
574.3		X81	2801	†Hunt_____W Va
576.0		X82	2601	†Landville____W Va
577.0		X83	2602	†Bruno_____W Va
577.7	3S2L	X84	2603	†Christian____W Va
578.7	3S1L	X85	2604	②†Wylo_____W Va
579.7		X86	2606	†Verner_____W Va
582.4		X88	2609	†Kimberling__W Va
583.6		X90	2810	†Tamcliff____W Va
585.2	2S1L1S	X92	2779	West Gilbert__W Va

MERRILL SUB-DIVISION

Dist. from Ft. Monroe	Tel. Calls	Station No.	Code No.	STATIONS
556.3		X62	2578	Henlawson____W Va
558.8				End of Line____W Va

ISLAND CREEK SUB-DIVISION

Dist. from Ft. Monroe	Tel. Calls	Station No.	Code No.	STATIONS
560.1		X65	2581	Logan_____W Va
560.8	2S	IC1	2650	②†Monitor Jct_W Va
561.1		IC1½	2651	†Gay_____W Va
561.3	1S2L1S	IC2	2670	②†Mud Jct.____W Va
561.5		IC2	2653	†Shamrock____W Va
562.9	1L2S	IC3	2654	②Whitman Jct.__W Va
564.3	1L3S	IC5	2658	②Holden_____W Va
565.7			2662	End of Track__W Va

LOGAN AND SOUTHERN SUB-DIVISION

Dist. from Ft. Monroe	Tel. Calls	Station No.	Code No.	STATIONS
560.8	2S	IC1	2650	†Monitor Jct.___W Va
561.7	1S2L	LS1	2680	†Wilkinson____W Va
563.5		LS3	2683	†Monaville____W Va
564.6	2S2L	LS4	2684	†Rossmore____W Va
566.3	3S	LS5	2686	†Switzer_____W Va
566.8		LS6	2692	†Micco_____W Va
567.9	1S2L	LS7	2889	†Chauncey____W Va
568.7	4S	LS8	2690	†②Omar_____W Va
569.5		LS9	2692	†Barnabas____W Va
571.0		LS11	2695	②Stirrat_____W Va
572.3		LS13	2697	†Sarah Ann____W Va

Legend:

4-Coupon Stations.

*-Day and Night Telegraph Office.

1-Junction with connecting line.

2-Junction of Sub-division shown elsewhere.

6-Established for operating purposes only-not a station for passengers or freight business.

3-Within switching limits of Newport News; carload freight should be waybilled to Newport News, Va.

†-No Siding.

‡-Private Siding only.

Dist. from Ft. Monroe	Tel. Calls	Station No.	Code No.	STATIONS	Dist. from Ft. Monroe	Tel. Calls	Station No.	Code No.	STATIONS	Dist. from Ft. Monroe	Tel. Calls	Station No.	Code No.	STATIONS
				PINE CREEK SUB-DIVISION					**BUFFALO SUB-DIVISION** Continued					**BIG SANDY SUB-DIVISION** Continued
568.7	4S	LS8	2690	†Omar_____W Va	578.6	1S1L1S	XC6	2768	‡Amherstdale___W Va	587.0	*BG	S73	4074	②④Prestonsburg___Ky
574.0		LSP6	2691	‡Pine Creek____W Va	579.5		XC7	2769	†Robinette_____W Va	590.7		S78	4081	Bull Creek_____Ky
					581.1	3L1S	XC8	2770	††Latrobe_____W Va	593.4				E. M. Cabin_____Ky
				LITTLE CREEK SUB-DIVISION	582.4		XC9	2771	†Crites_____W Va	594.0		S81	4085	†Emma_____Ky
571.0		LS11	2695	‡Stirrat_____W Va	582.9		XC9½	2773	†Stowe_____W Va	596.1		S83	4087	Dwale_____Ky
572.3				‡End of Line____W Va	583.2		XC10	2774	‡Lundale_____W Va	596.8	*BI	S84	4088	②†Beaver Jct____Ky
					583.8	2L	XC11	2775	†Craneco_____W Va	597.0		S85	4089	Allen_____Ky
				MUD FORK SUB-DIVISION	585.0	1S1L	XC12	2777	Lorado_____W Va	598.8		S86	4090	Banner_____Ky
561.3	1S2L1S	IC1½	2670	†Mud Jct_____W Va	586.3		XC14	2778	‡Pardee_____W Va	601.2	*X	S88	4091	Ivel_____Ky
562.7		MF2	2671	†Verdun_____W Va	588.9		XC17		†Saunders_____W Va	603.2		S89	4096	Tram_____Ky
563.5		MF3	2672	Manus_____W Va					**HUFF CREEK SUB-DIVISION**	604.9		S91	4093	‡Betsy Layne___Ky
564.4		MF4	2673	‡Argonne_____W Va	573.9	2S1L	X80	2598	†Huff Jct_____W Va	606.6	*HD	S93	4094	‡Harold_____Ky
					575.6		XD2	2800	†Mallory_____W Va	608.1		S95	4095	†Boldman_____Ky
				WHITMAN CREEK SUB-DIVISION	576.3		XD3	2802	‡Huffsville_____W Va	609.8		S96	4097	‡Broad Bottom__Ky
562.9	1L2S	IC3	2654	†Whitman Jct__W Va					**ELK CREEK SUB-DIVISION**	611.0		S97	4098	†Mossy Bottom__Ky
564.1		WC2	2655	‡Whitman_____W Va	578.7	3S1L	X85	2604	†Wylo_____W Va	612.9		S101	4104	‡Big Shoal_____Ky
567.5		WC5	2656	‡Mine No. 20___W Va	580.0		XE2	2605	‡Emmett_____W Va	613.6		S102	4105	‡Coalrun_____Ky
					582.4				End of Track___W Va	615.1		S103	4107	‡Pauley_____Ky
				TRACE FORK SUB-DIVISION						617.9	*KN	S104	4110	④Pikeville_____Ky
564.3	1L3S	IC5	2658	Holden_____W Va					**Ashland Division**	620.2		S107	4112	Island Creek___Ky
566.6		TC2	2659	‡Mine No. 21___W Va					**BIG SANDY SUB-DIVISION**	622.4	FO	S109		F. O. Cabin____Ky
					513.3	*BS	513	4000	Big Sandy Jct___Ky	627.7		S110	4113	‡Kewanee_____Ky
				DINGESS RUN SUB-DIVISION	516.5		S3	4003	‡Leach_____Ky	624.5	FD	S111	4115	‡Fords Branch___Ky
561.9	3S1L1S	X67	2583	‡Stollings_____W Va	517.9		S5	4005	Savage Branch__Ky	625.8		S112	4116	②†Shelby Jct____Ky
562.9		XA1	2709	‡Melville_____W Va	520.6		S7	4007	Lockwood_____Ky	626.3	*SY	S113	4117	④Shelby_____Ky
563.8		XA2	2710	†Fort Branch____W Va	520.9				W. D. Cabin____Ky	628.5		S115	4121	††Sutton_____Ky
565.0		XA3	2711	‡Wanda_____W Va	523.7		S11	4010	Burnaugh_____Ky	629.6	LJ			⑥②Levisa Jct____Ky
565.4		XA3½	2712	‡Rex_____W Va	526.1		S13	4013	Buchanan_____Ky	629.7		S116	4123	Millard_____Ky
565.9	2S2L	XA4	2713	②†Ethel_____W Va	529.0		S16	5016	Zelda_____Ky	631.6		S118	4125	†Winright_____Ky
567.3		XA5	2714	‡Ethel No. 2____W Va	530.8		S17	4017	††Catalpa_____Ky	633.5	*MA	S120	4127	②Marrowbone___Ky
567.5				End of Line____W Va	532.9		S20	4020	Fullers_____Ky	635.2		S122	4128	②R. C. Junction_Ky
					533.9		S21	4021	††Potters_____Ky	636.7		S123	4131	†Draffin_____Ky
				GEORGES CREEK SUB-DIVISION	537.9	*UX	S25	4025	④Louisa_____Ky	638.5		S124	4132	†Belcher_____Ky
565.9	2S2L	XA4	2713	‡Ethel_____W Va	540.3		S27	4027	Holt_____Ky	640.0		S127	4134	†Dunleary_____Ky
566.7		XAG1	2715	‡Freeze Fork___W Va	540.5		S28	4028	†Walbridge____Ky	640.1	DJ			⑥②Dunleary Jct___Ky
567.4		XAG2	2717	†Moran_____W Va	543.3		S30		Torchlight_____Ky	640.4		S127½	4135	Federal_____Ky
568.2		XAG3	2716	†Hetzel_____W Va	546.0	*CN	S33	4033	Chapman_____Ky	641.2	RO	S128	4136	①Elkhorn City___Ky
					546.9		S34	4034	†Gallup_____Ky	642.0	YD	S129	4138	①Elkhorn City Jct_Ky
				RUM CREEK SUB-DIVISION	549.2		S36	4036	†Beech Farm___Ky					
565.5	1L1S1L	X70	2586	††Rum Jct_____W Va	551.0		S38	4038	†Kise_____Ky					**ROAD CREEK SUB-DIVISION**
565.9		XB1	2730	‡Dabney_____W Va	552.1		S39	4039	‡Georges Creek_Ky	635.2		S122	4128	‡R. C. Junction__Ky
567.0	1L3S	XB2	2732	‡Dehu_____W Va	553.3		S42	4041	†Ben Bow_____Ky	637.9		SX3	4295	‡Republic_____Ky
567.5		XB2½	2733	†Hutchinson___W Va	555.9		S43	4043	Richardson_____Ky					
568.0		XB3	2735	‡Orville_____W Va	556.8				J. B. Cabin____Ky					**MIDDLE CREEK SUB-DIVISION**
568.5		XB3½	2734	Cham_____W Va	557.8		S44	4045	Patrick_____Ky	587.0	*BG	S73	4074	Prestonsburg____Ky
569.9		XB3¾	2736	†Argyle_____W Va	558.8		S45	4046	††Ray_____Ky	590.7		PE4	4077	†Whitaker_____Ky
570.2		XB4	2737	†Yolyn_____W Va	561.4		S46	4048	Henrietta_____Ky	593.0		PE6	4078	†Buckeye_____Ky
572.1	3L	XB6	2739	††Slagle_____W Va	564.2	*WN	S51	4051	White House____Ky	593.8		PE6½	4083	‡Samson_____Ky
					566.2		S53	4053	†River_____Ky	594.4		PE7	4080	†Permele_____Ky
				BUFFALO SUB-DIVISION	567.1		S54	4055	Offutt_____Ky	596.2		PE9	4075	‡David_____Ky
573.3	4S	X79	2597	Man_____W Va	569.2		S56	4057	††Bobbs_____Ky					
574.2		XC1	2760	‡Kistler_____W Va	570.5		S57	4058	†Buskirk_____Ky					**DAWKINS SUB-DIVISION**
575.8	2S1L2S	XC2	2762	††Lax_____W Va	571.1				B. U. Cabin____Ky	574.5		S62	4065	†Dawkins_____Ky
576.6	2L1S	XC4	2763	‡Accoville_____W Va	572.2		S59	4060	‡Thealka_____Ky	575.5		BSK1	4140	†Hager Hill____Ky
577.2		XC5	2764	‡Braeholm_____W Va	573.2	*CD	S60	4061	④Paintsville____Ky	577.0		BSK2½	4139	†Paints_____Ky
577.9		XC5½	2766	†Fanco_____W Va	574.5		S62	4065	②Dawkins_____Ky	577.4		BSK3	4142	†Collista_____Ky
578.2		XC5¾	2767	‡Becco_____W Va	575.0		S63	4067	②Van Lear Jct___Ky	579.5		BSK5	4145	†Denver_____Ky
					579.1		S66	4068	East Point_____Ky	580.5		BSK6	4147	‡Asa_____Ky
					580.4				⑥Johns Creek___Ky	581.0		BSK7	4149	†Fitch_____Ky
					580.7	*AR	S67	4069	Auxier_____Ky	582.0		BSK7½	4151	†Leander_____Ky
					581.6				O. X. Cabin____Ky	582.3		BSK8	4153	†Dobson_____Ky
					582.9		S70	4071	†Bays Branch___Ky	583.8		BSK9	4156	‡Riceville_____Ky
										588.5		BSK14	4162	††Ivyton_____Ky
										592.7		BSK18	4165	Royalton_____Ky

DAWKINS SUB-DIVISION Continued

Dist. from Ft. Monroe	Tel. Calls	Station No.	Code No.	STATIONS
594.5		BSK20	4168	‡West Royalton...Ky
595.5		BSK21	4170	‡Sublett...Ky
598.2		BSK24	4173	†‡Carver...Ky
599.5		BSK25	4175	‡End of Line...Ky

MILLERS CREEK SUB-DIVISION

Dist. from Ft. Monroe	Tel. Calls	Station No.	Code No.	STATIONS
575.0		S63	4067	Van Lear Jct...Ky
575.5		MC½	4354	†‡West Van Lear...Ky
576.6		MC1½	4362	Supply House...Ky
577.0		MC2	4372	‡Van Lear...Ky
577.7		MC3	4384	†Van Lear No. 4...Ky
578.8		MC4	4388	‡Van Lear No. 155..Ky
579.3		MC4½	4399	‡End of Line...Ky

ELKHORN AND BEAVER VALLEY SUB-DIVISION

Dist. from Ft. Monroe	Tel. Calls	Station No.	Code No.	STATIONS
596.8	*BI	S84	4088	†‡Beaver Jct...Ky
598.5		BV2	4086	†Colliver...Ky
599.8		BV3	4200	†Arkansas...Ky
601.6	*MN	BV5	4202	Martin...Ky
601.8				②⑥Martin Jct...Ky
603.0		BV6	4203	②Dinwood...Ky
604.4		BV8	4205	‡Warco...Ky
605.5		BV9	4206	Maytown...Ky
608.3		BV11	4210	†‡Eastern...Ky
609.4		BV12	4212	†Northern...Ky
610.0		BV14	4213	‡Midas...Ky
612.0		BV15	4215	Bosco...Ky
613.6		BV16	4217	‡Welco...Ky
614.0		BV18	4218	Garrett...Ky
614.2		BV17¼	4235	†Garrett Jct...Ky
614.7	PJ	BV17½	4226	†②Porter Jct...Ky
615.3		BV18	4219	Lackey...Ky
616.5		BV19	4220	Estill...Ky
616.9		BV20	4222	‡Glo...Ky
617.6	WK	BV21	4221	②Wayland...Ky

LONG FORK SUB-DIVISION

Dist. from Ft. Monroe	Tel. Calls	Station No.	Code No.	STATIONS
601.8				⑥Martin Jct...Ky
601.6	*MN	BV5	4202	Martin...Ky
602.9		LFB1½	4411	Hite...Ky
603.6		LFB2	4414	†Garth...Ky
604.7		LFB3	4416	Salisbury...Ky
606.6		LFB5	4417	†Hunter...Ky
607.6		LFB6	4422	‡Jump...Ky
608.6		LFB7	4424	Drift...Ky
609.6		LFB8	4430	†‡Lane Siding...Ky
610.0		LFB8½	4440	‡Gibson...Ky
611.5		LFB10	4445	‡McDowell...Ky
613.7		LFB12	4448	Orkney...Ky
616.5		LFB15	4449	†‡Price...Ky
617.7	CJ	LFB16	4450	②†Clear Creek JctKy
619.9		LFB18	4464	Buckingham...Ky
620.6		LFB19	4468	②Jack's Creek...Ky
621.4		LFB19½	4469	‡Burton...Ky
621.8	WJ	LFB20	4473	②‡WheelwrightJctKy
623.4		LFB22	4480	†Melvin...Ky
624.8	2S	LFB23	4495	Weeksbury...Ky
626.2		LFB25	4498	‡East Weeksbury..Ky

CLEAR CREEK SUB-DIVISION

Dist. from Ft. Monroe	Tel. Calls	Station No.	Code No.	STATIONS
617.7	CJ	LFB16	4450	†Clear Creek Jct..Ky
618.2		LFB16½	4463	Hi-Hat...Ky
619.7		CC2	4459	†Lambert...Ky
621.9		CC4	4460	Ligon...Ky

JACKS CREEK SUB-DIVISION

Dist. from Ft. Monroe	Tel. Calls	Station No.	Code No.	STATIONS
620.6		LFB19	4468	‡Jack's Creek...Ky
620.9				‡End of Line...Ky

WHEELWRIGHT SUB-DIVISION

Dist. from Ft. Monroe	Tel. Calls	Station No.	Code No.	STATIONS
621.8	WJ	LFB20	4473	‡Wheelwright Jct..Ky
623.4		WW1½	4475	Wheelwright...Ky
623.5				End of Line...Ky

STEPHENS SUB-DIVISION

Dist. from Ft. Monroe	Tel. Calls	Station No.	Code No.	STATIONS
603.0		BV6	4203	Dinwood...Ky
605.0		ST2	4224	‡Marrs...Ky

JONES FORK SUB-DIVISION

Dist. from Ft. Monroe	Tel. Calls	Station No.	Code No.	STATIONS
614.7	PJ	BV17½	4226	†Porter Jct...Ky
616.6		JF2		‡End of Line...Ky

STEELE CREEK SUB-DIVISION

Dist. from Ft. Monroe	Tel. Calls	Station No.	Code No.	STATIONS
617.6		BV21	4221	Wayland...Ky
619.1				‡End of Line...Ky

SANDY VALLEY AND ELKHORN SUB-DIVISION

Dist. from Ft. Monroe	Tel. Calls	Station No.	Code No.	STATIONS
625.8		S112	4116	†Shelby Jct...Ky
628.0		SV2½	4901	†Richam...Ky
629.2		SV3½	4903	‡Collins...Ky
629.8		SV4	4907	Yeager...Ky
631.4		SV5½	4910	‡Robinson Creek..Ky
632.0		SV6	4913	†Douglas...Ky
633.3		SV7½	4915	‡Esco...Ky
634.0		SV8	4918	Penny...Ky
636.5		SV10½	4922	Virgie...Ky
638.0		SV12	4925	‡Ellwood...Ky
642.0		SV15	4932	†Myra...Ky
643.1		SV17½	4933	Herman Sdg...Ky
643.6		SV18	4934	†‡Dorton...Ky
645.7		SV20	4939	†Elimer...Ky
648.5		SV22½	4944	Shelby Gap...Ky
648.9		SV23	4945	†28 Bridge...Ky
649.8		SV24	4946	†Adamson...Ky
651.5		SV25½	4953	†Burdine...Ky
652.2		SV26½	4956	†Gaskill...Ky
653.9	D	SV28	4965	④**Jenkins**...Ky
655.6		SV30	4980	‡Dunham...Ky
656.3		SV30½	4999	‡End of Track...Ky

MARROWBONE SUB-DIVISION

Dist. from Ft. Monroe	Tel. Calls	Station No.	Code No.	STATIONS
633.5	MA	S120	4127	Marrowbone...Ky
634.6		MB1	4275	†Wolf Pit...Ky
635.0		MB2	4276	‡Ratliff...Ky
636.8		MB3	4277	†Venters...Ky
637.7		MB4	4278	‡Rockhouse...Ky
639.3		MB6	4280	Lookout...Ky
639.7		MB6½	4281	‡Henry Clay...Ky
640.3		MB7	4283	‡Big Branch...Ky
641.3		MB8	4285	Hellier...Ky
641.5		MB8½	4286	‡Greenough...Ky
643.3		MB10	4288	‡Manco...Ky

LEVISA RIVER SUB-DIVISION

Dist. from Ft. Monroe	Tel. Calls	Station No.	Code No.	STATIONS
629.6	LV			⑥Levisa Jct...Ky
630.4		SR1	4180	Slones Branch ...Ky
642.2		SR13	4185	‡Rowe...Ky
644.0		SR14	4187	Lick Creek...Ky
649.5		SR20	4189	Nigh...Ky
652.3		SR22	4191	‡Dunlap...Ky

BEAVER CREEK SUB-DIVISION

Dist. from Ft. Monroe	Tel. Calls	Station No.	Code No.	STATIONS
640.1				⑥Dunleary Jct...Ky
643.9		BC4	4133	‡Mikegrady...Ky

LEXINGTON SUB-DIVISION

Dist. from Ft. Monroe	Tel. Calls	Station No.	Code No.	STATIONS
519.2	*AU	520	4509	④**Ashland**...Ky
	DS			" Dispr's Office...
519.5	*AX	521	4510	Ashland Jct...Ky
520.6		L1	4511	‡Gulfco...Ky
522.1		L2	4512	‡Winslow...Ky
524.3		L5	4516	‡Summit...Ky
526.3		L7	4518	Meads...Ky
527.9		L8	4520	†Hicarbon...Ky
528.2		L9	4519	†Bartell...Ky
528.8		L10	4521	Princess...Ky
530.4		L11	4522	‡Coalton...Ky
531.5		L12	4523	‡Bailey Mine...Ky
532.3		L13	4525	Kilgore...Ky
532.8	*KS	L14	4526	Rush...Ky
534.7		L15	4527	†Norton Branch..Ky
536.1		L17	4529	Grant...Ky
536.9		L18	4530	†Music...Ky
538.2		L19	4531	Williams Creek..Ky
539.0		L20	4532	†Burdette...Ky
540.6		L21	4533	†Denton...Ky
541.4		L22	4535	†Strait Creek...Ky
542.5		L23	4536	Mt. Savage...Ky

LEXINGTON SUB-DIVISION Continued

Dist. from Ft. Monroe	Tel. Calls	Station No.	Code No.	STATIONS
544.1		L25	4537	‡Little Fork...Ky
544.7	*JX	L26	4538	Hitchins...Ky
547.7		L28	4540	Leon...Ky
549.8		L30	4542	†Fultz...Ky
552.0	*A	L33	4544	Aden...Ky
553.0		L33½	4543	‡Oats...Ky
553.5	GN	L34	4545	‡Grahn...Ky
555.5		L36	4547	Corey...Ky
556.7		L37	4549	†‡Mountain Top...Ky
558.8		L39½	4551	‡Atlas...Ky
559.4	*OV	L40	4552	④**Olive Hill**...Ky
560.5		L41	4553	‡Parks...Ky
563.8		L44	4557	‡Lawton...Ky
564.2		L45	4558	‡Silica...Ky
565.7	RS	L46	4560	Enterprise...Ky
567.4		L48	4564	‡Hayward...Ky
567.9		L48½	4566	‡Bradmeyer...Ky
568.2		L49	4565	Soldier...Ky
569.8	HM	L51	4567	Haldeman...Ky
571.2		L52	4568	†Hayes Crossing..Ky
572.3		L53	4569	Gates...Ky
575.6		L56	4571	Rodburn...Ky
576.5		L57	4572	‡Christy...Ky
577.7	*RY	L58	4575	①④**Morehead**...Ky
578.5		L59	4576	†Brady...Ky
583.2		L64	4579	†Bluestone...Ky
585.7	FB	L66½	4582	Farmer...Ky
588.0		L68	4584	†Midland...Ky
589.4	ME	L70	4586	④Salt Lick...Ky
594.2		L75	4590	Olympia...Ky
597.6	*PN	L78	4593	Preston...Ky
602.1		L83	4598	Stepstone...Ky
606.4		L87	4601	Ewington...Ky
609.5	*GR	L90	4604	④**Mt. Sterling**...Ky
610.4		L91	4605	‡New Market...Ky
612.7		L93	4607	†Prewitt...Ky
613.6		L94	4608	†Klondike...Ky
615.5		L96	4610	†Thomson...Ky
616.8		L98	4611	†Hedges...Ky
617.8		L99	4612	L. & E. Jct...Ky
620.3		L102	4614	†Fox...Ky
624.4	*W	L105	4616	①④**Winchester**...Ky
626.5		L107	4619	†Nelson...Ky
629.3		L110	4621	†Colby...Ky
630.2		L111	4622	†Tebbs...Ky
632.2		L113	4624	Pine Grove...Ky
634.8		L115	4626	Chilesburg...Ky
636.1		L117	4628	†Walnut Hill...Ky
637.9		L118	4630	†Brighton...Ky
638.8		L		Sharon...Ky
693.3		L120	4631	Propane...Ky
641.8	*NS	L122	4633	Netherland...Ky
642.9		L124	4634	①②④**Lexington**...Ky
	VX		4632	" Union Station...Ky
			4633	" Baggage...

LOUISVILLE SUB-DIVISION

(Operate over leased L&N Tracks Lexington to Louisville)

Dist. from Ft. Monroe	Tel. Calls	Station No.	Code No.	STATIONS
642.9	VX	L124	4634	①④Lexington...Ky
646.4		L127		Viley...Ky
649.9		L131		Yarnallton...Ky
653.5		L134		Paynes...Ky
657.0	SU	L138		**Midway**...Ky
660.9		L142		Spring Station...Ky
663.9		L145		Duckers...Ky
666.4		L147		Jetts...Ky
671.3		L152		Cliffside...Ky
671.6	F	L153		**Frankfort**...Ky
672.5		L154		West Frankfort..Ky
677.3		L158		Benson...Ky
680.5		L161		†Hatton...Ky
681.0		L161½		Gath...Ky
685.0		L166		Bagdad...Ky
687.5	*CB	L168		Lewis...Ky
695.8		L177		**Shelbyville**...Ky
699.7		L181		Scotts...Ky
703.7		L185		Simpsonville...Ky
707.8		L190		Long Run...Ky
709.5		L192		Eastwood...Ky
712.5		L194		Avoca...Ky
714.9	*B	L196		**Anchorage**...Ky
715.7		L197		Lakeland...Ky
718.6		L200		Lyndon...Ky

Legend:

4-Coupon Stations.

*-Day and Night Telegraph Office.

1-Junction with connecting line.

2-Junction of Sub-division shown elsewhere.

6-Established for operating purposes only-not a station for passengers or freight business.

3-Within switching limits of Newport News; carload freight should be waybilled to Newport News, Va.

†-No Siding.

‡-Private Siding only.

Dist. from Ft. Monroe	Tel. Calls	Station No.	Code No.	STATIONS
				LOUISVILLE SUB-DIVISION — Continued
721.4	MA	L203		St. Matthews____Ky
725.2	MN	L206		East Louisville___Ky
726.9	*FH	L208	4635	1④Louisville____Ky
	*GI			" Yard Office_____
	AK		4638	" City Tkt. Office___
	*JA		4636	" Central Station___
			4637	" Baggage_____
				Russell Division
523.9		524	4705	④Russell_____Ky
524.5	*RU	524		R. U. Cabin____Ky
526.0	*MS	525		M. S. Cabin____Ky
526.1		526	4706	Raceland_____Ky
527.5		527	4707	Raceland Jct.___Ky
528.7		529	4710	Wurtland_____Ky
529.4		530	4711	Kico_____Ky
				Cincinnati Division
531.7	*M	532	4713	Riverton_____Ky
532.4	GK	533	4714	Greenup_____Ky
536.1		536	4716	Oliver_____Ky
537.7		538	4718	Gray's Branch___Ky
539.4		540	4720	††D. G. Cabin___Ky
540.3		540	4721	Edgington_____Ky
541.9		542	4723	Limeville_____Ky
542.9	*NJ	543	4724	②N. J. Cabin_____Ky
544.2		545	4725	Siloam_____Ky
546.1		546	4727	Frost_____Ky
547.9		548	4729	Taylor_____Ky
548.7		549	4730	Fullerton_____Ky
550.5	SV	551	4732	④So. Portsmouth_Ky
		551	4733	④Portsmouth___Ohio
553.3		553	4735	Kirkville_____Ky
554.2		554	4736	Fire Brick_____Ky
555.7	*GN	555		††G. N. Cabin___Ky
556.7		557	4740	St. Paul_____Ky
560.3		561	4742	Quincy_____Ky
562.1	KD	562	4745	Lloyd_____Ky
563.0		563	4746	Garrison_____Ky
567.6		568	4749	†Buena Vista___Ky
572.0		572	4753	④Vanceburg____Ky
576.8		577	4760	Rome (Stout, O.)Ky
579.4		580	4762	Carrs_____Ky
581.5		582	4764	†Chalkley_____Ky
	*CD	583		C. D. Cabin____Ky
583.8		584	4766	Concord_____Ky
586.7		587	4769	†Pence_____Ky
588.5		588	4771	†Irwin_____Ky
590.8		591	4774	Trinity_____Ky
592.0		592	4777	†Sand Hill_____Ky
595.9		596	4780	Springdale_____Ky
598.0		598	4782	‡Bates_____Ky
598.7		599	4784	Fair Grounds___Ky
601.0		601	4786	L. & N. Jct._____Ky
601.7	*RT	602	4787	1④Maysville____Ky
606.3		607	4792	††Duke_____Ky
610.1		610	4795	South Ripley___Ky
		610	4796	④Ripley_____Ohio (Via Ferry.)
612.4	DV	613	4798	Dover_____Ky

Dist. from Ft. Monroe	Tel. Calls	Station No.	Code No.	STATIONS
				CINCINNATTI DIVISION — Continued
617.0		617	4800	†Higginsport___Ky
618.9	AG	619	4801	④Augusta_____Ky
623.9		623	4805	†Rock Springs___Ky
624.6	WG	624	4806	Wellsburg_____Ky
627.0		627	4809	Bradford_____Ky
628.3		628	4810	‡Willow Grove___Ky
630.8		631	4813	Foster_____Ky
633.9		634	4814	Carntown_____Ky
635.1		635	4815	Ivor_____Ky
637.0		637	4817	Mentor_____Ky
637.9		638	4819	†Beagle_____Ky
639.5		639	4821	California_____Ky
642.3		642	4825	New Richmond__Ky
				New Richmond_Ohio
643.1		643	4827	†Dam No. 35___Ky
644.1		644	4829	Oneonta_____Ky
647.7		648	4831	Ross_____Ky
649.7		650	4833	Melbourne_____Ky
650.5	*CS	651		C. S. Cabin____Ky
651.1		652	4837	Stevens_____Ky
652.6		653	4838	Coney_____Ky
653.6		654	4840	Brent_____Ky
654.8		655	4841	Altamont_____Ky
655.6		656	4843	Water Works___Ky
658.8		659	4845	Dayton_____Ky
659.7		660	4847	Bellevue_____Ky
661.0	*NX	662	4850	①Newport_____Ky
662.6		663	4853	K. C. Jct._____Ky
663.4		663½	4855	①Covington (K. C. Junction)___Ky
	*DI			" Tel. Office_____
663.7		664	4856	④Covington (Pike St.)_____Ky
				(12th St.)_____
		666	4857	④Cincinnati____Ohio
664.9	*GC		5000	④ " Union Terminal_
			5001	④ " Baggage_____
	*MD		5002	" M. D. Tower Rose St_____
			5003	" City Ticket Office, 110 Dixie Terminal
				" 4th Street_____
1.5				B. & O. Jct., 8th St_____Ohio
				Dining Cars_____
3.2	*BI	CL3	7003	Brighton_____Ohio / Yard Office_____Ohio
6.9	*YD	CL6	7007	②Cheviot_____Ohio
				NORTHERN SUB-DIVISION
542.9	*NJ	542.9	4724	†N. J. Cabin____Ky
553.3		CN10	6007	Minford_____O
554.2	*WR	CN11	6005	††Wheeler_____O
561.0		CN17	6014	Stockdale_____O
566.5	RB	CN23	6018	Robbins_____O
569.7	G	CN26	6020	①Greggs_____O
576.8	*GB	CN34		††G. B. Cabin____O
583.8	*RA	CN40	6036	†R. A. Junction___O
588.4		CN44	6040	①Vauces_____O
589.8	*VA	CN46	6046	①V. A. Junction___O
596.5		CN54	6049	Hopetown_____O
600.8		CN57		K. N. Cabin_____O
612.4	*SC	CN69	6056	††Scippo_____O

Dist. from Ft. Monroe	Tel. Calls	Station No.	Code No.	STATIONS
				NORTHERN SUB-DIVISION — Continued
615.5		CN73	6064	‡Sturm and Dillard Siding_____O
624.7		CN81	6079	††Fite_____O
634.8	*CH	CN91		‡C. H. Cabin_____O
636.8	*PA	HV0	6089	②Parsons_____O
				Hocking Division
				TOLEDO SUB-DIVISION
636.8	*PA	HV0	6089	②Parsons_____O
637.7		HV1	6267	①South Columbus__O
640.0		HV3	6264	Columbus (Mound Street)_____O
			6092	④Columbus (City Office)_____
642.0	*RN	HV5	6091	④Columbus (Union Station)_____
641.6			6090	①Columbus (Freight Station)_____
645.7		HV9	6105	Ackerman_____O
647.3		HV11	6107	‡Jewetts_____O
650.0	OD	HV13	6111	Linworth_____O
655.0		HV18	6115	Powell_____O
656.6	*WY	HV20	6119	Powell Wye_____O
657.6		HV21	6121	‡Industrial Switch__O
659.1		HV22	6123	Hyatts_____O
664.8	*WA	HV28	6130	①④Delaware_____O
671.4	NA	HV35	6138	Meredith_____O
676.5	RS	HV40	6144	Prospect_____O
681.3		HV45	6149	Owens_____O
685.3	*MA	HV49	6154	M. A. Cabin_____O
686.2			6156	①Marion (Freight Station)_____
686.3		HV50	6157	④Marion (Union Station)_____
687.2	*MD	HV51	6159	M. D. Cabin_____O
694.0	*JS	HV57	6167	Morral_____O
698.1	FR	HV62	6173	Harpster_____O
704.6	*SA	HV68	6181	①④Upper Sandusky O
711.8		HV74	6190	Crawford_____O
714.4	*C	HV78	6193	①④Carey_____O
721.4	*VA	HV85	6203	Alveda_____O
728.5	*BD	HV92	6212	B. & O. Crossing___O
729.1	*FA	HV93	6213	①④Fostoria_____O
			6214	" Tkt. Office_____
736.6	RU	HV100	6224	Rising Sun_____O
740.4	*DN	HV104	6229	Bradner_____O
746.3	MR	HV110	6235	Pemberville_____O
752.4	*MN	HV116	6243	LeMoyne_____O
755.8	*VR	HV119	6247	V. R. Tower_____O
758.9	*WB	HV122	6251	①Walbridge_____O
760.9		HV124	6254	①Rockwell Jct.____O
764.0		HV127	6258	Toledo Docks____O
767.0	DK	HV130	6259	Presque Isle_____O
	H		6263	④Toledo (City Office)_____
			6260	①Toledo_____O
763.4	BR	HV125	6261	④Toledo Union Depot_____O
			6262	" Baggage_____

ATHENS SUB-DIVISION

Dist. from Ft. Monroe	Tel. Calls	Station No.	Code No.	STATIONS
636.8	*PA	HV0	6089	Parsons_____O
639.2	*SK	HVA2	6274	①Valley Crossing___O
641.8		HVA5	6277	‡Big Walnut_____O
643.6	G	HVA7	6280	①Groveport_____O
647.7	W	HVA11	6285	Canal Winchester__O
651.1		HVA14	6290	Lockville_____O
654.4	CA	HVA18	6294	Carroll_____O
663.3	*X	HVA26	6306	①④Lancaster_____O
665.8		HVA29	6309	‡Brewer_____O
670.1	SG	HVA33	6315	Sugar Grove_____O
670.5		HVA34	6316	‡Sharps_____O
673.9		HVA37	6320	Rockbridge_____O
677.1		HVA40	6325	Enterprise_____O
681.3	ON	HVA44	6330	②④Logan_____O
682.8	*WN	HVA46	6357	②Oldtown_____O
687.9	H	HVA51	6363	Haydenville_____O
693.7		HVA57	6371	②④Nelsonville_____O
694.3	*S	HVA58	6374	Nelsonville (Yard)__
695.9		HVA59	6518	Kimberly_____O
697.6		HVA61	6521	Floodwood_____O
699.4		HVA62	6522	Poston_____O
699.7		HVA63	6524	Hamley Run_____O
704.7		HVA68	6531	Valley_____O
706.4	*AN	HVA70	6534	①⑤Armitage_____O
707.7	A	HVA71	6536	①Athens_____O
708.0		HVA72	6537	④Athens (Union Depot)_____O

POMEROY SUB-DIVISION

Dist. from Ft. Monroe	Tel. Calls	Station No.	Code No.	STATIONS
682.8	*WN	HVA46	6357	Oldtown_____O
688.3		HVR5	6558	Union Furnace____O
690.6		HVR7	6561	‡‡Summit_____O
692.9	RA	HVR9	6564	②Starr_____O
695.2		HVR12	6567	New Plymouth____O
696.8	.	HVR13	6570	Orland_____O
702.3		HVR19	6576	Creola_____O
707.0	AU	HVR23	6582	④McArthur_____O
709.8	*UN	HVR26	6586	①②Dundas_____O
713.1		HVR30	6631	‡‡Eagle_____O
715.3		HVR32	6635	Oreton_____O
717.9		HVR34	6638	Radcliff_____O
720.2		HVR37	6641	Hawks_____O
722.3		HVR39	6645	Clarion_____O
724.1		HVR41	6647	Minerton_____O
728.1		HVR45	6652	Alice_____O
732.0	V	HVR49	6658	Vinton_____O
734.2		HVR51	6661	Glenns_____O
736.7	BW	HVR53	6665	Bidwell_____O
740.7	KS	HVR57	6671	Kerrs_____O
741.7		HVR58	6673	‡‡Blanc's_____O
742.9		HVR59	6675	‡Mills_____O
743.3		HVR60	6677	‡Bennett's_____O
746.2	GI	HVR63	6680	①④Gallipolis_____O
747.4		HVR64	6683	‡‡Fair Grounds___O
750.8	*CK	HVR67	6687	①Kanauga_____O
752.5		HVR69	6690	Addison_____O
756.9		HVR73	6695	Cheshire_____O
760.5	HO	HVR77	6701	Hobson_____O
762.4	BI	HVR79	6704	①④Middleport____O
763.7	MY	HVR80	6706	①Pomeroy (Freight)_____O
764.5		HVR81	6707	④Pomeroy (Pass.)_O
767.5				End of Line_____

MONDAY CREEK SUB-DIVISION

Dist. from Ft. Monroe	Tel. Calls	Station No.	Code No.	STATIONS
693.7		HVA57	6371	④Nelsonville_____O
696.6		HVM3	6378	Myers Crossing____O
698.6		HVM5	6381	②Snow Fork Jct.___O
701.0		HVM7	6384	Monday_____O
701.7		HVM8	6386	Longstreth_____O
703.1	CB	HVM9	6388	Carbon Hill_____O
703.9		HVM10	6390	Helm_____O
704.6		HVM11	6392	Sand Run Jct_____O
706.5		HVM12	6395	Greendale_____O
708.1		HVM14	6397	Dewey Jct._____O
711.0		HVS10	6342	Monday Creek Jct._O
713.2	SI	HVS13	6346	New Straitsville___O

SNOW FORK SUB-DIVISION

Dist. from Ft. Monroe	Tel. Calls	Station No.	Code No.	STATIONS
698.6		HVM5	6381	Snow Fork Jct.___O
699.8	B	HVF1	6421	Buchtel_____O
701.8		HVF3	6424	Orbiston_____O
702.5		HVF4	6426	Brush Fork Jct.___O
703.9	MC	HVF5	6428	Murray City_____O
704.3		HVF6	6431	Ward Jct._____O

COONVILLE SUB-DIVISION

Dist. from Ft. Monroe	Tel. Calls	Station No.	Code No.	STATIONS
692.8	RA	HVR9	6564	Starr_____O
694.8		HVC2	6565	Coonville_____O

JACKSON SUB-DIVISION

Dist. from Ft. Monroe	Tel. Calls	Station No.	Code No.	STATIONS
709.8	*UN	HVR26	6586	①Dundas_____O
714.5		HVW5	6592	Hamden_____O
717.6	WX	HVW8	6596	①Wellston_____O
718.3		HVW9	6598	Grand Crossing___O
722.7		HVW13	6605	Coalton_____O
727.1	J	HVW17	6611	①Jackson_____O

MIAMI SUB-DIVISION

Dist. from Ft. Monroe	Tel. Calls	Station No.	Code No.	STATIONS
6.9	*YD	CL6	7007	Cheviot_____O
8.9		CL9	7009	‡‡Mulligan_____O
9.3		CL9½	7010	Bridgetown_____O
11.5	*DL	CL11	7012	‡‡Dent_____O
16.1	*MO	CL16	7016	Miami_____O
19.3		CL19½	7020	‡Willys_____O
20.7	*FD	CL21	7021	Fernald_____O
24.0	*S	CL24	7024	Shandon_____O
27.5	*NA	CL28	7028	Okeana_____O
32.0	*NK	CL32	7032	Newkirk_____O
34.6	*PO	CL34	8000	Peoria_____Ind
37.6		CL38	8003	Raymond_____Ind
40.5	*BA	CL41	8005	Bath_____Ind
46.5	*CG	CL47	8007	①Cottage Grove_Ind
52.4	*K	CL52	8010	Kitchell_____Ind
54.5		CL54	8012	Witts_____Ind
56.4	*B	CL56	8015	Boston_____Ind
61.9	*DK	CL62	8019	‡Elkhorn_____Ind
64.5	*RI	CL64	8025	①④Richmond____Ind
			8024	" Tkt. Office____
65.2		CL65	8026	Mt. Auburn_____Ind
69.0	*WA	CL69	8029	‡‡Wayne_____Ind
70.5		CL70	8033	Webster_____Ind
75.4	*W	CL75	8037	Williamsburg____Ind
81.1	*ON	CL81	8040	Economy_____Ind
88.0	*DR	CL88	8046	①Losantville_____Ind
91.9	SN	CL92	8049	Blountsville_____Ind
94.0	*HN	CL94	8051	‡‡Henry_____Ind
98.2	*MF	CL98	8053	Medford_____Ind
103.5		CL103	8055	South Muncie____Ind
104.6	*MU	CL105	8057	①④Muncie_____Ind
			8058	", Tkt. Office____
106.9	*DW	CL107	8060	‡‡Drew (P.R.R. Xing)_____Ind
107.3		CL108	8062	‡Delser_____Ind
110.5		CL110	8064	‡Barker_____Ind
111.7		CL112	8065	‡Benadum_____Ind
115.1	*G	CL115	8068	Gaston_____Ind
120.0	*JN	CL120	8070	‡‡Janney_____Ind
122.5	*FO	CL122	8073	Fowlerton_____Ind
127.5	*GR	CL127	8077	‡‡Grey_____Ind
128.9	BR	CL129	8079	④Jonesboro-Gas City_____Ind
131.2	*DC	CL131	8081	①Deer Creek____Ind
134.0	*MA	CL134	8085	①④Marion_____Ind
			8086	" Tkt. Office____
135.5	*PX	CL135	8087	①‡‡Phoenix_____Ind
139.5	*WS	CL140	8090	Sweetser_____Ind
141.5		CL142	8093	‡Mier_____Ind
145.2	*CO	CL145	8095	④Converse_____Ind
148.3	*BY	CL148	8098	Amboy_____Ind
154.2	*FA	CL154	8104	Santa Fe_____Ind
162.0	*OX	CL162	8110	①④Peru_____Ind
162.0	*RU	CL162	8111	*Peru Pass. Sta.__Ind

WABASH SUB-DIVISION

Dist. from Ft. Monroe	Tel. Calls	Station No.	Code No.	STATIONS
162.0	*OX	CL162	8110	①④Peru_____Ind
162.0	*RU	CL162	8111	Peru Pass. Sta.__Ind
168.0		CL170	8115	‡Vicord_____Ind
171.6	*VR	CL172	8117	①‡‡Hoover_____Ind
176.0	*V	CL176	8120	Twelve Mile_____Ind
182.0	*UN	CL182	8123	Fulton_____Ind
191.4	*KN	CL191	8129	①④Kewanna____Ind
195.7	*BU	CL196	8133	Lake Bruce_____Ind
199.5		CL200	8137	Lawton_____Ind
204.2	*BN	CL204	8141	Beardstown_____Ind
211.3	*PK	CL211	8147	‡‡Park_____Ind
214.9	*J	CL215	8150	①④North Judson_Ind
219.1	*NG	CL219	8153	English Lake____Ind
224.0	*CS	CL224	8155	①④La Crosse___Ind

WABASH SUB-DIVISION
Continued

Dist. from Ft. Monroe	Tel. Calls	Station No.	Code No.	STATIONS
224.6	*QN	CL225	8157	①‡‡QN Tower____Ind
228.1		CL228	8159	‡Liberty View____Ind
232.4	*DN	CL232	8162	Malden_____Ind
236.4		CL236	8166	‡Sevier_____Ind
241.6	*BT	CL242	8170	Beatrice_____Ind
244.5		CL244	8172	‡Hornbeck_____Ind
250.3	*MV	CL250	8175	Merrillville_____Ind
255.7	*GF	CL256	8180	①Griffith_____Ind
258.6		CL259	8183	Highlands_____Ind
260.0		CL260	8184	‡‡‡Woodmar____Ind
262.4	*HY	CL262	8190	H. Y. Tower_____Ind
264.1	*HM	CL264	8195	④Hammond_____Ind
264.8		CL265	8197	‡Erie Jct._____Ind
265.1		CL265½	8199	‡State Line_____Ill
266.3		CL266	9003	①‡Burnham_____Ill
272.2		CL272		CalumetrYard___Ill
272.8		CL273		93rd St. Stony- Island_____Ill
274.0		CL274		*I. C. Jct._____Ill
				①Chicago_____Ill
283.5	KD	CL283	9000	" Foot So. Water St._
			9001	①U. S. Yards Chicago_____Ill

NOTE: Lines of the former Pere Marquette Railway are not included here. To obtain this information consult *C&O Officers, Agents, Stations, Etc. No. 82, August 1948.*

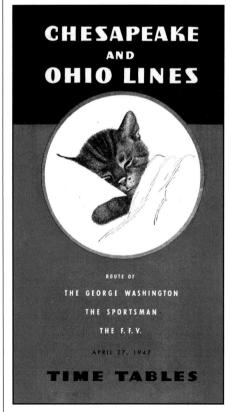

CHESAPEAKE
AND
OHIO LINES

ROUTE OF
THE GEORGE WASHINGTON
THE SPORTSMAN
THE F.F.V.

APRIL 27, 1947

TIME TABLES

Front cover of a C&O public timetable from April 17, 1947. (C&OHS Collection, COHS 22810)

THE CHESAPEAKE AND OHIO RAILWAY COMPANY — TUNNEL DATA

NAME OF TUNNEL	M.P. AT EAST END	NEAREST STATION	TOTAL LENGTH	NO. OF TRACKS & CENTERS	TANGENT LENGTH	CURVE LENGTH	BRICK	CONCRETE	TIMBER	NAT ROCK
MAIN LINE										
Brookville	201	Greenwood	1051'	1	1051'					1051'
Little Rock	202	Afton	100'			100'		100'		
Blue Ridge	204	Afton	3979'		3979'					3979'
Millboro	260	Millboro	1335'			1335'		1335'		
Lick Run ★	261	Millboro	290'			2'02" 290'				
Mason's	262	Millboro	326'		84'	4° x 299'	196			326'
Coleman's	271	Griffith	368'				368'			368'
Mud	294	Callaghan	634'		27'		634'	27'		634'
Moores	301	Callaghan	331'			331'		331'		
Lakes	301	Backbone	712'		712'		712'			712'
Kelleys	302	Backbone	467'	2 (14')	467'		467'			467'
Lewis W.B. (old)	304	Jerrys Run	3788'			2°55' 289'	3055			
Lewis E.B. (new)	304	Jerrys Run	3055'	2 (14')	3055'		3055'			
Lewis E.B. (old)	307	Alleghany	4743'			3°-100'	22C	2242		
Alleghany W.B. (new)	307	Alleghany	4751'		4751'		4751'			
White Sulphur	311	White Sulphur	300'	2 (14')		3°57½'-300'	300'			
Second Creek	327	Rockland	2067'	2	2067'		2067'			
Mann's E.B. (old)	330	Fort Spring	982'		903'	3°3'-79'	465'			
Mann's W.B. (new)	330	Fort Spring	916'		916'	4°38'-11'	916'			
Big Bend W.B. (new)	348	Hilldale	6500'		6500'		23			6477
Big Bend E.B. (old)	348	Hilldale	6168'		6168'		6168'			
Little Bend E.B. (old)	350	Hilldale	692'		692'		692'			
Stretchers Neck	380	Prince	1588'	2 (14')		3°22% 1588	1588'			1588'
JAMES RIVER LINE										
Wasp Rock (James River S.D.)	193	Dillon	102'			4°45'-12'	102'			
Bells	208	Lyle Saltsbury	307'			7°-307'	189'	223'		
LEXINGTON SUB-DIVISION										
Ashland	520	Ashland	975'		947'		241'	16'	344'	373
Princess	529	Princess				1970'	1969'		34'	374'
Williams Creek	538	Williams Creek	2003'							
Aden	552	Aden	382'		382'		382'			
OTHER SUB-DIVISIONS										
Droop Mountain (Greenbrier S.D.)	31	Rorer	402'		402'	12°-402'			23'	
Sharps	65	Harter	511'		511'	8°- 511'				511'
Carnifex (N.F.& G.R.R. Sub-Div.)	49	Shawvers Bridge	942'		942'	8°- 942'				
Koontz (Bend)	58	Woods Ferry	3164'		3030'	16°-134'	3164'			
Piney No.1	19	Burks	1210'		1210'					
Piney No.2 (Piney Cr. S.D.)	20	Burks	483'		483'	8°-485'				42
Piney No.3	7	Affinity	272'		272'		272'			230
Winding Gulf No.1 (Winding Gulf S.D.)	8	Diehl	588'			8°-569'	588'			588'
Winding Gulf No.2	16	Tunnel Siding	3955'		3487'	8°-472'	3955'			569'
Seng Creek (Seng Cr. S.D.)	2	St. Albans	1472'		1472'	8°-190'	1472'			
St. Albans (Coal River S.D.)	3	Calvert	400'		400'	7°-400'			400'	
Armstrong (new)										
Sproul (Coal River S.D.)	16	Sproul	951'		485'	7°-466'		951'		
Blue Tom	16	Blue Tom	403'		403'	8°-403'		403'		
Pinnacle	2.5	Altman	310'		310'	8°-310'		238'	72'	
Buffalo (Big Sandy R.R.)		Woodville	409'		409'			409'	409'	
Gun Creek (Dawkins S.D.)	15	Ivyton	632'		632'	2°36'-404'		178'	454'	
Koontz (Bend)	58	Buskirk	404'		404'					
E. & B.V. No.1 (E. & B.V. S.D.)	6	Dinwood	241'		241'	8°-241'		241'		
E. & B.V. No.2	7	Dinwood	806'		806'	7°-401'		806'		
E. & B.V. No.3	10	Maytown	388'		388'	8°-366'		388'		
E. & B.V. No.4	14	Bosco	514'		514'	8°-514'		285'	219'	
Long Fork No.1 (S.F.& E.S.D.)	4	Salisbury	350'		113'	7°-237'		350'		
Long Fork No.2 (Long Fork S.D.)	13	Borders	812'		780'	4°- 32'		812'		
Long Fork No.3	17	Clear Creek	552'		552'			352'		
Long Fork No.4	17	Clear Creek	424'		424'			424'		
Long Fork No.5	17	Clear Creek	216'		216'			216'		
Robinsons Creek (S.F.& E.S.D.)		Robinsons Creek	744'		578'	7°- 166'		744'		
Eagle (Pomeroy S.D.)	11	Virgie	283'		101'	7°- 182'	110'			283'
Campbell	C-84	Oreton	343'		343'					233'
Quinwood (40 Min/1 Creek S.D.)	C-88	Hawks	896'		896'			896'		
★ STONE LINING 10	9	Crichton	968'		968'			968'		667'

C&O Drawing X-7105-A showing tunnel data as of 1935. Update data is printed below, showing tunnels eliminated and new ones added. This drawing was made following the huge 1930-1935 tunnel upgrade program. It has been updated through 1945. (COHS collection)

Additions include:

Meade Fork SD - Pine Mountain Tunnel; Built 1948; Length 3,621 ft; 854 ft. concrete, 2,767 ft. timber. Island Creek SD - Holden Tunnel; Built 1948; Length 2,869 ft.; Steel & timber lining. Dawkins SD - Carver Tunnel; Built 1949; Length 1,400 ft.; Steel & timber lining. Alleghany SD - Ft. Spring Tunnel; Built 1948; Length 2,806 ft.; concrete lined.

Eliminated:

Brookville (daylighted); Mason's (bypassed); Coleman's (bypassed); Little Bend (bypassed); Lewis westbound (old) (track removed); Big Bend westbound (old) (track removed); Williams Creek, Aden (Lexington SD abandoned); Droop Mountain, Sharps (Greenbrier SD abandoned); Seng Creek (Seng Creek SD abandoned)

Chief Engineers Office — Richmond, Va. Nov. 27, 1935. Drawing No. X-7105-A.

Additional Sources of Information for C&O's Route, Stations, Divisions, Yards, and Terminals

- *The Chesapeake & Ohio Railway in West Virginia: Huntington Division*, William R Sparkmon, C&O Historical Society, 1988.
- *Chesapeake & Ohio Railway in West Virginia: Photos 1940-1960*, by Thomas W Dixon Jr., TLC Publishing, 2005. 80 pgs. Available from www.chessieshop.com (Catalog number BK-04-393)
- *Chessie's Road*, by Charles W. Turner, updated by Thomas W. Dixon, Jr. and Eugene L. Huddleston (Richmond 1956, Clifton Forge 1986 and 1993), publishing in final expanded form by C&O Historical Society, Clifton Forge, Va. 323 pages. Reprint available from C&O Historical Society (Catalog No. BK-10-539) – The first part of this book, which is the 1956 book, gives a good corporate history of the C&O.
- *Chesapeake and Ohio Superpower to Diesels*, Thomas W. Dixon, Jr., Carstens Publications Inc, 1984
- *The Pere Marquette in 1945*, Second Edition, Clifford J. Vander Yacht, Arthur B. Million, Chesapeake & Ohio Historical Society (BK-08-466)
- *West Virginia Railroads - Vol 2 - Chesapeake & Ohio*, Thomas W. Dixon, Jr., T L C Publishing, Inc. 2010 (Catalog No. BK-10-509)
- *Virginia Railroads - Vol 2 - Chesapeake & Ohio*, Thomas W. Dixon, Jr., T L C Publishing, Inc. 2010 (Catalog No. BK-11-605)
- *C&O Officers, Agents, Stations, Etc. No. 82, Aug. 1948.* C&O Historical Society, Clifton Forge, Va. (Catalog No. DS-12-349)
- *Pere Marquette Officers, Agents, Stations, Etc. No. 17, Feb. 1945* C&O Historical Society, Clifton Forge, Va. (DS-12-350)

CHAPTER FOUR

Passenger Service and Equipment

C&O's early passenger trains were powered by tiny 4-4-0s and consisted of a few wooden cars. Without diners, the trains made 20-minute meal stops along the route. Here a C&O train is stopped in front of the Alderson Hotel in Alderson, W. Va. long enough for its passengers to get some sandwiches or small meal. (C&OHS Collection, COHS 5376)

Passenger Service

Although the C&O didn't have a large population in its region, it was always inordinately interested in running passenger trains and providing a high level of service. Even though it operated only a few trains in comparison with the major passenger-carrying railroads, its trains gained wide fame and acclaim. C&O's advertising and publicity operations for its passenger service, especially in the era 1900-1950, gave its trains a broad reputation and made them well known far beyond their area of operation.

In the early years, Virginia Central ran mixed trains that consisted of both passenger and freight cars, and it began hauling mail early in its career. As the major express companies were organized, that business was added. Adams Express was the company that used C&O trains until the organization of the American Railway Express (later the universal Railway Express Agency).

As business in the region and the railroad grew, separate passenger trains began to operate. As an example, in 1858, Virginia Central was operating a passenger and mail train between Richmond and Jackson's River, leaving at 6:45 am, and arriving Jackson's River at 5:30 pm, covering the 195 miles in just under 12 hours for an average of about 16 miles per hour over the entire route. It made 26 stops en route, or an average of a stop every 7½ miles! The eastbound train left Jackson's River at 3:10 am, arriving Richmond at 2:30 pm. There was also a second all-passenger "accommodation" train that operated between Richmond and Charlottesville leaving Richmond at 5:45 pm arriving Charlottesville 10:30 pm, and leaving Charlottesville 11:00 pm, arriving Richmond 4:30 am.

For overnight trains Virginia Central experimented with its own crudely-built sleeping berths. By the 1870s C&O had several cars with sleeping accommodations in them. It wasn't until 1880 that it contracted with the Pullman Com-

This 1903 view shows the FFV leaving Huntington, W. Va. with class A-6, 4-4-0 American-type No. 75 for power and seven wooden cars, about the average for the era.
(C&OHS Collection, COHS 23864)

pany to supply and operate its Palace Sleeping Cars. With this arrangement the best and most modern equipment was supplied to the company's first class customers.

The Virginia Central and C&O built most of their cars in their own shops until the early 1870s, when C&O began to buy cars from the major manufacturers of the era, although the first Louisa passenger run of 1847 was community, built by Harlan and Hollingworth.

There was no change in service until the beginning of the C&O era in 1869, when service was extended to White Sulphur Springs, eliminating the need for people to take stages from Jackson's River to the Springs. From the 1840s up until this time stage coaches operated on the James River & Kanawha Turnpike (that was built to connect the end of the James River and Kanawha Canal with the Ohio River at Guyandotte (Huntington). When the Virginia Central reached Jackson's River, that became a stage connection, where passengers bound for the west could change from the trains to the stage coaches for the trip across the mountains, and down to the Ohio River.

On May 5, 1873, the first regular C&O train was placed in service over the entire new route between Richmond and Huntington. The line had been open for several months, but was considered too unstable to allow for passenger operations west of White Sulphur Springs, but after a great deal of additional ballasting, and other work the passenger and through freights began operations on that date.

Two mail trains operated on the main line, one from Richmond to White Sulphur Springs, and another one on the western portion of the line. The new through train over the whole route was called the *Cincinnati Express*, leaving Richmond at 10:00 pm, arriving Huntington at 5:10 pm the next day, where it connected with C&O's line of Ohio River steamboats for the trip to Cincinnati. The boat left Huntington at 5:20 pm and arrived at Cincinnati the next morning at 6:00 am. So, the first named train on the C&O was the *Cincinnati Express*, and it didn't even go to Cincinnati! Accommodation trains continued to operate between Richmond and Gordonsville. Stagecoach connections were made at Staunton, Goshen, Millboro, Covington, Alleghany, and Talcott for the many mountain springs resorts, and at Kanawha Falls for Raleigh Court House (today's Beckley, W. Va.). Direct connections were available over what was later the Southern Railway at Charlottesville for Lynchburg and at Gordonsville for Washington.

In 1881, passenger service was extended down the peninsula from Richmond to Newport News when C&O completed that line. Also in 1881, connections were made in the west over Huntington-controlled Elizabethtown, Lexington and Big Sandy, via the L&N to Louisville, and via Huntington's Kentucky Central between Winchester, Ky., and Cincinnati. However, the Ohio River steamboat connection also was retained from Huntington to Cincinnati, until the C&O's own Cincinnati Division line was completed along the south bank of the Ohio River in 1888. Beginning then, for the first time, C&O could actually run its own train on its own line into Cincinnati, and there make connections for its passengers to a number of roads for midwestern, southern, and western points.

Also by 1881, the C&O had regularly established through connections to and from New York over both the Pennsylvania Railroad and the Baltimore & Ohio.

A 1905 postcard view showing women selling food to passengers on a C&O train at Gordonsville, Va., a practice that dated from the pre-Civil War days before diners.
(C&OHS Collection, COHS 16154)

By 1885, C&O's service had expanded and two more sets of trains were placed into operation, the *Washington Express*, the *Cincinnati Express*, as well as the *Virginia Springs Express*. Both through trains carried Pullman drawing room and sleeping cars. Local trains also operated over several portions of the mainline. Other names used during this time included *Louisville & Cincinnati Fast Line*, and *Night Express*. About this time the Pullman buffet cars were added, with limited food service offered to the Pullman passengers. Coach passengers still had to get off the train at designated stops to take a fast meal at a line-side hotel. Some of the hotels that were used "to feed the trains" were the American Hotel in Staunton, the Alderson House and Monroe House hotels in Alderson, W. Va., and the Kanawha Falls Hotel in Kanawha Falls, W. Va. Trains stopped for 20 minutes during which passengers rushed to the hotel food bars and bought sandwiches and other portable food.

The year 1889 represents a major watershed in C&O passenger service, heralded by the inauguration of the *Fast Flying Virginian* (also known as the *FFV*). The train consisted of the most modern Pullman-built cars, and C&O conducted a very extensive advertising and publicity program including keeping people guessing as to the meaning of the *FFV* initials.

When the *FFV* went into service on May 10, 1889, it was certainly one of the most luxurious and modern trains in American railroading. The seven-car consists were built by the Pullman Company and were comprised of a combination baggage/coach, coaches, a full dining car, and sleeping/lounge cars. The cars were equipped with electric lights and fans powered by a generator located in the baggage compartment of the combination car, steam heat from the locomotive, and the most opulent of appointments within. The exterior of the train was painted bright orange. The letter board was maroon with gold-leaf lettering, including the railroad or Pullman name and the train name at the car end. Car wheels were red with gold striping. The innovation getting the biggest attention, however, was the vestibule. Every car was connected by a narrow passageway, joined by a flexible rubber diaphragm which allowed passengers to pass from car to car easily, safely, and out of the weather. The *FFV* was one of the first trains to have this convenience throughout, and it was often called, in its early days, "The Fast Vestibule," or "Vestibule Limited."

Additionally, the *FFV* was run through from Washington to New York as a solid train, with only the exchange of a Pennsylvania locomotive for the C&O locomotive. At Cincinnati, direct connections were made over the Big Four (CCC&St.L.) for Indianapolis, St. Louis, and Chicago, but the train was not run through to any of these points.

At this time, the pattern was established that would be standard to the end of C&O passenger service, whereby a "Virginia Section" of the train traveled from Newport News to Charlottesville, and there was added to the train coming

Front cover of Summer Homes and Mountain and Seashore Resorts, Season 1984. *(C&OHS Collection)*

from (New York) Washington, and then would travel over the C&O to Huntington, (later Ashland, Kentucky), where it was parted again, with the main section going through to Cincinnati, and a "Kentucky section" going through to Louisville (via the L&N from Lexington). At the time of the *FFV*'s introduction, the other through trains operated from Washington to Cincinnati with a Virginia section but no Kentucky section. Locals operated over different sections of the line as traffic warranted.

It was with the *FFV* that C&O began its own dining car service, and though Pullman Buffet service continued for a short time, it was soon eliminated, and C&O acquired diners for all its name trains over the next decade, eliminating the traditional meal stop.

Throughout the 1890s, C&O passenger business grew not only because of its good connections east-west, but in local business as the coal towns grew up along its main and new branch lines. In 1897, C&O was still operating two sets of through name trains, the *FFV* and the *Cincinnati-Washington Fast Line*. Additional local trains had been added so that most stations had at least four and up to eight trains

The narrow vestibule was introduced on C&O in 1889 by the FFV. (C&OHS Collection, COHS 35095)

per day. Mail and express business had become one of the most important aspects of C&O passenger operations, and the company built or bought ever larger cars to accommodate this business. Around 1900 the wide vestibules replaced the narrow, and C&O quickly populated the *FFV* and other trains with the new cars. Many new sleeping cars were also placed in service by Pullman during the era 1890-1908.

Concurrent with the *FFV* introduction in 1889, C&O acquired the James River line (the old R&A) down the James River between Clifton Forge and Richmond via Lynchburg. This was a sparsely settled farming area as well and C&O picked up the old R&A local service and continued it usually running two local accommodation trains each way during daylight hours over the line, connecting with mainline trains at Richmond and Clifton Forge. The service never grew in status and ended in 1957 much as it had begun as a rural local operation. In this era the new coal branches were built, and they each received a local passenger train at least once per day. The 101-mile-long Greenbrier branch was put into service in 1901 and got its rather longer-distance local train, which also lasted to the late date of 1957. As the number of coal branches grew, so did the number of local trains being operated, so that by about 1920 C&O had scores of pas-

senger trains in operation running routes as short as 10 miles, terminal-to-terminal, mainly to bring people to stations where they could connect with mainline trains, or to take them to towns where they could do business not possible in the small coal camps or rural villages.

It was in the 1890s that C&O really began to promote its line as a way to reach tourist destinations. This had begun in the 1880s when the railway issued fancy timetables and brochures featuring the historic and scenic wonders along the line. But most importantly it was the Virginia and West Virginia mountain mineral springs resorts that attracted people to the C&O. In the age before air-conditioning, well-to-do people who lived in the coastal eastern cities sought refuge in the mountains during high heat of summer. C&O began to attract these people with through New York-Springs area trains, especially with the introduction of the *FFV*, with its through, high-luxury cars and dining service. Over the next few decades, tourist publicity programs became more and more intense, with the issuance of more and better quality brochures, timetables, newspaper and magazine ads, all touting the wonders of the C&O line.

By 1908 C&O was still operating only two through trains, the *FFV* and the *C&O Limited*. Like the *FFV*, the *C&O Limited* came with its name emblazoned on the side of its cars, but this time only on the blind side of the combination baggage/coach car at the head of the train. It was in this era that tail signs began to be used showing the train's name on the rear of the last car, which was usually had an observation platform.

About 1910, C&O began advertising itself as "The Rhine, the Alps, and the Battlefield Line" in timetables, ads, and brochures. People of the era were used to the idea of the wealthy making a trip to Europe and taking the "Grand Tour" to historic and scenic sites, so C&O advertising men decided to advertise their railway as an alternative. The idea was that C&O's rivers: the James, Greenbrier, New, Kanawha, and Ohio were comparable to the Rhine, that the scenic mountain ranges (Blue Ridge, Shenandoah, and Alleghany) equated to the Alps, and the colonial and Civil War battlefields were like those of Europe. This could all be done right here in the eastern U. S., on the C&O! This was the first of many slogans C&O would use to advertise itself in the next half century.

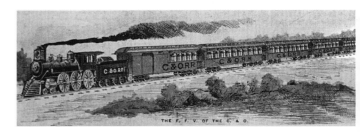

This early woodcut shows the C&O's Fast Flying Virginian of 1889. (C&OHS Collection)

This superbly ornate dining car was used on the FFV *in the 1890s. Imagine it set with white table cloths, china, and silver! (C&OHS Collection, 35096)*

In 1910, C&O acquired the Chicago Division line between Cincinnati and Chicago and to expand its service. Two of the mainline train sets were routed over this line while still retaining connections with The Big Four at Cincinnati for the same destination. This arrangement lasted until about 1920, when service on the Cincinnati-Chicago line became strictly a local accommodation service, first with two sets of trains and later one, which lasted until 1949.

World War I saw much troop traffic on C&O trains, especially transport of troops to Baltimore, New York, and Newport News for embarkation to Europe. During this period the United States Railroad Administration seized and operated American railroads including C&O. Service remained essentially unchanged, except advertising and publicity ceased, and tourist business decreased in favor of military and immediate postwar demobilization traffic.

However, following the war, the second golden era of C&O passenger service opened. The first era was inaugurated by the *FFV* and the wooden cars in 1889. This second great era was heralded by the steel car, air-conditioning, and new services. During the 1920s some of the name trains were: the *FFV*, the *West Virginian*, the *Old Dominion Limited*, the *Mid-West Limited*, and the *Kentuckian*.

C&O began acquiring its first all-steel passenger cars in 1911, and by the early 1920s all mainline trains were equipped with steel cars. The pattern of three sets of name trains over the mainline was now settled. Each of these would have a main section Washington-Cincinnati, connecting at Charlottesville with through cars on a Virginia section, and at Ashland with a Kentucky section. Connections east and west remained essentially as they had always been, via trackage rights over the Southern Railway Orange-Washington and via the PRR to New York, and via the Big Four (NYC) at Cincinnati to Chicago and St. Louis.

As an example, in 1912 the relatively small town of Waynesboro, Va., had service from 10 trains per day. Even tiny towns such as Alderson, W. Va., (about 1,000 people) had eight trains per day.

Interline connections continued to be built up. Typical of sleeping cars operating to and from off-line points were the following, shown in 1925 timetables:

New York - Louisville
New York - Cincinnati
New York - White Sulphur Springs
New York - Virginia Hot Springs
Washington - St. Louis
Newport News - Chicago
Richmond - Chicago

Other cars operating to and from on-line C&O points included:

Washington - Cincinnati
Washington - Huntington
Richmond - Cincinnati
Richmond - Huntington
Newport News - Cincinnati
Richmond - Louisville
Washington - Louisville
Clifton Forge - Louisville

Through the 1920s C&O adopted the new slogan "The Route to Historyland" in its tourist brochures and print advertising.

It was in 1930, at the onset of the Great Depression, that C&O began the next phase of its passenger service . On March 30, 1930, C&O inaugurated a new train named the *Sportsman*. It ran from Newport News to Detroit. The idea of the train was as a tourism vehicle, connecting the Virginia seashore resorts with the Virginia and West Virginia Springs resorts, and the Michigan resorts (via the Pere Marquette Railway out of Detroit). This was a new route because C&O had just completed the last link in its connection of the Cincinnati Division mainline with the C&O-owned Hocking Valley between Limeville, Kentucky, and Columbus, allowing for a through all-C&O operation as far as Toledo and over the C&O-controlled PM to Detroit. The big innovation of the train was its *Imperial Salon Car*, with

The Sportsman *was introduced by C&O in 1930 with great fanfare. Here the westbound train pauses at White Sulphur Springs in about 1935. Smoke from a special train is seen behind the depot. (C&OHS Collection, COHS 5581)*

the two-and-one rotating bucket seats. Later Washington-Charlottesville and Cincinnati-Ashland sections were added.

In 1932, C&O introduced a new flagship for its fleet of trains, the *George Washington*. This tied in with the country's celebration of the 200th anniversary of Washington's birth. Of course, C&O immediately gave up *Route to Historyland* and took on the slogan "George Washington's Railroad." The introduction of the *George Washington* was a comparable event to that of the *FFV* back in 1889, and for the first time that ancient name was eclipsed (though retained) in the C&O stable of passenger trains. C&O spared no expense in equipping the new train with amenities and niceties that would set it apart from all other trains and concurrently giving it one of the most intense advertising campaigns in railroad passenger train history. The train became one of the best known named trains in America. From its decorated locomotives to its famous wordless tail sign (just the portrait of Washington), it was a class act and people appreciated it. It was the second all-air-conditioned-long distance train in America (following the B&O's *National Limited* by a week).

With the introduction of "The George," C&O passenger service was set up in the following way:

The *George Washington*: No. 41-Newport News-Charlottesville
No. 1 - Washington-Charlottesville
No. 1 - Charlottesville-Ashland
No. 21 - Ashland-Louisville
No. 1 - Ashland-Cincinnati
The *George Washington*: No. 2/22/42/2 - reverse of above.
The *Sportsman*: No. 47 - Newport News-Charlottesville
No. 5 - Washington-Charlottesville
No. 5/47 - Charlottesville-Ashland
No. 47 - Ashland-Columbus-Detroit
No. 5 - Ashland - Cincinnati
The *Sportsman*: No. 4/46/4/46 - reverse of above
plus No. 24 Louisville-Ashland
The *FFV* No. 43 - Newport News-Charlottesville
No. 3 - Washington - Charlottesville
No. 3 - Charlottesville - Ashland
No. 23 - Ashland - Louisville
No. 3 - Ashland -Cincinnati
The *FFV*: No. 6 - Cincinnati-Washington only

During World War II, traffic expanded exponentially, especially carrying troops to the Hampton Roads Port of Embarkation at Newport News-Norfolk.

During the war, in 1942, C&O came under the control of Robert R. Young as its board chairman. He instituted a wide variety of innovations, and among his top priorities was

The Chesapeake & Ohio Railway - A Concise History and Fact Book

In 1932, C&O introduced the George Washington *as its flagship train. This image of the train pausing at White Sulphur Springs, with its understated tail sign (drumhead) shining in the night, was used in timetables, brochures, and in countless books since. (C&OHS Collection, COHS 5578)*

the upgrade of passenger service. He conceived a new ultra-luxury coach train over the C&O mainline, to be called the *Chessie*, to go into service right after the war. It was meticulously planned with the very best accommodations, and was to show other railroads how customers could be attracted back to the rails with the right level of service. The train was to be powered by the new M-1 class steam-turbine-electrics. The cars and M-1s were received just as C&O was experiencing not only a precipitous decline in passenger traffic (1948), but also disastrous coal strikes, resulting in the first financial distress on the railway in memory. The *Chessie* was cancelled just before the arrival of the equipment. Some of the cars went into regular trains for a while, and the bulk inaugurated the new *Pere Marquette* trains between Grand Rapids and Chicago, but they were nearly all sold by 1951.

In 1946, C&O's wholly-owned Pere Marquette instituted the nation's first all-new postwar streamliners in the form of the *Pere Marquettes* operating between Detroit and Grand Rapids. The new, seven-car, train sets powered by E7 diesels were a big success and increased ridership on the route over 80%. They remained successful for several years, but gradually declined as new roads were built, and the Interstate Highway System give them the *coup de grace*.

Concurrent with this operation, enough lightweight cars were ordered from Pullman-Standard Car Manufacturing Company to completely reequip all mainline trains, but by the time they were ready in 1950, the need was less than half what had been ordered. Many cars were sold before delivery and others spun off to other railroads after delivery. How-

ever, the C&O retained enough cars to reequip all its trains except for diners and head-end cars. A new yellow/blue/silver scheme was adopted, and E8 diesels took over as power a year after the cars arrived.

From 1950 onwards, C&O would retrench its passenger services overall, but the decline was generally slow. Because C&O President Walter J. Tuohy believed that passenger service was the best advertisement C&O had, he refused to make wholesale cuts even when the service was losing considerable amounts of money.

On the mainline, the three sets of trains (*George Washington*, *Sportsman*, and *FFV*) continued in their normal patterns, supplemented by a single set of mail and express/local passenger trains. In 1949, most branch line passenger service was discontinued, leaving trains only on: James River Line, Greenbrier Branch, Hot Springs Branch, Big Sandy Branch, Logan Branch, Coal River Branch, and a few mixed trains.

The mainline mail/express/locals disappeared in 1958, and the first set of name trains: No. 6 the *FFV*, and Nos. 47/5/47, the *Sportsman* disappeared in 1962. From that time onward service was in steep decline. The post office removed the mail in 1968, which essentially killed any remaining chance at covering the majority of passenger train costs. In May 1968, Nos. 43/3/23, the *FFV*, and Nos. 46/4/46, the *Sportsman*, were discontinued, leaving only the *George Washington*, Nos. 41/1/21/47 and 22/2/42/46 left on the old main line. The Detroit section of the *Sportsman* spent its last couple of years as a connector for Nos. 1 and 2.

On May 1, 1971, Amtrak took over American passenger train service. C&O's entire remaining Michigan service was cancelled, and one train was retained, the remnant of "The George." After much tumult under Amtrak the Virginia sections were discontinued, the entire route eliminated but revived, and became the three-days-a-week *Cardinal*, which operates today (2012) Washington-Cincinnati on the C&O, and on to Chicago on other lines.

M-1 class steam-turbine-electric No. 500 with Train No. 4, the Sportsman, *at Clifton Forge, Va. station in 1948. Photograph by Gene Huddleston. (C&OHS Collection, COHS 7205)*

C&O's first post-war passenger experiment was on subsidiary Pere Marquette when two of these fine sets of seven cars powered by a new EMD E7 were put in service as the Pere Marquettes, *on a fast schedule between Detroit and Grand Rapids. They were a huge success initially. C&O Ry. Photograph, C&OHS Collection, CSPR 1583A)*

C&O E8s led by No. 4013 were photographed on the westbound Sportsman *at White Sulphur Springs, always a favorite location for passenger publicity photos. This view was used on timetables for many years and in many ads and articles about the C&O. (C&O Ry. Photograph, C&OHS Collection, CSPR 2810)*

The Chesapeake & Ohio Railway - A Concise History and Fact Book

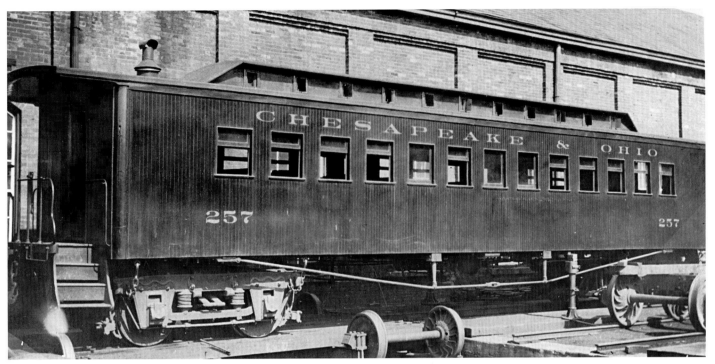

Early C&O cars were simple affairs such as this coach built by Va. Central shops in 1860. It survived into the 1900s and was finally used in the 1930s as an employee car to shuttle workers a few miles from Huntington to the shops. (C&OHS Collection, COHS 23236)

Passenger Equipment

C&O followed the general trends in passenger car construction and development. The old Louisa and Virginia Central began with the common open-platform wooden cars of about 40 feet in length in the Antebellum era. After the War Between the States the C&O continued buying its passenger stock from the bigger builders of the era, including Gilbert & Bush, Pullman, Jackson & Sharp, and Barney & Smith. In the 1920-1950 era, cars were built by Pullman-Standard Car Mfg. Co., Standard Steel Car Co., Pressed Steel Car Company or Bethlehem Shipbuilding.

The designs and accommodations were hardly different from the early cars of the 1850s until 1889 when C&O made a drastic departure from the past by ordering the newest designs from the Pullman Company to equip its new *Fast Flying Virginian* (*FFV*) trains. These cars were still of all-wooden design, but for the first time featured a vestibule, a narrow, enclosed corridor between the cars, electric lights, steam heat, etc., described previously in this chapter. These were all innovations that within a decade or two became standard everywhere. It's interesting that this occurred on C&O, a line with relatively few passenger trains, operating in a sparsely populated territory.

By the 1880s C&O was buying passenger cars from outside builders such as this coach built by Jackson & Sharp in 1881. It was, however, hardly changed from those of 30 years before in accommodation. It was longer, heavier, better built, but the passenger felt the same riding it. (C&OHS Collection, COHS 26237)

By the 1890s C&O was running high class trains, including observation lounge cars on the rear with open platforms such as this parlor car, photographed at Clifton Forge in 1915. It was built by Pullman in 1902. (C&OHS Collection, COHS 26238)

The C&O contracted early with Pullman to operated the sleeping cars on its lines, so cars owned and maintained by Pullman were used. This persisted to the end of the Pullman Company in 1969. After the breakup of Pullman in the post-World War II era into an operating company and a car building company, C&O, like other railroads, owned and maintained its sleepers, but Pullman operated them.

In the 1890s, passenger cars began to be built with steel under-frames and ends, though the car body remained wood. C&O bought many of these "composite" cars in the first decade of the 20th Century. These cars also had their vestibules extended flush with the sides of the cars and were called "wide-vestibule" cars. These were used to re-equip the premier named trains on the C&O main line in the 1905-1910 era.

The greatest innovation in passenger car design came in the early 1900s when cars began to be built entirely of steel. Within a very short time the public demanded the new steel cars because of the perception that they offered a much greater margin of safety in accidents, which, in fact, they did. C&O acquired its first steel cars in 1911, and by the mid-1920s all mainline name trains consisted of steel cars, from RPO, express, and baggage cars to coaches, diners, parlors, and sleepers. These cars became so common in American railroading that were called "standard" cars, but today are more commonly called "heavyweight" because of the lighter cars that followed them in the "Streamlined Era."

The heavyweight cars were of a fairly standard design except for the *Imperial Salon Cars* of 1930 (described previously) with their 2 and 1 bucket seating.

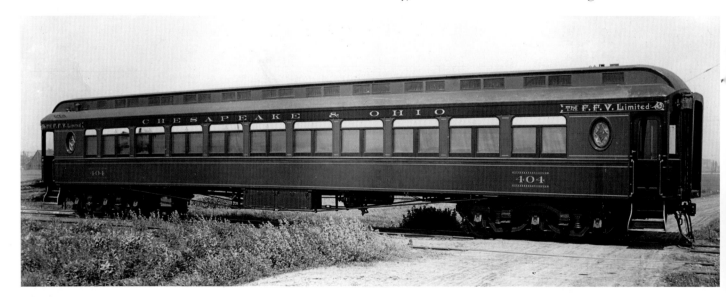

Cars such as this coach were the very top of the line when it was built in 1906 for service on C&O's premier train, the Fast Flying Virginian. *This black and white photograph nonetheless gives a good idea of the orange body and maroon letter board. (C&OHS Collection, COHS 26239)*

The best of the heavyweight coaches on C&O were the Imperial Salon cars introduced in 1930 with the Sportsman. *This photograph of No. 742 was taken in 1948, and shows the bubble along the clerestory that was the air-conditioning duct. Note also the sealed windows. (C&OHS Collection, COHS 26240)*

The *George Washington* of April, 1932, introduced air-conditioning and by 1934, all C&O mainline trains were fully air-conditioned.

During the 1930s many of America's railroads introduced new "streamliners" consisting of lightweight, ultra-modern cars, often pulled by new diesel locomotives, but C&O didn't opt for any of these. C&O did finally go for the streamliner concept following World War II. A new ultra-luxury, all-daylight train to be called the *Chessie*, was planned for a fast run over the old mainline, with accommodations that were unequalled. Its services ran family cars with children's theatres featuring Disney movies, to 36-seat coaches each with an eight-seat lounge, several types of food service cars, lounges and domes (all of stainless steel design built by the Budd Company). But because of financial problems occasioned by coal strikes and a sharply declining passenger traffic, the railway cancelled the train before it was actually inaugurated. The cars were used on several regular trains for a while, and most of the lot was used to create a new streamliner service in Michigan, the new *Pere Marquettes* between Grand Rapids and Chicago (the *Pere Marquette* streamliners of 1946 ran between Detroit and Grand Rapids).

While planning the *Chessie* with cars from the Budd Company, C&O also ordered nearly 300 new lightweight cars from Pullman-Standard Car Manufacturing Company, aimed at re-equipping all its mainline name trains as they existed at the end of the war. However, by 1948 the cars had not been delivered, and the number of trains to be re-equipped had fallen by almost half, so many of these cars were sold off to other roads before they were delivered to C&O, or were disposed of soon after arriving on the line. Likewise, the cars for the *Chessie* were sold by 1951, with C&O keeping only a few. The much decreased order of Pullman-Standard light-

The interior of an Imperial Salon Coach, showing the individual and dual, rotating bucket seats, that made it such a high-class and much remarked-upon car. (C&OHS Collection, COHS 26235)

C&O rebuilt three of its lightweight 5-Bedroom/Buffet/Lounge cars into diners that replaced the old heavyweights in the C&O trains. These cars, Alleghany Club, Blue Ridge Club, and Bluegrass Club, were used to the end of service. Here patrons enjoy a meal on one of these cars soon after its 1962 rebuild at C&O's Huntington shops. (C&O Ry. Photo, C&OHS Collection, CSPR 11332.8)

weight cars, delivered in mid-1950, was sufficient to cover the sleeping car, coach, and lounge needs for the remaining trains. Old heavyweight cars, repainted to the new blue/yellow/silver (gray) scheme were retained and used to cover dining services. All head-end service (mail, express, and baggage) continued to be handled in old heavyweight stock. This situation remained until the end of C&O-operated passenger service on May 1, 1971, when Amtrak took over. By that time C&O operated only one mainline train, the *George*

Washington, and only a few one or two car trains were left on the old *Pere Marquette* routes in Michigan.

C&O's remaining passenger cars were sold or scrapped, only a few going to Amtrak because it preferred stainless steel cars and most C&O cars were not. A few were rebuilt for company service, and a few others retained for B&O Baltimore-Washington area commuter service for a few years before that was taken over by public companies.

Many old heavyweight head-end cars were repainted the new 1950 C&O lightweight car colors and retained in service to the end of passenger operations. Here is Railway Post Office No. 105, built in 1911, rebuilt in 1938 and was in service into the 1960s. Seen here at Cincinnati in 1952. (C&OHS Collection, C&OHS 7494)

Pullman-Standard Car Manufacturing Company built most of C&O's postwar lightweight cars. Principal among them were the coaches like this one seen new at the builder's plant in 1950. (COHS Collection, COHS 26242)

The Chesapeake & Ohio Railway - A Concise History and Fact Book

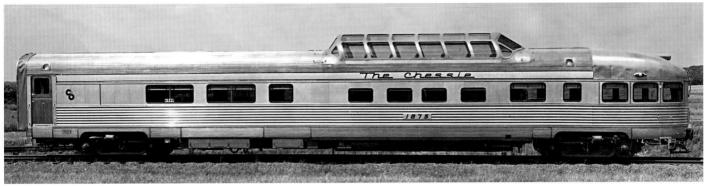

Stainless steel cars were built by the Budd Company for the proposed Chessie *train in 1948, but were soon sold off when the train never ran. Here is the ultimate luxury dome lounge observation car lettered for the train that never ran. (C&OHS Collection, COHS 26241)*

The interior of the 1600-series coaches was broken into two compartments with a nice curved partition in the center that displayed a route map, timetable rack, and water fountain. (C&O Ry. Photograph, C&OHS Collection, CSPR 11332.050)

Advertisement touting the new C&O lightweight sleepers and coaches, from 1950. (C&OHS Collection, AD 117)

One of the Sleeper-Lounge-Observations built for C&O's postwar trains is Allegheny Club, *with a flat end observation section. C&OHS Collection, COHS 26243)*

One of the 56 lightweight 10-Roomette/6 Double-bedroom sleeping cars that graced C&O's trains is City of Beckley. *They were all named for line-side cities and towns. (C&OHS Collection, COHS 26244)*

The first Chessie calendar, printed in the fall of 1933 and issued for the year 1934, featured the simple Gruenwald etching that had attracted so much attention in the September, 1933 Fortune *magazine and other publications. At this point, she still hadn't been named, so the first calendar doesn't have her name on it. © 1934 CSX Transportation, used with permission.*

Chessie the Railroad Kitten

The original image of Chessie was the creation of Viennese artist Guido Gruenwald, who specialized in the copperplate engravings of cats. She was featured in a national magazine ad campaign designed by C&O Public Relations Chief Lionel Probert and the Campbell-Ewald ad agency in September, 1933. The ad was intended to communicate the comfort of the newly air-conditioned passenger cars on the C&O. Chessie was an immediate hit with the public. Requests poured in from all over wanting to see more of her. With some reluctance to use a kitten to symbolize a railroad, the C&O decided to use her as the image for the 1934 calendar. The C&O printed 40,000 calendars and demand far exceeded supply. The rest is history.

Over the years, Chessie was featured in the same pose in many different situations. She had kittens, an "Old Man," slept in the lower 9, and delighted millions. She has been honored with a distinctive popularity that extends far beyond her original role. Her fanmail reached moviestar proportions. Requests for her picture were received from almost every part of the globe. Children adopted Chessie as their Number One pin-up.

Chessie is probably the most endearing and certainly one of the most successful corporate symbols in American advertising history. She became the Chesapeake and Ohio Railway's passenger and public relations salescat, and used as the corporate symbol and namesake for Chessie System Railroads.

The success of the 1934 calendar was so great that C&O continued its newspaper and magazine ads featuring the kitten. For the 1935 calendar, two small look-alike images were added, named "Nip" and "Tuck." © 1935 CSX Transportation, used with permission.

The Chesapeake & Ohio Railway - A Concise History and Fact Book

In 1933, L. C. Probert, a C&O official charged with public relations and advertising, saw an etching in a newspaper of a cuddly little kitten sleeping under a blanket with a paw thrust contentedly forward. At the time, he was developing an ad campaign to popularize C&O's new air-conditioned sleeping car service, and hit upon the notion of using the kitten with the slogan "Sleep Like a Kitten and Wake Up Fresh as a Daisy in Air-Conditioned Comfort" for the C&O passenger ads, the first of which appeared in September, 1933. Chessie's first appearance on behalf of C&O was in the September 1933 issue of *Fortune Magazine*, in an ad that carried "Sleep Like a Kitten" as its slogan. The etching, executed by Guido Gruenewald, a Viennese artist who specialized in cats and other animals, was purchased for $5 for the railway's use.

The C&O's advertising agency built a whole campaign around the kitten and chose the name "Chessie" from the railroad's name. In 1934, 40,000 calendars were printed and ads featuring her appeared in most national magazines. Her popularity grew, as did her family. She got two look-alike kittens in 1935, and a mate, "Peake" (from the railroad name as well- Chesapeake = "Chessie-Peake") in 1937. Soon Chessie, "America's Sleepheart," was the talk of the railroad world, and propelled C&O to the top ranks of rail advertising.

Chessie Goes to War

In late 1941, C&O produced its 1942 calendar. Since thousands of men had already left home for military service, it was appropriate that the designers dress up Peake in the main illustration in an Army visor cap and add a letter he had penned to Chessie describing how he was now helping "national defense" (since war hadn't come when the calendars went to press). The letter noted that C&O was helping, too, moving men and materiel where and when needed. Chessie, the letter said, was doing a good job, also, representing C&O and acting as a symbol of enduring peace.

Then the day of infamy came and America was plunged into the long night of war, and Chessie picked up the mantle on the home front while Peake went off to serve in other climes.

As soon as the ads showing Peake in uniform appeared, a flood of mail poured into the Terminal Tower C&O offices in downtown Cleveland, this time addressed not only to Chessie, but also to Peake. Within 96 hours of publication of the calendar ads in the national magazines, the C&O Advertising Department under Walter S. Jackson (C&O's advertising manager and chief administrative coordinator of ad agency work) received thousands of letters ... twice as many as in the same period the previous year.

Peake - "Chessie's Old Man" - was first introduced in a C&O advertisement on Father's Day 1937, and he appears in the 1938 calendar. It featured three pages, Chessie on the first, Peake on the second, and Chessie and Her Kittens on the third. At last, the whole family was together, riding the C&O's air-conditioned fleet of trains! Peake would be a major feature of the calendars through 1948. © 1938 CSX Transportation, used with permission.

Peake is doing his part for the war and his country, portrayed here in a jaunty army "overseas cap" and pack, somewhere in a war zone. He looks at a photo of his girl Chessie on his barracks wall while he reads a letter from her that says she eagerly awaits his return. © 1944 CSX Transportation, used with permission.

Postwar

In 1947 the Chesapeake & Ohio Railway embarked on a program of improvements, innovations, and experimentation like no other railroad in any era before or since. Under the personal leadership of Robert R. Young ,C&O's mercurial and visionary chairman of the board, the railroad was moving ahead on all fronts to capture as much of the postwar boom traffic as possible. Young's main thrust, and the most public manifestation of his new drive, was the improvement of C&O's passenger service that resulted in the advertisements that have become legend in the public relations world.

One of Young's pet projects was the introduction of a new super-luxury coach train between Washington and Cincinnati, to be called, of course, the *Chessie*. The rear marker (called a "drumhead" in railroad terms) for the train would be a portrait of Chessie in her usual pose. It would have cars of the most modern design, including dome coaches, cabin cars with private rooms, luxurious coaches with leg-rest reclining seats, superior diners, and lounges, as well as family cars with children's theaters and facilities to assist the traveling mother.

Chessie System

Probert's creative genius blossomed again across the generations. The Chessie System paint scheme for locomotives and cars was introduced to the public and employees

in the summer of 1972. Each new bright yellow 4100-series GP40-2 locomotive cost an estimated $800 more to paint than the previous scheme of blue with simple "C&O" or "B&O" letters. But the image was so striking and the kitten still so popular that Chessie System soon became the darling of railfan photographers and the general public. The introduction of this new logo and paint scheme for locomotives and cars was a PR coup second only to the original introduction of Chessie herself nearly 40 years before.

In an era less sophisticated than our own, Chessie became the darling of millions, helping bolster the spirit of a Depression-ravaged people, and then seeing them through the great conflict of World War II. Chessie lead the way as "America's Sleep Warden," and gave up her Pullman berth for traveling soldiers. After the war, she returned to her passenger promotional work for the railway that had itself become widely known as "Chessie." After the takeover of passenger service by Amtrak in 1971, Chessie took on a new role, giving her name to the combined C&O, Baltimore & Ohio and Western Maryland Railways under Chessie System, and helped them sell their freight service.

Today, Chessie no longer appears in timetables or on locomotives and railroad cars, but she nevertheless is alive in the hearts of millions who grew up during her life's work on the C&O and successor lines. Interest in her and her history is perhaps as great now as when she was the foremost advertiser of railroad passenger travel.

Pullman Service

C&O operated a sleeping car service fairly early in its life and continued until the end of passenger service and Amtrak's take over in 1971. During most of this time

This is the Chessie art work for the 1956 calendar, showing a little girl telling the conductor to be quiet because Chessie is asleep. She is no longer in the "Lower 9" berth of the heavyweight era, but now in one of the comfortable bedrooms in the sleek new lightweight C&O sleeping cars. (C&OHS Collection)

This GE B30-7 locomotive shows how a stylized Chessie image was used to create the "Ches-C" letter "C" which was used as both the logo and the first letter in the road name. Photo taken at at Huntington, WV Sep. 23, 1983. (C&OHS Collection, COHS 33071)

it contracted with The Pullman Company to operate this service. Most railroads did this. The Pullman Company (and some competitors in the early years) built and staffed the cars, and the railroads just carried them. In the 20th Century Pullman had become a monopoly in this business, running almost all the sleeping cars on American railroads. It worked in this way: The railway would sell the passenger a first class ticket, which was more expensive than a coach ticket. Then, the passenger would be sold space on the sleeping car as a "space charge." When he/she got on the train, the tickets were presented to the C&O conductor and the Pullman Conductor. The C&O conductor lifted the railroad ticket and the Pullman conductor took the space ticket. A porter working for Pullman was assigned to handle the passengers' needs in each car. A Pullman conductor was required if one or more Pullman cars operated on a train. The cars were cleaned and maintained by Pullman employees except in emergencies and shopped at Pullman shops located around the country. They were lettered Pullman rather than the railroad name. In fact, not only did Pullman own and operate the cars, it built them. Congress required the breakup of the Pullman monopoly just after WWII and as a result two companies were formed. The Pullman Company continued to operate the cars, but was now owned jointly by all the railroads that used the service. The car building portion of the company continued building railroad cars until recent times as a separate private company, as Pullman-Standard Car Manufacturing Co.

C&O was not a large user of Pullman cars as with roads which had large passengers services and never operated a regularly scheduled all-Pullman train except the seasonal *Resort Special*. It did have Pullman cars on all its mainline

Broadside view of a C&O steel coach built by Pullman in 1917 shows a typical early steel car. (C&OHS Collection, COHS 7437)

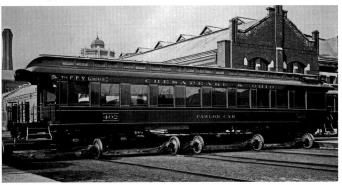
Fancy wooden observation lounge car 402 is decorated with the FFV name on its letter board and was used in the train in the 1890s. (C&OHS Collection, COHS 7434)

trains and as was described above had a number of Pullman lines running to and from locations not only on the C&O but to many destinations off-line (see material earlier in this chapter).

Mail and Express Operations

One of the important components of passenger service was mail and express. This is often called "head end" business or traffic because it was always carried in cars at the head end of passenger trains.

Express was handled by independent express companies that operated on many different railroad by contract. In World War I many of these were consolidated under the "American Railway Express Company," which later became "Railway Express Agency." By the early 1930s almost all of the other express companies were gone, and Railway Express Agency (REA) handled all the business up to the end. The C&O's agent at a particular location was usually also the REA agent and did the paperwork and labor associated with the express business. Express consisted of generally smaller parcels (what we would give to UPS today), headed to various locations across the country. Just like the LCL operation, this was often sorted at major terminals, etc. It was sent in sealed cars that looked like what we would normally call "baggage cars" with large side doors or, for local work, at least one car on the train would have an REA employee called a "messenger" who put the packages off at the right station or picked them up from the station. At very large cities a separate agent was employed to handle express business. The C&O was paid a set price for carrying the car(s)

The interior of the George Washington's observation car had all the modern conveniences of the era including radio. Houdin's bust of Washington in the alcove above the door was a salute to the Great Man whose name the train took as well as the "Crossing the Delaware" painting on the bulkhead. (C&OHS Collection, COHS 7432)

in its trains and for handling the paperwork and labor of the business. The cars were owned by the railway and not the express company. So, as can be seen it was a hybrid, part C&O, part REA operation. As passenger service decline express declined and eventually was replaced by today's FedEx, UPS, DHL, etc.

U. S. Mail

Almost from the outset in the 1830s, mail began to be carried by the railroads. In the early years it was given to the railway's personnel abroad the train (usually the baggage man on a train) who saw to it that the sealed pouch was put off at the proper station. In this case the post office employees came to the station and exchanged the mail. The C&O's agent had nothing to do with it.

As things became more sophisticated, a postal employee was put on the train called an "agent" who not only handled the sealed pouches, but also put on and took aboard local mail as well. This eventually developed into the "Railway Post Office" (RPO) in the 1880s. The RPO was staffed by regular mail clerks from the post office and run entirely by then, delivering and picking up with postal employees at the various stations. C&O's only responsibility was to carry the car. The car was owned by the railway and was rated and carried at a set rate per mile paid by the Post Office. By the 1920s this was a very highly developed, complicated, and superbly efficient operation. Mail was taken on at each station and sorted immediately while the train was traveling, and the dispatched to stations, other trains, post offices to be forwarded, etc. A letter put on at one station could often be sorted in time to be put off at the next. Many believe it was the pinnacle of postal operations.

The other type of mail carried was "closed pouch," or "storage mail." This consisted of closed or sealed pouches of mail that were not opened or sorted en route but carried to specific stations or terminals as partial car loads

or even full sealed cars. The railway's baggage man usually handle closed pouch mail for local station, whereas through traffic went in sealed cars.

In 1950 there were about 10,000 intercity passenger trains in the U. S., almost 6,000 of which carried mail. As trains were discontinued the network began to falter, caused by the rise of good roads and airmail. By the early 1960s the RPO was doomed and most were discontinued in 1966-1969 era. The last on the C&O were on Trains 1 and 2, the *George Washington*, up through 1969. A RPO did run on the old PM lines until 1970, as the Detroit-Grand Rapids Line.

Mail was a good source of revenue and often the mail contract was the determining factor in a train's profitability, especially in the later years.

Station workers load mail on a C&O RPO in a time-honored tradition from the days when Mail by Rail was the finest postal service on Earth. (C&O Ry. Photo, C&OHS Collection, COHS 35938)

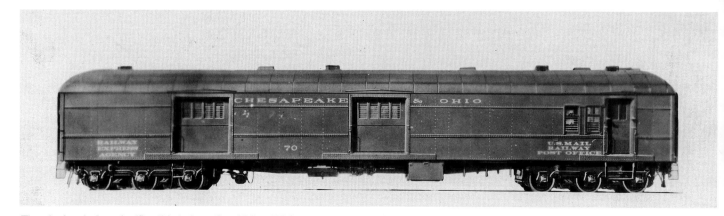

The single window signifies this to be a tiny 15-foot RPO section in the combination RPO and Express (M&E) car No. 70 (built by the ACF in 1930). The 15-foot space was one of the most common RPO authorizations on the C&O, appearing on scores of branch lines. (C&OHS Collection, COHS 22035)

Typical wooden-era C&O full combination RPO/Express "M&E" car No. 77 was built by C&O Huntington Shops in 1909 seen here at Clifton Forge in 1915. (C&OHS Collection, COHS 3839)

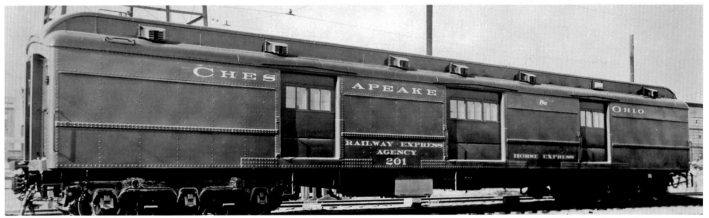

Horse Express car No.201 is shown here now at St. Louis in 1937, ready to be delivered to C&O to handle the high class horse business occasioned by its line to Lexington, Kentucky. When not in horse service the car was used in regular express work and was liked by the express messengers because of the 3-door configuration. (C&OHS Collection, COHS 7710)

Postal clerks work the mail in C&O RPO car No. 110 on its last week of service as the WASH & CIN ED RPO. A week after this May 1, 1968, photo, the trains that hauled it (Nos. 3 & 4) were discontinued and this became the last RPO route on the old C&O main stem. T. W. Dixon, Jr. photograph. (C&OHS Collection, COHS 7710)

Early C&O RPO Routes

Richmond & Clifton Forge (1882 - ?)
Clifton Forge & Huntington (1882-1889) (1897-1909)
Richmond & Huntington (1882-86) (1888-1890) (1907-1917)
Richmond-Ashland (1886-1888)
Washington & Hinton (1890-1917)
Richmond & Hinton (1890-93)(1907-08)
Richmond, Gordonsville & Clifton Forge (1893-1907)(1908-1909)
Richmond & Clifton Forge (Via Lynchburg) 1892-1957)
Others during era operating over James River Line (R&A and then C&O)

Some Modern Main Line C&O RPO Routes

Ft. Monroe & Richmond (1903-1941)
Newport News & Richmond (1954-59)
Newport News & Charlottesville (1959-64)
Richmond & Charlottesville (1931-59)
Hinton & Cincinnati (1890-1935)
Washington & Cincinnati ED (1935-1968)
Washington & Cincinnati WD (1935-1968)
Washington & Cincinnati MD (WWII years)

Many Short Routes Operating on Most Branches

Shortest of all RPO routes - Thurmond & Price Hill (1917-1949)
Huntington & Logan (1949-1959)
Quinnimont & Lester (1909-1949)
Durbin & Ronceverte (1942-1957)
St. Albans & Monclo (1933-1948)
Richmond & Clifton Forge (via Lynchburg) (1892-1957)
Toledo & Huntington (1932-1952)
Detroit & Huntington (1952-1962)
Columbus & Pomeroy (1889-1949)

A typical C&O passenger train of the 1950-1951 era with an ultramodern J-3a 4-8-4 steam locomotive (built 1948) and a train made up of heavyweight cars still in green paint and lightweight cars in the new scheme. No. 612 is in charge of what is probably No. 4, the Sportsman *on North Mountain near Blue Ridge Tunnel, May 10, 1951. By the beginning of 1952, steam had been supplanted by E8 diesels on C&O mainline trains. Photo by Bob Collins. (C&OHS Collection, COHS 35098)*

Roster of C&O Lightweight Passenger Cars

The *Pere Marquette* Equipment (Built 1946)

10-11	Diner (Retained until 1968-69)
20-21	Coach: 58 seats/10 in Lounge (Sold 1951)
22-23	Coach: 58 Seats/10 Lounge (Sold 1951)
30-33	Coach: 56 Seats/10-Lounge (Sold 1951)
50-51	RPO/Baggage (Retained until 1967)
60-61	Full Baggage (Retained until 1969 and 1967 respectively)

The *Chessie* Equipment (Built 1948)

1400-1402	Coach/Baggage Combine (1401-02 sold, 1403 To Amtrak 1971)
1500-1501	Coach-Lounge: 36 Seats/8-Lounge Seats (Sold 1951)
1600-1609	Coach-Lounge: 36 Seats/8-Lounge Seats (Sold 1951)
1700-1702	Family Coach: 32 Seats + Facilities for Children (Sold 1951)
1850-1852	Dome/Cabin/Drawing Room Car (Sold 1950)
1875-1877	Dome/Coach/Observation Car (Sold 1949)
1900-1902	Lunch Counter/Tavern/Lounge (6 lunch, 8 snack, 10 lounge, 25 diner seats) (Sold 1951)
1920-1922	Lunch Counter/Diner/Obsv. (Retained in service sold Amtrak 1971)
1940-1942	Lunch Counter-Kitchen-Dorm Twin Unit Diner
1970-1972	Dining Room/ Theater Car in Twin Unit Set (all sold 1949-1950)

Pullman-Standard Equipment Built for Main Line Reequipping (Built 1950)

1403	Coach/Baggage Combine (Sold 1955).
1600-1668	Coach: 52 Seats with Divider at Center (Some sold, most remained until 1971: remainder sold or scrapped.) (1610-11 rebuilt as Coach/Diner - Sold 1971.)
1800-1803	Parlor for Michigan Service (Sold 1959)
1903	"Chessie Club" Lunch Counter/Buffet/Lounge (Sold 1971)
1950-1957	
1973-1980	Twin Unit Diners (Sold 1950)
2500-2507	5-Bedroom/Buffet/Observation (Nos. 2500,01,04,05,07 Sold 1951; Nos. 2500, 2503, 2506 Rebuilt and Diner/Dorm 1962, sold 1971)
2600-2655	10-Roomette/6-Double Bedroom Sleeper (Several sold 1950, balance retired 1971)
2800-2804	11-Double Bedroom Sleepers - Retained in Service, sold 1969-70)

The Chesapeake & Ohio Railway - A Concise History and Fact Book

C&O Passenger Equipment 1948

These pages from the 1948 C&O Consist Book, show the car roster as well as the assignment of Pullman Sleeping Cars and whether or not they were lettered for the George Washington. Regular assignment are also shown for these cars as well as diners, and postal cars. Full postal cars are shown with 60-foot RPO authorizations, the combined express, baggage and RPO cars are shown with either a 30-foot or 15-foot RPO authorization. The end points of the RPO routes are annotated. This represents the last assignments of the fully heavyweight fleet of Sleepers, Diners, and Postal Cars.

THE CHESAPEAKE AND OHIO RAILWAY COMPANY

C. & O. PASSENGER EQUIPMENT

A.A.R. M.E. B.H. Designation.	KIND.	SERIES OF NUMBERS.	SEATING CAPACITY.	LENGTH OF CAR.	No.	A.A.R. M.E. B.H. Designation.	KIND.	SERIES OF NUMBERS.	SEATING CAPACITY.	LENGTH OF CAR.	No.
PV	Business	1 to 8			8	PB	Passenger	555 and 556	Under 70	60 ft. & under 70 ft.	2
PV	Business	27 to 29			3	PB	Passenger	600 to 606	Over 70	70 ft. and over.	7
MB	Mail and Express	60 to 91		70 ft. and over.	32	PB	Passenger	607 to 627	80 to 85	70 ft. and over.	21
MA	Postal	105 to 112		60 ft. & under 70 ft.	8	PB	Passenger	635 to 718	80 to 86	70 ft. and over.	66
BH	Express	200 to 212		70 ft. and over.	12	PB	Passenger	719 to 722	Under 70	70 ft. and over.	4
BX	Express (Box)	220 to 226		Under 60 ft.	7	PB	Passenger	723 and 724	85	70 ft. and over.	2
BE	Express	230 to 231		60 ft. & under 70 ft.	2	PB	Passenger	725 to 754	Under 70	70 ft. and over.	29
MR	Express	240 to 249		70 ft. and over.	10	PB	Passenger	800 to 861	80 to 83	70 ft. and over.	45
BE	Express	258 to 271		70 ft. and over.	14	PB	Passenger	862 to 876	Under 70	70 ft. and over.	15
BE	Express	273 to 278		70 ft. and over.	6	PB	Passenger	659	80	70 ft. and over.	1
BE	Express	280 to 291		70 ft. and over.	12	PBA	Passenger	1500 to 1511	Under 70	70 ft. and over.	12
BE	Express	296 to 317		70 ft. and over.	18	PBA	Passenger	1600 to 1609	Under 70	70 ft. and over.	10
BE	Express	379 to 380		60 ft. & under 70 ft.	2	PBA	Passenger	1700 to 1702	Under 70	70 ft. and over.	3
BE	Express	385 to 399		70 ft. and over.	15	PS	Sleeping	1850 to 1852	Under 70	70 ft. and over.	3
BX	Express	217 and 218		Under 60 ft.	2	PBO	Passenger	1875 to 1877	Under 70	70 ft. and over.	3
CO	Pass., Mail & Express	400 to 404	Under 70	70 ft. and over.	5	DC	Cafe	1900 to 1902	Under 70	70 ft. and over.	3
CA	Pass. and Express	407 to 412	Under 70	60 ft. & under 70 ft.	5	DCL	Lunch Counter	1920 to 1922	Under 70	70 ft. and over.	3
CA	Pass. and Express	413 to 420	Under 70	70 ft. and over.	6	DC	Cafe	1940 to 1942	Under 70	70 ft. and over.	3
CA	Pass. and Express	439 to 481	Under 70	70 ft. and over.	39	DA	Diner	1970 to 1972	Under 70	70 ft. and over.	3
CA	Pass. and Express	550 to 552	Under 70	70 ft. and over.	3	DP	Club Diner	916 and 917	Under 70	70 ft. and over.	2
CA	Pass. and Express	1400 to 1402	Under 70	70 ft. and over.	3	PSA	Dormitory	920 to 925		70 ft. and over.	6
PB	Passenger	540 to 544	Over 70	70 ft. and over.	5	DA	Diner	959 to 972	Under 70	70 ft. and over.	13
DA	Diner	900 to 901	Under 70	70 ft. and over.	2	DA	Diner	912 to 915	Under 70	70 ft. and over.	4
DCL	Lunch Counter	902 to 903	Under 70	70 ft. and over.	2	DA	Diner	930 to 931	Under 70	70 ft. and over.	2
	Pass. & Express (Motor)	9050 to 9055			6	DA	Diner	980 to 981	Under 70	70 ft. and over.	2
PB	Passenger	586 and 587	Under 70	60 ft. & under 70 ft.	2		Total				493

(margin: 193)

This roster of in-service equipment shows the fleet as it was operated in August, 1948. Cars numbered 1500 through 1972 represent the recently-arrived equipment intended for the Chessie. This shows the fleet just before the arrival of the new Pullman-Standard cars in 1950. (C&OHS Collection, from page 193 of C&O Agents, Stations, Etc. No. 82, August 1948.)

DINING CAR ASSIGNMENTS (ALL AIR-CONDITIONED)   Revised 5-16-48

(*) Cars so designated are stenciled "THE GEORGE WASHINGTON" on letter board

Car	Class	Assignment Between	Trains
(W) 900	Military Diner	EXTRA SERVICE	
901	Military Diner	EXTRA SERVICE	
902	Cafeteria	EXTRA SERVICE	
903	Cafeteria	EXTRA SERVICE	
(S) 912 (Brent's Tavern)	Diner	Washington and Hinton	4 & 5
(S) 913 (Harrodsburg Tavern)	Diner	Detroit & Columbus	46 & 47
(S) 914 (Golden Eagle Tavern) PA	Lounge Diner	EXTRA SERVICE	
(S) 915 (Elbert's Tavern)	Diner	Washington & Hinton	4 & 5
916 (William Grayson)	Lounge Diner	Ashland & Louisville	23 & 24
917 (William Byrd)	Lounge Diner	Ashland & Louisville	23 & 24
959 (Ashby's Tavern)	Diner	Richmond to Huntington	47
961 (Old Homestead)	Diner	Huntington to Hinton	14
963 (Old White)	Diner	Hinton to Richmond	46
960 (Union Tavern) PA	Diner	EXTRA SERVICE	
962 (Michie's Tavern)	Diner	Cincinnati-Clifton Forge-Huntington	6 & 43-3
(*) 964 (Raleigh Tavern) PA	Diner	EXTRA SERVICE	
(*) 965 (Gadsby's Tavern)	Diner	Ashland & Louisville	21 & 22
966 (Sutter's Tavern)	Diner	EXTRA SERVICE	
(*) 968 (Fraunce's Tavern) PA-M	Diner	EXTRA SERVICE	
969 (Mkt. Sq. Tavern) M	Diner	Cincinnati & Phoebus	41 & 42
(*) 970 (City Tavern) M	Diner		
971 (Hanover Tavern)	Diner	Cincinnati & Clifton Forge-Huntington	6-43-3
972 (Swan Tavern)	Diner		
930 (Stuart Kitchen)	Twin Unit		
980 (Stuart House) M	Twin Unit	Cincinnati-Washington	1 & 2
931 (Carlyle Kitchen)	Twin Unit		
981 (Carlyle House) M	Twin Unit		

(S) Steam Ejector Type A. C.   M-Equipped with movie projectors.
(W) Waukesha Type A. C.   PA Equipped with public address system.

DINING CAR OPERATIONS

Three Cars operate:
No. 6—Cincinnati-Clifton Forge
No. 43—Clifton Forge-Huntington.
No. 6—Huntington-Clifton Forge.
No. 3—Clifton Forge-Cincinnati.

Two Units operate:
No. 2—Cincinnati-Washington.
No. 1—Washington-Cincinnati.

Two Cars operate:
No. 41—Phoebus-Cincinnati.
No. 42—Cincinnati-Phoebus.

Two Cars operate:
No. 4—Hinton-Washington.
No. 5—Washington-Hinton.

Three Cars operate:
No. 47—Richmond-Huntington.
No. 14—Huntington to Hinton.
No. 46—Hinton-Richmond.

One Car operates:
No. 46—Detroit-Columbus.
No. 47—Columbus-Detroit.

One Car operates:
No. 21—Ashland-Louisville.
No. 22—Louisville-Ashland.

Five Cars—EXTRA SERVICE.
One Car—EXTRA SERVICE. (Military Diner)
Two Cars—CAFETERIA.

LOUNGE DINERS

Two Cars operate:
No. 23—Ashland-Louisville.
No. 24—Louisville-Ashland. (Following day)

CAFE-COACH

One Car operates:
No. 36—Ashland-Shelby.
No. 39—Shelby-Ashland.

POSTAL AND MAIL APARTMENT CAR AUTHORIZATION

Trains	BETWEEN	Authorization	Daily Except as Noted
1	Hinton to Cincinnati	60 ft. R.P.O.	
2	Hinton to Charlottesville	30 ft. Apt.	Ex. Monday
3-4 & 6	Washington to Cincinnati	60 ft. R.P.O.	
5	Washington to Hinton	60 ft. R.P.O.	
15 & 16	Hinton to Huntington	15 ft. Apt.	Ex. Sunday
15 & 16	Cincinnati to Huntington	30 ft. Apt.	Ex. Sunday
9 & 10	Richmond to Clifton Forge	15 ft. Apt.	Ex. Sunday
11 & 12	Richmond to Lynchburg	15 ft. Apt.	Ex. Sunday
13	Charlottesville to Hinton	30 ft. Apt.	Ex. Sunday
13 & 14	Hinton to Huntington	30 ft. Apt.	Ex. Sunday
19 & 20	Cincinnati to Peru	15 ft. Apt.	Ex. Sunday
21 & 24	Ashland to Louisville	30 ft. Apt.	
22 & 23	Louisville to Ashland	30 ft. Apt.	Ex. Sunday
30-130	Columbus to Pomeroy	30 ft. Apt.	Ex. Sunday
33 & 34	Clifton Forge to Lynchburg	15 ft. Apt.	Ex. Sunday
35 & 36	Columbus to Toledo	15 ft. Apt.	Ex. Sunday
36 & 39	Ashland to Elkhorn City	30 ft. Apt.	Ex. Sunday
37 & 38	Elkhorn City to Ashland	15 ft. Apt.	Ex. Sunday

POSTAL AND MAIL APARTMENT CAR AUTHORIZATION Continued

Trains	BETWEEN	Authorization	Daily Except as Noted
141 & 44	Charlottesville to Richmond	15 ft. Apt.	Ex. Sunday
42 & 47	Richmond to Charlottesville	15 ft. Apt.	Ex. Sunday
46 & 47	Phoebus to Richmond	30 ft. Apt.	Ex. Sunday
46-146 & 47	Huntington to Toledo	30 ft. Apt.	Ex. Sunday
50 & 51	Lorado to Huntington	30 ft. Apt.	
49 & 52	Huntington to Logan	15 ft. Apt.	Ex. Sunday
58 & 59	Wayland to Allen	15 ft. Apt.	Ex. Sunday
113 & 114	Cabin Creek Jct. to Ameagle	15 ft. Apt.	Ex. Sunday
130 & 131	Ameagle to Colcord	15 ft. Apt.	Ex. Sunday
134 & 135	Mt. Hope to Thurmond	15 ft. Apt.	Ex. Sunday
136 & 137	Mt. Hope to Thurmond	15 ft. Apt.	Ex. Sunday
137-37	Pomeroy to Columbus	30 ft. Apt.	Ex. Sunday
141 & 42	Phoebus to Richmond	30 ft. Apt.	
142 & 143	Durbin to Ronceverte	15 ft. Apt.	Ex. Sunday
155 & 156	Lester to Quinnimont	30 ft. Apt.	Ex. Sunday
214 & 215	Monclo to St. Albans	15 ft. Apt.	Ex. Sunday
218-219	Whitesville to St. Albans	15 ft. Apt.	Ex. Sunday

ASSIGNED SLEEPER CAR OPERATION — Revised 5-10-48

(*) Cars so designated are stencilled "THE GEORGE WASHINGTON" on letter board

Car	Class	Between	Trains
(*) Commander in Chief	8 sec. obs. buffet lounge	Washington & Cincinnati	1 & 2
(*) American Revolution		Washington & Cincinnati	1 & 2
(*) Washington Elm			
(*) Midland Trail	8 sec. 1 DR lounge	Phoebus & Chicago	41-42
(*) Continental Congress			
Ohio Valley	8 sec. 1 DR buffet lounge	Washington & Cincinnati	3-43
Kentucky Home		Cincinnati & Washington	4
Sea Breeze	6 sec. 1 DR lounge	Hinton & Toledo	47
Sea View		Toledo & Hinton	46-14
Fort Washington	8 sec. 1 DR buffet lounge	Huntington & Phoebus	6-42
Port Union			43
Kanawha	6 sec. 1 DR 2 Compt. 2 DBR	Clifton Forge & Cleveland	46 & 47
Greenbrier		Clifton Forge & Cleveland	46 & 47
Homestead	6 sec. 1 DR 2 Compt. 2 DBR	New York & Hot Springs	3 & 6
Hot Springs			
(*) Williamsburg	8 sec. 1 DR 3 DBR	New York & Louisville	1-21-22-2
(*) Yorktown			
(*) Valley Forge			
(*) First Citizen		Cincinnati to New York	6
(*) Mount Vernon	8 sec. 1 DR 2 Compt.	New York to Cincinnati	3
(*) Potomac		Cincinnati to New York	6
Centcroft		New York to Washington (Local)	PRR
Stonewall Jackson		Washington to Cincinnati	1
Glen Trail	6 Compt. 3 DR	New York to White Sul. Spgs.	3-6
Glen Almond			

ASSIGNED SLEEPER CAR OPERATION Continued

Car	Class	Between	Trains
Wadsworth Oak	8 sec. 1 DR 2 Compt.	New York to Huntington	3-6 tri weekly
(*) James Craik			
(*) Tobias Lear	10 sec. 1 DR 1 Compt.	Washington & St. Louis	3 & 4
(*) James Harrod			
John Witherspoon	10 sec. 1 DR 1 Compt.	Washington & Ashland	3-43
Alexander Spotswood			2
David Mossom	10 sec. 1 DR 1 Compt.	EXTRA SERVICE	
Cape Flattery	10 sec. 1 DR 2 Compt.	New York & Huntington	3 & 6
Cape Romano			
(*) Simon Kenton			
(*) Sam Houston			
(*) William Clark	10 sec. 1 DR 2 DBR	Washington to San Antonio	1-NYC-MP-T&P
(*) Meriwether Lewis		San Antonio to Washington	T&P-MP-NYC-2
(*) Isaac Shelby			
(*) Jack Jouett		Washington to Louisville	1-21
(*) Governor Nelson		Louisville to Washington	24-4
(*) Pierre L'Enfant	10 sec. 1 DR 2 DBR	Washington to Louisville	3-43-23
(*) Charles Thomson		Louisville to Washington	22-2
(*) Chancellor Livingston			
(*) Brother Jonathon	12 sec. 1 DR	Richmond to Louisville	41-21
(*) Ferry Farm			22-42
Camp McCoy		Phoebus to Chicago	43
Fort Stevens	10 sec. 1 DR 2 Compt.	Chicago to Phoebus	46
Windom			
Neshuga	12 sec. 1 DR	Hinton-Pittsburgh	47-B&O-14
Securitas			

Additional Sources of Information for C&O Passenger Service and Equipment

Cars:

Wooden and Heavyweight Era: There are no good rosters of cars from the wooden and heavyweight era that give complete details. A complete heavyweight roster is being developed as this is written that may be available at a future date. The best information on these cars is in the C&O Historical Newsletter/C&O Historical Magazine published 1969 to present. Available on fully searchable CD from C&O Historical Society as Catalog No. AV-08-102. A compendium of heavyweight articles from the magazine was published as a softbound book:
• *Chesapeake & Ohio Heavyweight Passenger Cars* by C&OHS (118 pages) in 2006 and is available as Catalog No. BK-06-423).

Lightweight Era: A complete, detailed roster for all C&O lightweight cars ordered for the *Pere Marquettes*, the *Chessie*, and the mainline equipment including details on cars not delivered to C&O, and dispositions on all cars up to 1990 in the book:
• *Chesapeake & Ohio Streamliners - Second to None - Vol. 1, The Cars*, by James K. Millard and published by the C&O Historical Society in 1994. It also includes drawings/diagrams and scores of photographs of all the cars. Now out of print, but as of this writing a reprint is expected soon (contact C&OHS at address shown in the font of this book).
• *Chesapeake & Ohio Passenger Cars in Color* by Harry Stegmaier, TLC Publishing, Lynchburg, Va., 100-pages, hardbound, 2001. Full color photograph with details on both lightweight and heavyweight cars in the 1950-1971 era; also includes consists and train photographs.
• *C&O Passenger Car Diagram Book, 1949* (Reprint of 7x14 inch detailed C&O mechanical diagrams of each heavyweight and lightweight passenger train car in the – C&O fleet as of this date. Available from C&OHS as Cat. Number DS-08-081.
• *C&O Passenger Car Diagram Book, 1952* -Ditto (DS-07-047)
• *C&O Passenger Car Diagram Book, 1965* - Ditto (DS-07-050)

Passenger Service:
• *The George Washington, The Most Wonderful Train in the World, 1932-1950*, by Edgar Parke Billups, Hardbound, 304 pages. Published by C&O Historical Society 2012. Massive study of C&O's premier train in the Heavyweight Era. (Limited printing, consult C&OHS for availability.)
• *Chesapeake & Ohio Streamliners - Second to None, Vol. 1 , The Cars*, by James Kemper Millard, Published by C&O Historical Society 1994, Hardbound, 126 pages. No operational data, but details on the cars and background historical treatment.
• *Chesapeake & Ohio's Pere Marquettes* by Thomas W. Dixon, Jr. TLC Publishing, Lynchburg, Va. and C&OHS, 2004, softbound, 92 pages, order from C&OHS Catalog No. BK-03-348)
• *Instructions for Passenger & Freight Train Handling*, C&O Ry., 1952 - C&OHS Reprint (Catalog No. DS-00-191) Information on how enginemen were expected to handle passenger trains.
• *Rules and Regulations for Passenger Train Personnel*, C&O Ry., 1952 - C&OHS Reprint (Catalog No. DS-09-185) Complete instructions for all passenger train operations by conductors, brakemen and porters.
• *C&O Passenger Train Consist Book - 1938* (C&OHS Catalog No. DS-12-351)
• *C&O Passenger Train Consist Book - 1948* (C&OHS Catalog No. DS-7-039)
• *C&O Passenger Train Consist Book - 1952* (C&OHS Catalog No. DS-00-199)
• *C&O Passenger Train Consist Book - 1956* (C&OHS Catalog No. DS-00-198)
• *C&O Passenger Train Consist Book - 1965* (C&OHS Catalog No. DS-8-138)
• *C&O Historical Magazine*, various issues 1969-Present. (Catalog No, AV-08-102)

CHAPTER FIVE

Freight Train Service and Operations

Making a good show of exhaust, K-4 Kanawha 2-8-4 No. 2749 is moving a fast freight at Meads, Kentucky, on the Lexington Subdivision, about 1949. Gene Huddleston photograph. (C&OHS Collection, COHS 21060)

C&O's Freight Train Operation falls into two broad categories: coal and other. By far the bulk of C&O freight operation was the movement of coal from mine to market. This accounted to about 70% of the line's business until the 1947 merger with the Pere Marquette. The PM had a mainly "merchandise" (a term used to deal with traffic that was not originated in mines) traffic based on its heavy industry centered around the automobile manufacturing, and the carriage of completed autos. Once the merger occurred, the new, expanded post-1947 C&O was about 50% coal and 50% other in its traffic patterns. However, the "old" C&O lines in Virginia, West Virginia, Kentucky, and Ohio, were still mainly coal haulers.

This pattern of traffic influenced everything about the railway. The C&O tended to build its engines to specific purposes, as with most railroads in the steam era. Therefore, the carrying of coal east from West Virginia and Kentucky to Newport News was an important factor, especially the route of the Alleghany Subdivision over the 0.56% 13-mile long grade over Alleghany Mountain. C&O's mainline power was almost always measured against this operation. In the west it was the forwarding of very heavy (usually about 14,000 ton) trains of coal from West Virginia and Kentucky fields to Toledo, Cincinnati, and other points in the Midwest.

Coal, of course, traveled in non-scheduled extra trains. The C&O supplied empty cars to the mines, then picked them up, assembled them into trains at marshalling yards which were located in the coal fields, then took them to mainline classification terminals (Russell for west and eastbound coal, and Clifton Forge for eastbound coal). Once blocked into cars for specific destinations, the trains were then forwarded to final terminals.

Almost all the coal classified at Clifton Forge was sent to Newport News piers via the low-grade James River and Rivanna Subdivisions (informally known together as the "James River Line"). Some coal was sent over the Mountain Subdivision, especially after the arrival of diesels, but generally coal headed for the Northern Virginia/Maryland, and Washington market was sent down the James River Line to Strathmore on the Rivanna Subdivision, where it was sent over the short Virginia Air Line Subdivision northward to a connection with Lindsay on the Washington Subdivision and thence eastward. This avoided the heavy grades of the Mountain Subdivision. Most of this coal came from West Virginia mines, with some also from Kentucky mines.

Russell yard classified westbound coal and some eastbound, out of both West Virginia and Kentucky mines. Most of the coal traffic from here went over the Northern Subdivision to Columbus, and over the Hocking Division to Toledo, where it was dumped into Great Lakes freighters for further transport to the consumers around the Lakes. A large amount was also handed over to connecting lines north of Columbus for shipment to Midwestern points, including Nickel Plate, Pennsylvania, and New York Central. East-

In July 1947, K-3 2-8-2 Miakdo No. 1261 switches the eastbound Alleghany Subdivision local freight at White Sulphur Springs. Note the brakeman standing on to last car. A full signal bridge controlled the tracks at its point. (J. I. Kelly Photo, C&OHS Collection, COHS 375)

bound coal from Russell went to Clifton Forge where it was reclassified and forward to final terminals. Some coal also went down the Cincinnati Division from Russell to Cincinnati. The C&O was involved as well in forwarding a considerable quantity of interchange coal received from the Virginian Railway at Deepwater and Gilbert, West Virginia. Since the Virginian had no lines west of these points, it relied on C&O to transport a good amount of its westbound coal, along with neighbor N&W.

C&O maintained marshalling yards in the coal fields that consisted of an engine terminal for locomotives used in 'mine run' or 'mine shifter trains' (both terms are found), and numerous yard tracks. From these points empty cars were taken to mine by the mine run trains, and loads returned to the marshalling yard. These loads were then assembled into large trains and sent to one of the mainline classification terminals.

Freight trains carrying non-mine products were usually called "manifest freights," and sometimes "fast freights," and were operated at expedited speeds on a regular schedule according to a published timetable. They had precedence below passenger trains and above coal trains. In general, C&O did not have a large quantity of through fast freight, but it did carry an appreciable amount. From the west the primary terminals for gathering and beginning eastbound manifest service (called so because the consists of the trains were telegraphed ahead to then next terminal, thus "made

manifest"), were Chicago and Cincinnati, and in a smaller extent Louisville, Detroit, Toledo, and Columbus. Trains with through traffic from foreign roads originated at these points, and were reshuffled (set off and picked up cars) at various intermediate terminals including Russell, Huntington, Charleston, Hinton, Clifton Forge, and Charlottesville. Eastern terminals were Potomac Yard (near Washington, D. C.) for the northeastern points, and Newport News (traffic to and from oceangoing and coastwise ships).

Lowest in precedence among freight operations were the local freight trains. These trains delivered box car loads and less-than-carload (LCL) freight to various local stations along the C&O lines. LCL freight was also called "package freight," and consisted of any shipments that didn't require a full car to transport. This could be as small as a 50 pound barrel of nails to several thousand pounds of refrigerators, etc. The LCL freight was assembled in freight stations at various terminals and then loaded in cars to be sent out on the local freights. Some of this freight was headed for destinations on foreign railroads, and full cars of many different shipments were regularly sent to major gateway terminals for further sorting and forwarding, and vice versa. Large LCL freight assembly stations included Newport News, Charlottesville, Clifton Forge, Hinton, Charleston, Huntington, Ashland, and Cincinnati, as well as Columbus, Toledo, and Louisville. Local freights usually were sent in each direction daily from the major divisional terminal. For example one

K-2 Mikado No. 1189 is switching the Rivanna Subdivision eastbound local freight beside the C&O depot at Bremo, Virginia, November 3, 1950. The station is typical of those built by the Richmond & Alleghany RR before it merged into C&O in 1890. K-2s were standard on almost all trains on this line, local and through. (J. D. Welsh Photo, C&OHS Collection, CSPR 1233)

train was started west from Clifton Forge to Hinton each weekday with stops to drop off and receive LCL and full car freight to all the stations in between. At the same time a westbound local would start from Hinton headed for Clifton Forge. An eastbound train would also start from Clifton Forge for Charlottesville and another westbound from that point to Clifton Forge, and so on all across the system.

Some coal branches had enough non-coal traffic to warrant a regular local freight train, but most did not, so the cars were often simply put on an empty coal train headed up the line and brought back on a loaded coal extra. This is why one sometimes sees a box car or two on the front in photos, right behind the locomotive, an operation many modelers seem not to know about.

Finally, extra freights were sometimes run when cars had to be moved but a regularly scheduled train wasn't available. Coal trains were run "as needed" as extra trains.

If a full car load was destined to a consignee at one of these stations, then it was taken by the local and placed on the customer's private siding or "team track" at the depot. The team track was located so that the customer could bring

his "team" (motor truck in later days) and pick it up directly using his own labor. If the customer got LCL freight he came to the freight depot (or the freight section of a combination station), and picked it up there in his own conveyance. Customers with large business getting many carloads of freight per day were usually located in and around major terminals and their traffic was handled by special switchers operating from the terminal yard.

Although a lot of attention was given to passenger operations and those trains were the pride of the line, it was the freight business (coal and other) that made all the money. In general, passenger revenue accounted for less than 5% of income and freight 95%. Yet, we know so much more about passenger trains because of the public appeal and at the advertising and other attention given them. Little concrete data has survived about the prosaic freight trains.

In the years following World War II C&O decided to emphasize its fast freight service and gave names to its two fastest manifest freight train, the *Speedwest* going west and the *Expeditor* going east, and gave these trains priority attention in getting over the road. This, however lasted

This 1942 photo show an eastbound fast freight train with a number of refrigerator cars ready to leave MX Cabin (in the distance) at the east end of Hinton's Avis yard. No. 1602 has just arrived on the C&O, fresh from Lima Locomotive Works. *(C&O Ry. Photo, C&OHS Collection, CSPR 256)*

only short time before the pattern settled into a couple of manifests each way each day over most of the main stems. Emphasis during the 1950s and early 1960s was given to the "Car Ferry Route." This was an expedited service across Michigan on the old Pere Marquette lines connecting with the C&O's fleet of huge freight car carrying ferry boats (actually ships by any measure since they were most about 400 feet long), which connected with railroads in Wisconsin at the ports of Milwaukee, Kewaunee, and Manitowoc. In the east, the trains crossed into Canada on tackage rights on the New York Central, allowing through C&O traffic to reach Buffalo, New York, creating it as a new fast freight gateway for C&O well into the 1960s era.

With the C&O and B&O affiliation and essential merger into Chessie System in 1963 and 1972 respectively, the pattern of fast freight trains gradually changed, with more of the through traffic going via B&O lines and C&O lines becoming more and more coal-oriented.

In addition to coal and general merchandise (box car) traffic, agricultural products were an important business for C&O, more in the early era than in the latter. Stock pens and chutes were available at almost every station and cattle especially were important. C&O maintained a stock yard resting facility at Hinton since rules required stock to be fed, watered and rested en route.

F7 ABA set of road diesels is powering manifest freight No. 92 eastbound at Blue Hole, W. Va. in the New River Gorge region in April 1956. Note the many tank cars in the train, probably originating with the big chemical plants at Charleston. *(Gene Huddleston Photo, C&OHS Collection, COHS 2382)*

The Chesapeake & Ohio Railway - A Concise History and Fact Book

C&O GP9 diesels 5962 and 6022 with a north-bound coal train on the Big Sandy branch near Paintsville, Kentucky in 1964. (C&O Ry. Photo, C&OHS Collection, CSPR 5023)

Lynchburg was the largest city on the James River line between Clifton Forge and Richmond, and the point which C&O crossed the N&W and Southern Railways. This huge freight station served the city's needs during the era of LCL freight. It burned in the late 1980s. (T. W. Dixon, Jr. photo).

The C&O had two large Cincinnati area yards. One was at Cheviot, Ohio, about seven miles west of the city. The predominance of merchandise freight reflects the amount of traffic on the Chicago Division, Cincinnati-Chicago. Here Mikado No. 1123 shifts in the yard in June 1948. (C&O Ry. Photo, C&OHS Collection, CSPR 1469)

This 1945 photo shows laborers transferring, loading, and unloading Less-Than-Carload (LCL) freight at the Huntington freight station. (C&O Ry. Photo, C&OHS Collection, CSPR 57.14)

In 1957, the C&O introduced a new special paint scheme for the cars that it dedicated to handling its declining LCL business. But by 1962, the business was gone, completely overtaken and eclipsed by motor freight within a decade after WWII. (C&O Ry. Photo, C&OHS Collection, CSPR 4031)

The huge H-8 Allegheny type locomotives, pride of the C&O in the 1940s, were standard for Manifest Freight trains, especially operating in the mountain districts. Here one passes Alleghany while another of the type is ieastbound with an empty coal train in 1948 (C&O Ry. Photo, COHS Collection, CSPR 2244).

K-4 No. 2736 has an eastbound freight in tow on the mainline just east of Russell in the summer of 1956, at the very end of steam operations. (Gene Huddleston Photo, C&OHS Collection, COHS1680)

TRAIN No. 94-194-294-394-494-894

Through Time Freight Train

SCHEDULE

Chicago (Rockwell Street)		* 8:30 P. M.
+Burnham		*10:00 P. M.
○Peru		*12:30 A. M.
+Peru		* 1:45 A. M.
+Muncie		* 3:15 A. M.
○Cheviot		* 6:15 A. M.
Stevens		3:30 P. M.
○Russell		7:45 P. M.
Toledo	(190)	8:00 A. M.
+Fostoria		9:05 A. M.
○Columbus		12:45 P. M.
+Columbus	(194)	4:30 P. M.
Russell		8:30 P. M.
Louisville	(394)	* 9:45 A. M.
○Lexington		*12:45 P. M.
+Lexington	(394)	* 2:01 P. M.
○Ashland		* 7:00 P. M.
Russell		8:25 P. M.
Russell	(294)	10:15 P. M.
+Ashland		10:40 P. M.
○Shelby		2:50 A. M.
Elkhorn City		5:00 A. M.
+Russell	(94)	10:30 P. M.
○○+Ashland		10:53 P. M.
○○+Huntington		11:35 P. M.
○○+Charleston		1:05 A. M.
Handley		2:00 A. M.
○Hinton		5:00 A. M.
+Hinton	(94)	6:30 A. M.
○○Ronceverte		7:30 A. M.
○○Covington		9:30 A. M.
○Clifton Forge		10:30 A. M.
Clifton Forge	(494)	1:00 P. M.
Fordwick (See Note 2)		2:22 P. M.
○+Staunton		4:05 P. M.
○+Waynesboro		4:35 P. M.
○+Waynesboro (U. S.)		4:59 P. M.
○Charlottesville		7:40 P. M.
+Charlottesville	(894)	8:40 P. M.
○+Gordonsville		9:35 P. M.
Potomac Yard		1:30 A. M.
+Clifton Forge	(94)	1:15 P. M.
○Lynchburg		3:40 P. M.
○Gladstone		5:35 P. M.
+Gladstone		6:35 P. M.
+Strathmore		8:00 P. M.
○Richmond		11:45 P. M.
+Richmond	(94)	12:45 A. M.
○Penniman		2:30 A. M.
Newport News		3:45 A. M.
Norfolk (Sewalls Point)		8:45 A. M.
Norfolk (C. & O. Terminal)		‡10:30 A. M.

Note 1.—Handles time freight from Chicago Stock Yard District, Clearing, Rockwell Street and Burnham for Cincinnati Connections.

Note 2.—No. 494 picks up only freight at Fordwick not ready on departure of No. 56.

*Indicates Central Standard Time.
+Indicates Pick-up Point.
○Indicates Set-off Point.
○○Indicates Set-off point. Perishable only.
‡Daily except Sunday and Holiday.

TRAIN No. 94-194-294-394-494-894

Cut Off Time by C. & O. from Connections.

Burnham	* 9:00 P. M.
Columbus	12:01 P. M.
Cincinnati	9:00 A. M. from P. R. R.
Cincinnati	10:30 A. M. from Sou. Ry.—Perishables only.
Louisville	* 7:45 A. M. Perishables.

Cut Off Time by Connections from C. & O.

Columbus	2:00 P. M. for N. & W. No. 84.
Richmond	11:00 P. M. for A. C. L. No. 99.
Richmond	5:00 A. M. for S. A. L. No. 27.

Special Instructions.

Greggs	Cars handled to Russell ahead of No. 194.
Russell	Cars on Lexington No. 394 and Northern No. 194 for destinations served by No. 98 are cut out and moved on No. 98.
Russell	Cars for Ashland and Huntington cut out Russell and handled in train immediately following.
Lynchburg	Picks up Perishables for points via Potomac Yard Gateway, Richmond and East.

*Indicates Central Standard Time.

This schedule (Right column and above) shows one of C&O's "hottest" manifest freights, No. 94 from Chicago, with cars coming in from Columbus and Louisville. Taken from the 1954 C&O Time Freight Book) (C&OHS Collection)

C&O H-8 No.1624 with train pulling away from the coaling station at Thurmond, W.Va. September, 1955. This is obviously a coal train, but it has several covered hoppers up front. Photograph by Gene Huddleston. (C&OHS Collection, COHS 1203)

C&O station at Alleghany, Va. with local freight switching September, 1950. A car is being left on the team track. Photograph by Gene Huddleston. (C&OHS Collection, COHS 1512)

The Chesapeake & Ohio Railway - A Concise History and Fact Book

CHAPTER SIX

C&O Freight Train Equipment   This Chapter Written by Al Kresse

One of the earliest photographs showing C&O freight cars is this showing 4-wheel and 8-wheel C&O flat-bottom gondola cars loaded with coal stagged on a siding at Quinnimont, West Virginia, in 1882. (C&OHS Collection, COHS 714)

Freight Equipment

The post-reorganization Chesapeake & Ohio Railway Company documents, of the 1880s, began to differentiate between more than four- or eight-wheeled, and "open" or "closed" freight cars. From 1880 through the turn-of-the-century, there was a stepped growth of car capacities from 15-ton to eventually 40-ton and 50-ton wooden coal cars. Coal car designs eventually changed from flat-bottom gondola cars with drop-bottom doors, to hopper-bottom gondola cars with internal slopes that didn't require men to hand-shovel the last of the coal out through the doors. Many of the images that you will see of the early wooden freight cars are builder's photographs of rebuilt, damaged cars equipped with "modern" Jenny couplers, put back into service 15-20 years after optimal-periods of usage. In the early-1900s, the industry and the C&O made the difficult transition from all-wood, to steel-underframes and wooden upper structures, then to all-steel freight cars. Just prior to the First World War, the genesis of the "modern" freight car would be brought into service. The solid, cast sideframe for four-wheel trucks made possible the 70-ton capacity coal cars. They were built with various "saw-tooth" and "clam-shell" shaped hoppers, with quick-disconnect doors, as car became the "utility player" that worked well at small mines with winding tracks, at the local coal yards, and either the Lake or Tidewater

outlets. Box cars also grew over this era, from 36-feet inside lengths to 40-feet, to even 50-feet. The C&O also purchased ventilated and ice-bunker box cars to haul fruits and vegetables, and stock cars for hauling livestock, from the booming local agricultural communities it then served. All-steel box cars began replacing wooden-sheathed box cars in the early-1930s. The largest infusion of box cars into the C&O came with absorption of the Pere Marquette Railway, can be seen in todays' flood-unloading coal cars. The all-wooden freight car understructure was supported by a "queen-post and tension-rod" truss system. They also utilized fabricated "arch-bar" trucks. "closed" cars of the era were essentially, open-car platforms with tops or diagonal and vertical truss

Builder's photograph of a replacement wooden 30-ton hopper bottom gondola car, C&O 11519, with a rachette and chain drop-door system, circa 1888. (Ensign Manufacturing Company collection, Huntington NRHS Chapter)

Newport News and Mississippi Valley Company - Eastern Division (holding company for the C&O) 25-ton wooden hopper car No. 26068 circa 1889.

superstructures. Flat cars had sideboards for driving up carriages on them or restraining shifting cargo. Coke cars of the era were equipped with both drop-doors and side-doors. Up to World War One, the coal fleet was comprised of a fairly even mixture of flat-bottomed and hopper-bottomed gondola cars. Local power and steam plants, and coal going West primarily utilized flat-bottom gondolas. Coal going to Tidewater, or east to the Newport News piers, where ship-loading times were paramount, utilized rapid-discharge hopper-bottom gondolas, or hopper cars. After the war, the ties to the Lakes, the Hocking Valley docks, Brown-Hoist coal car dumpers were established, the high-sided 50-ton gondola car became standard for coal going west and the

70-ton hopper car to Tidewater. The 50-ton hopper primarily in Michigan, in 1947. The Second World War brought mass production and weight-savings techniques to the freight car building process. The new coal car purchases were 70-ton capacity cars with subtle design differences. A temporary surplus of new 70-ton cars in the early-1950s would allow the Raceland, Kentucky, and Wyoming, Michigan, car shops to recondition thousands of the C&O's venerable 50-ton off-set-side and World War II composite hopper, and high-side gondola cars. Next, the 1930s era all-steel box cars would be reconditioned. The late-1950s also brought conversion of older flat and gondola cars into specialized bulkhead pulp-wood and gypsum-board cars. The late-1950s, along with

C&O 40-ton wooden flat car with side-boards No. 11528 circa 1890.

C&O 40-ton wooden coke-car with side and bottom-drop doors circa 1890.

C&O 55-ton all-steel drop-door, flat-bottom gondola car 33000, circa 1907. (Kieth Retterer collection)

C&O 40-ton wooden "house" or box car No. 2123 circa 1900.

C&O 70-ton all-steel ribbed-side, saw-tooth, clam-shell, saw-tooth hopper car No. 75000 circa 1923. (Keith Retterer collection)

the end of steam locomotives, brought in the era of specialized freight cars . . . and new paint schemes, reflecting the modern era. Modern freight cars of the 1950s and 1960s had a mixture of bulk hauling cars shooting for efficiency and specialized merchandise designs aiming at avoiding damage to their cargos. Coal car designs stayed essentially the same, but they received non-serif Futura Demibold markings, first in yellow and later, back to white paint. These cars, as rebuilt, were eventually upgraded from 50- and 70-tons, to

60- and 80-tons respectively. New gondola cars were built to the needs of specific markets and would come in lengths up 65-feet long and would have specific cargo tie-down features built into them. Box cars grew in capacity from 40- and 50-tons to 70-tons. End-of-car and underframe cushioning systems were added. Many would be equipped with interior load restraining devices. Specialized automobile parts cars grew to 86-feet in length and also become taller.Flat cars, designed for "piggyback" trailer service would grow to 85-feet

C&O 30-ton wooden live-stock car No. 10112 circa 1900. (All images are from the Ensign Manufacturing collection of the Huntington NRHS Chapter)

C&O 50-ton high-side, stamped extended end gondola car circa 1943. (Jay Williams collection)

C&O 70-ton, 86-foot "Cushion Underframe and excess height" automobile parts box car no. 301001, circa 1964. (C&OHS Collection, CSPR 5220)

C&O 50-ton high-side, stamped extended end gondola car circa 1943. (Jay Williams collection)

C&O 50-ton, 48-foot, low-side gondola car no. 32955 built 1958, circa 1970. (Photograph by Thomas Dixon)

C&O 50-ton, 40' 6" all-steel box car n. 4249 built in 1937, circa 195X. (Photograph by Wilber Whittaker, Arnold Menke collection)

C&O 70-ton ribbed-side hopper car, circa 1956. (Photograph by Philip Shuster)

A string of C&O 80-ton "unit train" hopper cars in dedicated service to the Inland Steel mills in Indiana, circa 1964. (C&OHS Collection, CSPR 11369.13D)

No. 90872 is a typical C&O wooden caboose, built in 1926 by Standard Tank Car Company, and shown here after repainting to the new Advisory Mechanical Committee C&O standard paint scheme of red with white Roman lettering in 1931. Cars such as this were standard on C&O until the steel cabooses began to arrive in 1937, relegating them in large part to local runs and branch lines. C&O numbered most of its cabooses in the 90000 series until the 1970s. (C&OHS Collection, COHS 35122)

Cabooses

The Chesapeake & Ohio Railway Company , in the late-1800s, had a modest fleet of 4-wheeled and a few 8-wheeled "cabin" cars, which today we know as cabooses. The latter were sufficient for branch line pickups, or drop-offs, of coal cars. The 8-wheeled "cabins" were utilized for faster mainline freight service. In 1913, the State of Ohio, after numerous accidents, legislated 4-wheel "bobber" cabin cars, and cabooses with less than 24 feet inside length out of interchange service. Soon, a "standard" C&O configuration, with a centered copula, evolved. We are unsure when the livery of these cars changed from C&O Freight Car Brown, or Metallic Brown, to the classic Caboose Red. However, changes happened under

the cars' exteriors: Steel-frames with wooden-sheathing (in 1924), cast-steel truck sideframes (in 1926), and then all-steel construction (in 1937).Cabooses from the Hocking Valley and Pere Marquette railroads, with different configurations, would be merged into the C&O fleet in 1929 and 1947. Wooden-sheathed cabooses would have decaying boards replaced and then repainted in the current livery. One would see cabooses of various era paint schemes. They carried white markings on Caboose Red liveries until 1956 or 57, when the body color was changed to Signal Yellow. This familiar office and home for the conductor and brakemen would remain a freight train fixture past the end of this C&O era.

C&O 8-wheel steel frame, wooden-sheathed caboose circa 1926. (C&OHS Collection, COHS 18068)

C&O 4-wheel wooden caboose No.504, circa 1906. (From Huntington NRHS AC&F collection)

In 1949 C&O bought 100 new steel cabooses from American Car & Foundry Company, numbered 90200-90299. They are as typical of a C&O steel caboose as can be found. The photographs show 90299 broadside and one end. These cars were in service until the end of caboose use. Many were unmodified except in interior details until their end, while others were rebuilt and modernized. They were the first to bear the C&O for Progress herald even though they retained the old Roman lettering and red body paint.
(ACF Photographs, C&OHS Collection, COHS 8227 and COHS 8229)

An interior view of 90299 shows fixtures about the same as had been in use on wooden cabooses back to the 1920s or before. The ice box at right allows use of ice for drinking water and food storage, stove at left for heat, as is the wash basin just barely in the photograph at left. A bunk is at right just out of photograph. Beyond the high cupola seats is a bunk (left) and a Pullman-style section with two facing seats and table than could be converted to a bunk. No rest room was provided. (ACF Photograph, C&OHS Collection, COHS 8230)

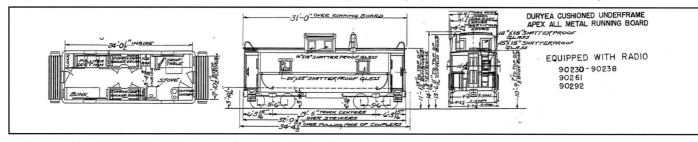

A diagram of the C&O 90200-90299 series caboose. (C&OHS Collection, DS-7-032)

C&O hauled a considerable traffic in pulpwood from the forests along its line to numerous paper mills that it served. This was carried in box cars before about 1950 when bulkhead flats came into use as shown here, next to a huge stack of wood. (C&O Ry. Photo, C&OHS Collection, CSPR 3603)

C&O used a small number of Ventilated Box Cars, which were generally needed for fruit and things that needed to have air circulation. Note the vents at the side and end of this car shown at Russell in 1931. These cars were gone by the 1950s. (C&OHS Collection, COHS 35864)

C&O's fleet of box cars was at about 12,000 in 1941 when this car (part of series 10000-10249) was built. C&O's box car fleet standard was the 40-ton, replaced by the 50-ton car in the 1920s-30s. Larger and specially designed cars came into play by the late-1950s and throughout the 1960s. This is the pre-1948 paint scheme. (C&OHS Collection, COHS 35865 and COHS 35866)

By 1948 C&O started using a new paint scheme with the "For Progress" logo, but the road name in the old Roman lettering (later replaced by modern "Futura Demibold). This double door car was built in 1948 by Pressed Steel Car Co. and was used for automobile haulage. Racks, as shown, allowed one auto to be elevated and another placed under it, so that the car could handled 4 automobiles. This inefficient operation was eliminated in the mid-1950s, when automobile rack cars came into use. (C&OHS Collection, COHS 35867 COHS 35869 and COHS 35868)

C&O acquired its first "Dry Bulk" cars (commonly called "covered hoppers") in the late 1930. This is an example of the earliest cars. Before this sand, grain, etc., were carried in box cars. The covered hopper was a drastic improvement. (C&OHS Collection, COHS 8147 (top) and COHS 8627)

Additional Sources of Information for C&O Freight Train Service and Equipment

- Chesapeake District Time Freight Book, 1949 (C&OHS Catalog No. DS-08-139)
- Chesapeake District Time Freight Book, 1953 (DS-08-068)
- Schedules of Fast Freight Trains, 1952 (DS-08-140)
- Northern Region Manifest Schedules (DS-08-127)
- Schedule of Package Cars, 1930 (DS-02-218)
- Schedules LCL Package Freight (DS-08-132)
- Code of Rules for Perishable Freight, 1940 (DS-03-240)
- Switching Instructions, 1950 (DS-03-232)
- C&O/B&O Train Handling Instructions, 1964 (DS-02-230)
- Instructions for Freight & Passenger Train Handling, 1952 (DS-00-191)
- C&O/B&O Piggyback Trailer Service, 1965 - (DS-03-259)
- C&O List of Businesses & Industry, 1950 - Part I List by Station (DS-217)
- C&O List of Businesses & Industry, 1950 - Part II List by Commodity (DS-217)

(The latter two Guides are of huge value to anyone interested in how C&O did freight business. Each station is listen along with its population, etc., how many sidings in hand, private, C&I owned, and team or yard, and all the businesses that shipped or received by rail. The Part II shows this by commodity rather than by location. - These are invaluable to modelers wanting to operate prototypically.)

For Freight Cars, the following are good sources:

- *Freight Car Equipment of the Chesapeake & Ohio Railway August 1, 1937*, with updates and background data by Carl Shaver, C&O Hist. Society, Clifton Forge, Va. 1980 and 1989. (About to be reprinted,expanded and updated as of this writing, 2012.)
- *Chesapeake & Ohio Freight Cars 1937-1965, Vol. 1 - Hoppers & Gondolas*, by Alfred Kresse, C&O Hist. Society, Clifton Forge, Va. 1996. Superb detailed 206 page book with hundreds of illustrations covering cars in great detail. Available from C&OHS Catalog No. BK-7-023.
- *Chesapeake &and Ohio Color Guide to Freight and Passenger Equipment*, by David H. Hickcox, Morning Sun Books, Scotch Plains, NJ , 1998. Great all color photography showing huge variety of C&O freight with some passenger and work train equipment.
- *Chesapeake & Ohio Steel Cabooses 1937-2010*, by Dwight Jones, C&OHS 2010, available at Catalog No. BK-10-528 (Encyclopedic history of all C&O steel cabooses with hundreds of drawings, photos, and rosters.)

Chesapeake & Ohio Freight Car Diagram Books - generally 7x14 inch diagrams that give all dimensions of cars as well as a great deal of technical data. Originally distributed to all mechanical and operating personnel on the railway for general reference and guidance. Available from C&OIHS as follows:

- 1922 (Catalog No. DS-00-192)
- 1938 (Catalog No. DS-09-182)
- 1960 (Catalog No. DS-00-196)
- 1964 (Catalog No. DS-09-183)
- 1969 (Catalog No. DS-07-049)
- 1970 (C&O and B&O Combined, 8-½ x 11 size) (Catalog No. DS-07-038)

Other C&OHS Reprints:

- Merchandise Freight Equipment Fleet Roster, 1967 (DS-03-236)
- Chessie System Equip. Fleet Roster 1979 (DS-03-258)

CHAPTER SEVEN
Steam Locomotives

C&O H-8 No.1637 with eastbound coal drag at Alleghany, Va. June, 1949 Gene Huddleston photograph. (C&OHS Collection, COHS 1131)

C&O steam locomotives have the reputation of being some of the biggest, most modern, and most powerful. Certainly this was the case for those that the railway purchased after 1910, and especially those built to the "Super Power" concept after 1930.

Part of the interest people express in C&O is the fact that it always had large locomotives, hauling large trains, in all types of beautiful scenery: through the narrow valleys and gorges of Kentucky and West Virginia, across the great mountain ranges of Virginia, through the fertile fields of Ohio, and the plains of Tidewater Virginia, passing by some of the most historic scenes in early American history.

It is not often considered that C&O also had a wide range of smaller steam locomotives, many of them long lived, that it used in various specific traffic areas up to the very end of steam. In the 1940s it was still common to see 4-4-2s and 4-6-2s built in 1902 handling passenger trains on some branches and in Indiana, or to find 2-8-2s from the 1911 era still in service. C&O is reputed to have had more different wheel arrangements (18) of locomotives in operation at one time than any other railroad except the Santa Fe, and it's likely true.

In the early years of the Virginia Central and the first years of the C&O, the standard locomotive for freight and passenger work was the reliable, flexible, 4-4-0 American type. It was so named because it was by far the most

C&O 4-4-0 No. 36 was a class A-6, built by Schenectady Loco. Works (later Alco) in 1873, just as C&O was being completed to the Ohio. This photograph shows it in about 1877 with giant pilot, fancy brass domes, Gothic cab and diamond stack, all typical of the era. (C&OHS Collection, COHS 5337).

Other than 4-4-0s, early C&O freight was hauled by the 4-6-0 Ten Wheeler type. Here No. 167 is pausing with a freight at Alderson, W. Va., in about 1910. It was built in 1881 as C&O Class F-4. (C&OHS Collection, COHS 35789)

widely used type on early American railroads. There were also some specialty locomotives including some odd 0-6-0 "Tank" engines (the water and coal were carried on the engine, and there was no tender) which were used in some of the construction work, and to take cars over the very steep temporary tracks that were initially used around some tunnels during their construction. Initially the fuel was wood, but by the mid-1880s C&O locomotives were burning coal.

After the C&O began to grow, it acquired some 4-6-0s in addition to the 4-4-0s, but it was not until 1881 that the first of the 2-8-0 Consolidation types arrived for use in the

heaviest freights service. They were the first locomotives that tackled the eastbound Alleghany grade with solid coal trains bound for the coast.

C&O liked the type and continued to enlarge its fleet in the following years until it had the heavy G-7 and G-9 classes of 1903 to 1909. These locomotives were capable of carrying a train of 40 of the then current 40-50-ton wooden and early steel hopper cars eastward over the Alleghany grade.

However, it was during this time that C&O was building coal branches and opening vast new coal fields and this type of operation wasn't acceptable any longer. In 1909 Clifton Forge Yard was receiving about 1,000 cars of coal per day. In trains of 40 cars, that amounted to 25 trains, in addition to 20 or so empires returning, plus the regular merchandise freight trains and about 12 passenger trains, all of which had to be dispatched over the road at some kind of reasonable speed and efficient organization.

The only solution was bigger power. In 1910 C&O received its first Mallet compound articulated locomotive, with a 2-6-6-2 wheel arrangement. Its tractive effort was about 82,000 pounds and it was able to move a coal train eastward with about twice as many cars as a G-7 or G-9 Consolidation. From that time forward, C&O loved the articulated locomotive design, first as a compound, and later as a "simple" design. The articulated design means that one boiler supplies steam to two sets of cylinders and drivers, one set of which is rigidly attached to the boiler, and the other of which swivels freely around curves. This reduced the rigid wheelbase but delivered the same power. "Compound" means that high pressure steam was sent to the rear set of cylinders and once it was used there, was exhausted to a set of larger cylinders on the front engine and was used again at the lower pressure before going up the stack as exhaust. The simple articulated

After C&O finished with its 4-4-0s and 4-6-0s, it adopted the 2-8-0 as a standard freight hauler. This is a builder's photograph of class G-5 No. 355 with its classic 1890s clerestory cab roof, and clean boiler. It was built by Richmond Locomotive Works in 1895. (C&OHS Collection, COHS 35788)

The Chesapeake & Ohio Railway - A Concise History and Fact Book

Most numerous of all C&O steam locomotives were its 2-6-6-2s, used widely on branch line mine runs. Here H-6 No. 1482 is headed out of Prince, W. Va. with empties for the Piney Creek Branch in September 1952. (Gene Huddleston photograph, C&OHS Collection, COHS 1585)

locomotives differed in that the steam was delivered directly from the boiler to both sets of cylinders at the same time, and when used, exhausted directly up the stack into the atmosphere. This allowed for a much more powerful locomotive, but also required a much larger boiler and firebox.

C&O stuck with the compound articulated (called "Mallet" after the name of their Swiss inventor), with the 2-6-6-2 wheel arrangement through the era from the first class H-1 in 1910 through the class H-6 of 1921. They were used in the heaviest of the road's traffic not only on the Alleghany Subdivision but in other areas as well.

At the same time that C&O acquired its Mallets, it also began buying 2-8-2 Mikado types with the class K-1 in 1911. A very powerful locomotive in its own right with a tractive effort of 63,000 pounds, the Mikado was used in all types of service.

After World War I, C&O experienced a boom in traffic, and developed new and bigger, more powerful locomotives. Included in this were larger, more powerful Mikado 2-8-2 types bought in 1924 through 1926. With 67,000 pounds of tractive effort, these were the final development of the 2-8-2 type on the C&O. They persisted in all kinds of service right

up to the end of steam in the early 1950s. At the same time, C&O mechanical engineers perfected the design of a 2-8-8-2 simple articulated locomotive that was to rule the Alleghany grade for almost two decades. This new ruler of Alleghany was the H-7 class, received between 1923 and 1926. These

The 2-8-0 Consolidation type served the C&O to the end of steam. Though it was soon eclipsed for mainline work, the sturdy G-7s and G-9s worked in yards, on locals, and up branches for nearly half a century. Here No. 975 and 990 switch in the Thurmond, W. Va. Yard after bringing in a train of coal from the Keeney's Creek Branch in September 1953. (Gene Huddleston photograph, C&OHS Collection, COHS 1205)

Powerful looking K-2 Mikado No. 1230 powers a heavily loaded train of coal leaving Clifton Forge for Richmond via the James River line. The Mikados were general purpose locomotives that handed coal, fast freight, locals, and even passenger trains when needed. (Bruce Fales Photograph, Jay Williams Collection)

cylinders. The Texas type really proved the concept and at its construction was the largest and most powerful non-articulated locomotive in the world. For the next 18 years C&O bought mainly Super Power locomotives and mainly from Lima Locomotive Works, though some also came from the other major builders American Locomotive Company (Alco), and Baldwin Locomotive Works.

Captive to the Russell, Kentucky - Columbus - Toledo, Ohio route, the giant 2-10-4s hauled 14,000+ tons coal trains like a conveyor belt, delivering a river of coal to the Toledo docks and to connecting lines north of Columbus.

The largest of all C&O motive power was the H-8 2-6-6-6 Allegheny type, of which the road had 60, built between 1942 and 1948. These giants could exert over 6,900 horsepower and are rated as the most powerful of all steam locomotives ever built when using sustained horsepower delivered to the train as the measure. They were also among the heaviest. They came just in time to supplant the old H-7 2-8-8-2s on the Alleghany grade, and they were workhorses in the World War II traffic that reached all-time highs.

Not wanting to give up steam, C&O received its last batch of H-8s in 1948. They were all out of service by 1956!

C&O got its first 2-8-4s in 1943 and called them "Kanawha" type after the river in West Virginia. They were powerful, versatile locomotives that were used in main line and branch line service, for fast freight, coal trains, local freights, and even passenger trains. By 1948 when the last arrived, C&O had 90 of the comely giants.

45 giants are considered the first class of simple articulateds to see successful service in the United States. They set the stage for the biggest and best in steam.

In 1930 C&O bought 40 2-10-4 Texas types from Lima Locomotive Works that were built using the new concept of "Super Power," whereby a huge free-steaming boiler with massive firebox supplied virtually limitless steam to large

The C&O's first Super Power locomotive, the T-1 2-10-4 Texas type, is shown here eastbound crossing the famous Limeville Bridge heading toward Russell with empties from Toledo. The T-1s were used exclusively on the Russell-Toledo route until the last year of their life. Photograph by Gene Huddleston (C&OHS Collection, COHS 1210)

The Chesapeake & Ohio Railway - A Concise History and Fact Book

Of all C&O steam, the H-8 2-6-6-6 is the most commented on. It was by any measure the very pinnacle of steam locomotive design. Here No. 1643 is just out of Big Bend Tunnel at Talcott, W. Va. with a coal train eastbound in September 1947. Charles H. Kerrigan photograph. (C&OHS Collection, COHS 35787)

One of the best all-purpose C&O locomotives was the K-4 class 2-8-4 Kanawha. No. 2700, the first of the class, is seen here at Handley, W. Va. in 1956. (C&O Ry. Photograph, C&OHS Collection, CSPR 3789)

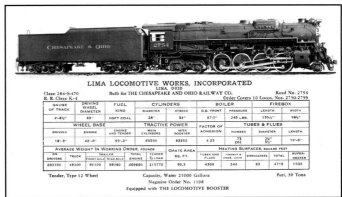

This builders card shows the compact, powerful appearance of the K-4 well. (C&OHS Collection, COHS 28866)

C&O F-19 Pacific No. 492 is ready to take the George Washington *east from Cincinnati in this 1934 photograph. The train's name is on the board hanging from the tender side. Later this locomotive was also fitted with a portrait of Washington on the front.*
(C&OHS Collection, COHS 2192)

It is interesting that the very last new steam locomotives bought by C&O were the 10 class H-6 2-6-6-2 Mallets that were built basically to a 1920 standard. But C&O needed them for its coal branches, to replace H-4 and H-6s that dated from the early 1920s. The new H-6s arrived in September 1949.

For passenger trains, C&O used 4-4-0s until 1889 when it introduced its glamorous *FFV* passenger train, and bought large 4-6-0s for its power. Small by later standards they were giants in their time, when the *FFV* comprised seven light wooden cars.

Satisfied with Ten Wheelers of this design until after the turn of the 20th Century, C&O bought 4-4-2 Atlantic types which were just an enlargement of the 4-4-0, and 4-6-2 Pacific types, which were a further development of the Ten-Wheeler. Both these types came in 1902 and were assigned

When the C&O inaugurated the FFV it acquired new, heavy 4-6-0 Ten-Wheeler type locomotives for the mountainous portion of the run. No. 129 was one of these It was considered a huge locomotive in its time, but by later standards was tiny.
(C&OHS Collection, CSPR 2787)

to the fastest of the road's passenger trains over the steepest grades. But with their high drivers they could make speed over the low-level lines as well.

The 4-6-2 was steadily enlarged and developed over the next 25 years, culminating in the fabulous and famous F-19 class heavy Pacifics of 1926. C&O began buying all-steel passenger cars in 1911 and by the early 1920s, all its mainline named trains were comprised of ever longer strings of steel cars, therefore bigger power was constantly needed. The larger Pacifics supplied this. But the mountain grades required a bit more, so in 1911-12 C&O acquired three locomotives of a new type, the 4-8-2, which it called Mountain type. Seven more came in 1919 and 1923. They were used largely between Charlottesville and Clifton Forge and Clifton Forge and Hinton on the heaviest of the passenger trains, sometimes doubleheaded with Pacifics.

In 1935 C&O placed the first post-Depression locomotive order with Lima Locomotive Works, when it ordered five large 4-8-4 types which it christened "Greenbrier" after the river, county, and C&O resort hotel in West Virginia. Named for famous Virginia statesmen, these huge-boilered, massively built locomotives with giant 25-ton, 22,000 gallon tenders, could haul the heaviest of the passengers over the grades in Virginia and West Virginia on time.

For switching work, C&O initially used 0-6-0s, but by the turn of the 20th Century heavy switching of coal cars at Clifton Forge required bigger locomotives, and Alco supplied the C-8 class 0-8-0s. C&O stuck with the 0-8-0 type right through the end of steam, buying its last in 1948. However, it did acquire a group of 0-10-0s, among the heaviest switchers ever built, again for coal switching and hump yard service. They lasted to the end of steam in coal fields and at big

This builder broadside photograph gives a good idea as to the compact and powerful build of C&O J-3 class 4-8-4 Greenbriers. This is No. 610, first of the J-3A class, received in 1948. They had only about three years of service before the passenger trains they were intended to handle were taken on by diesels. (C&OHS Collection, CSPR 810.78)

hump yards. Over the years, especially before 1930, many of the older 2-8-0s were downgraded to switcher service and helped out in smaller yards.

C&O's unwillingness to give up on steam and its interest in proving that coal-fired locomotives were still viable (because 33% of the coal it hauled in the late 1940s went to other lines as locomotive fuel), the new Research Department, in combination with others in the coal and locomotive industries, came up with a Steam-Turbine-Electric locomotive that used a conventional boiler to power a turbine that generated electricity to be used by traction motors mounted on the axles (just like diesel-electrics). C&O bought three of these complex, expensive, largely experimental giants from Baldwin/GE. They were to handle the line's new all-daylight Washington-Cincinnati coach train to be called the *Chessie*. But circumstances resulted in cancellation of the *Chessie*, so the Steam-Turbine-Electrics went to work in regular passenger trains in 1948. After just a year they were returned to

the builders and the experiment was over. By then C&O was buying diesel-electrics for yard work and soon after that for road work in areas not serving the coal fields, and then finally in the coal fields. By 1956 C&O had dropped the last fires on its steam and diesels ruled, as they did on other American railroads in the era.

Among the shortest lived and most talked about of all C&O steam was the Steam-Turbine-Electrics of 1947-48. Here No. 500, just received new at Clifton Forge, is being readied at its specially designed and built coaling station in December 1947. Giants by any measure, they were a great, but failed, experiment. (C&O Ry. Photograph, C&OHS Collection, CSPR 1325)

Unheralded and unsung were the switching locomotives. C&O had many of the heavy 0-8-0 types that were used on all its yards. Here C-15 class No. 110 poses between labors at Richmond's Fulton Yard August 9, 1946. (Charles T. Felstead Photograph, C&OHS Collection, COHS 26344)

C&O Condensed and Simplified Steam Roster

Type	Class	Numbers	Qty	Builder	Built	Retired	Notes
0-6-0	C-3	15	1	Baldwin	1900	1951	Ex-OSL 1
0-6-OT	C-5	13	1	Brooks	1905	1934	Ex-HV 119
0-6-0	C-6	125-129	4	Brooks	1907	1934.1951	Ex-HV 125-129
0-6-0	C-7	25-34	10	Richmond	1905-1906	1930-1952	C&CER&T&B
0-6-OF	C-8	35-37	3	Porter	1949		Fireless
0-6-0	C-13	35	1	Brooks	1906	1929	Ex-AM
0-8-0	C-8	80-82	3	Richmond	1903-1911	1929-1931	
0-8-0	C-9	40-49	10	Pittsburgh	1918		Ex-PM 1300-1309
0-8-0	C-10	50-59	10	Baldwin	1921		Ex-PM 1330-1339
0-8-0	C-11	360-369	10	Lima	1920		Ex-PM 1401-1410
0-8-0	C-13	340-359	20	Cooke	1923		Ex-PM 1310-1329
0-8-0	C-14	90	1	Baldwin	1910		
0-8-0	C-14	60-69	10	Lima	1925	1949-1952	Ex-C&O 100-109
0-8-0	C-14	70-79	10	Lima	1926	1950-1953	Ex-HV 100-109
2-8-0	G-6	351-425	75	Richmond	1899-1901	-1935	
2-8-0	G-7	790-994	205	Rich., BLW	1903-1907	-1961	
2-8-0	G-7	996-1001	6	Pittsburgh	1916		
2-8-0	G-8	710,711	2	Richmond	1907	1952	
2-8-0	G-9	1010-1059	50	Richmond	1909	-1961	
2-8-0	G-10	680-689	10	Baldwin	1900	1930	Ex-HV 212-224
2-8-0	G-11	1060-1081	22	Baldwin	1903-1909	-1934	Ex-CC&L 201-222
2-8-0	G-12	299	1	Richmond	1907	1924	Ex-White Oak 99
2-8-0	G-12	1080-1082	3	Baldwin	1906-1907	1935	Ex-HV 280-282
2-8-0	G-14	785,786	2	Brooks	1907	1930	Ex-AC&I 15, 16
2-8-0	G-15	1085	1	Pittsburgh	1916	1951	Ex-AC&I 17
2-8-0	G-17	1095-1098	4			1929-1935Ex-SV&E;	nee B&O
2-8-2	K	1089-1099	11	Richmond	1912-1913	1935-1952	Ex-HV 180-190
2-8-2	K-1	1100-1155	56	Richmond	1911-1914	1935-1953	
2-8-2	K-2	1160-1209	50	Rlchmond	1924		
2-8-2	K-3	1210-1259	50	Richmond	1924		
2-8-2	K-3-A	2300-2349	50	Richmond	1925-1926		
2-8-2	K-5	1060-1069	10	Schen	1927	1952	Ex-PM 1041-1050
2-8-2	K-6	1070-1074	5	BLW	1911-1913	1949	Ex-PM1095-1099
2-8-2	K-8	2350-2379	30	Lima, Schen.	1918-1919	1949-1951	Ex-PM 1011-1040
2-8-4	K-4	2700-2789	90	Alco, Lima	1943-1947		
2-8-4	N-1	2650-2661	12	Lima	1941		Ex-PM 1216-1227
2-8-4	N-2	2670-2681	12	Lima	1944		Ex-PM 1228-1239
2-8-4	N-3	2685-2699	15	Lima	1937		Ex-PM 1201-1215
2-10-2	B-1	2950-2959	10	Baldwin	1919		
2-10-2	B-1	2960.2961	2	Baldwin	1919	1952	
2-10-2	B-2	2000-2005	5	Baldwin	1918	1951	Ex-C&EI 2000-2005
2-10-2	B-3	4000.4001	2	Alco	1917	1949	
2-10-2	B-4	2975-2989	15	Brooks	1918	1949-1952	Ex-PM 1101-1115
2-10-4	T-1	3000-3039	40	Lima	1930	1952-1953	
2-6-6-2	H-1	1301	1	Schen	1910	1930	
2-6-6-2	H-2	1302-1325	24	Richmond	1911	1935	
2-6-6-2	H-3	1300	1	Brooks	1910		Ex-Chicago & Alton

Type	Class	Numbers	Qty	Builder	Built	Retired	Notes
0-8-0	C-15	110-124	15	Baldwin	1929	1952-1953	Ex-class C-1 5A
0-8-0	C-16	175-239	65	Alco	1930	1954-1957	
0-8-0	C-16	380-394	15	Alco	1930	1953	Ex-PM 240-254
0-8-0	C-16-A	240-254	15	Lima	1942-1943		To VGN, 1950
0-8-0	C-16	255-284	30	Baldwin	1948		To N&W, 1950
0-10-0	C-12	130-144	15	Richmond	1919-1923	-1956	
2-6-0	E-5	427,428	2	Baldwin	1908	1935.1946	"Ex-Virginia Air Line"
2-6-0	E-6	425,426	2	Richmond	1907.1908	-1930 Ex-Island	Creek Coal
2-8-0	G-1	725-749	24	Brooks	1911	-1951	Ex-PM 901-925
2-8-0	G-2	750-774	25	Rich, Brks	1910.1911	1949-1951	Ex-PM 601-625
2-8-0	G-3	150-159	10	Brooks	1910	1934-1949	Ex-HV 150-159
2-8-0	G-4	160-169	10	Brooks	1910	1935-1951	Ex-HV 160-169
2-8-0	G-5	170-179	10	Richmond	1911	1935	
2-6-6-2	H-3	1275-1299	25	Schen,Rich	1917-1918	1935-1952	Ex-HV 200-224
2-6-6-2	H-4	1325-1474	150	Rich,Schen	1912-1918	1930-1955	
2-6-6-2	H-5	1520-1539	20	Schen,BLW	1919	1952	USRA
2-6-6-2	H-6	1475-1519	45	Rich.Schen	1920-1923	1952-1957	
2-6-6-2	H-6	1300-1309	10	Baldwin	1949	-1957	
2-6-6-6	H-8	1600-1659	60	Lima	1941-1948		
2-8-8-2	H-7	1540-1565	25	Alco	1923-1924	1952	
2-8-8-2	H-7-A	1570-1589	20	Baldwin	1926	1952	
4-4-0	A-5	230-232	3	Baldwin	1903-1904	1925-1929	Ex-CC&L
4-4-0	A-8	210.211	2	Manch	1900	1926-1929	Ex-CC&L
4-4-0	A-14	83	1	Brooks	1905	1935	Ex-HV 83
4-4-0	A-15	84.85	2	Brooks	1907	1935	Ex-HV 84, 85
4-4-2	A-16	275-294	20	Alco	1902-1916	1936-1949	
4-6-0	F-7	370,371	2	Manch	1900	1926-1929	Ex-CC&L101, 102
4-6-0	F-11	375-387	13	Baldwin	1902-1904	1925-1952	Ex-CC&L 103-115
4-6-0	F-12	86-88	3	Brooks	1910	1935	Ex-HV 86-88
4-6-0	F-13	89-92	4	Brks,Rich	1912.1913	1931-1949	Ex-HV 89-92
4-6-2	F-12	405-409	5	Baldwin	1914	1948-1949	Ex-PM 725-729
4-6-2	F-14	410-421	12	Brooks	1920	1949	Ex-PM 711-722
4-6-2	F-15	430-456	27	Alco	1902-1911	1936-1952	
4-6-2	F-16	460-467	8	Baldwin	1913	1951-1952	
4-6-2	F-17	470-475	6	Richmond	1914	1951-1952	
4-6-2	F-18	480-485	6	Richmond	1923	1952	
4-6-2	F-19	490-494	5	Richmond	1926		Rebuilt to 4-6-4
4-6-2	F-20	486-489	4	Baldwin	1927	1952 Ex-RF&P	325-328
4-6-4	L-2	300-307	8	Baldwin	1941-1942	1955	
4-6-4	L-1	490-494	5	C&O	1946-1947	1953-1955	Rebuilt from F-19
4-6-4	L-2-A	310-314	5	Baldwin	1948	1955	
4-8-2	J-1	540-542	3	Richmond	1911-1912	1951-1952	
4-8-2	J-2	543-549	7	Alco, BLW	1918-1923	1951-1952	
4-8-4	J-3	600-606	7	Lima	1935.1942	1953	
4-8-4	J-3-A	610-614	5	Lima	1948		
	M-1	500-502	3	Baldwin	1947-1948	1950	
Shay	C-10	16	1	Lima	1911	Sold 1921	3-truck
Shay	C-9	1-15,20	16	Lima	1903-	1923	4-truck

The A-16 class 4-4-2 Atlantics were the first to bring C&O into the modern era of steam locomotives for its passenger trains, starting in 1902. Eventually C&O had 20 of these small and fleet-of-foot locomotives. They soon lost their place on the big name trains, but found work on locals and branch lines right up to the end of steam. No. 288, shown here in 1948 at St. Albans, W. Va. (where it handled the 2-car Coal River branch trains) looks very different from when it arrived in 1902. Charles Felstead photograph. (C&OHS Collection, COHS 35099)

C&O was widely known for its classy 4-6-2s, especially the heavy F-16, 17,18 and 19 classes, which handled the name trains east and west of the mountain districts, though they were no strangers to this territory either. Here F-16 No. 462 is seen at Cincinnati in the mid 1930s with its Vanderbilt tender and "donut" tender herald. Charles Foster photograph. (C&OHS Collection, COHS 35100)

The Chesapeake & Ohio Railway - A Concise History and Fact Book

In 1911 the C&O created the 4-8-2 type for use between Charlottesville and Hinton. Here No. 546, built in 1919, is about to take a heavy Sportsman *train west from Charlottesville in 1939. Ted Gray photograph. (C&OHS Collection, COHS 35102)*

In 1935 the 4-8-4 type came to C&O in the form of the 600-series class J-3. Called Greenbrier by C&O they stuck to the territory between Charlottesville and Hinton until the last years of steam. No. 601 is resting at the Charlottesville terminal in the late 1940s photograph. H. Reid photograph. (C&OHS Collection, COHS 35103)

. The K-3a was another highly successful C&O 2-8-2 class and No. 2302 is seen here fresh from the shops at Clifton Forge Oct. 15, 1938, ready for work on the James River Subdivision with coal trains east from the town. (C&OHS Collection, COHS 35132)

In 1946-47 C&O took its 20-year-old F-19 4-6-2s and rebuilt them as streamlined 4-6-4s for use on the never-run Chessie. Here No. 492 rests at the Ivy City engine terminal in Washington in about 1950. In a stainless steel and yellow jacket, they presented a startling appearance. No. 490 is preserved today at the B&O Railroad Museum. C. T. Felstead photograph. (C&OHS Collection, COHS 35105)

C&O began using 2-8-0 Consolidation type in 1881, and they were the backbone of the fleet for decades, supplanted later by Mallet articulated and Mikados. However, the fleet of more modern 2-8-0s lasted to the end in all kinds of shifter and local work, even in branch line passenger trains. Here No 982, a G-9 class, built by Baldwin 1904 is shown at Richmond in 1947, still at work. (C&OHS Collection, COHS 35106)

The 2-8-2 Mikado wheel arrangement gained great favor on C&O, which had 217 such locomotives in several classes. "Maids of all work," these versatile locomotives were used in all kinds of service about everywhere on the system. Here No. 1186, a K-2 class is at Chicago in 1951, still in service on the C&O's line between Cincinnati and Chicago across Indiana, which was being dieselized even as this photograph was taken. (C&OHS Collection, COHS 35107)

Class: 2666-S-725
R. R. Class: H-8

Built for CHESAPEAKE & OHIO RY. CO.

Road No. 1633
Order Covers 15 Locos. Nos. 1630-1644

GAUGE OF TRACK	DRIVING WHEEL DIAMETER	FUEL KIND	CYLINDERS		BOILER		FIREBOX	
			DIAMETER	STROKE	DIAMETER	PRESSURE	LENGTH	WIDTH
4'-8½"	67"	SOFT COAL	22½"	33"	109"	260 LBS.	180"	108¾"

WHEEL BASE			MAXIMUM TRACTIVE POWER	FACTOR OF ADHESION	TUBES AND FLUES		
DRIVING	ENGINE	ENGINE AND TENDER			NUMBER	DIAMETER	LENGTH
34'-8"	62'-6"	112'-11"	110200	4.27	48 278	2¼" 3½"	23'-0"

AVERAGE WEIGHT IN WORKING ORDER, POUNDS					GRATE AREA SQ. FT.	HEATING SURFACES, SQUARE FEET				
ON DRIVERS	TRUCK	TRAILER	TOTAL ENGINE	TENDER ⅔ LOAD		TUBES AND FLUES	SYPHONS	FIREBOX & COMB. CHAM.	TOTAL	SUPER-HEATER
471000	64500	189000	724500	341600	135.3	6478	162	600	7240	3186

Tender, Type 14 Wheel

Capacity, Water 25000 Gallons

Fuel 25 Tons

Negative Order No. 1188

The H-8 2-6-6-6 was the pinnacle of C&O locomotive development. It was, in the opinion of many the best of steam anywhere. This LIMA builder card shows its huge size and powerful arrangement. It is the only steam locomotive ever to use a six-wheel trailing truck. (LIMA photograph, C&OHS Collection, COHS 28867)

The C&O ordered 10 2-6-6-2 H-6s from Baldwin, the last of which arrived in August, 1949. No. 1309 was the last steam locomotive commercially built for American railroads. (Baldwin photograph, C&OHS Collection, COHS 28703)

The following four mechanical diagrams on pages 99 and 100 show typical C&O steam locomotives of the 20th Century. Full books showing all locomotives in operation are available from the C&O Historical Society (see note at the end of this chapter.) Mechanical diagrams are 7x14 inch sheets issued in updateable books that were issued to all mechanical personnel, as well as official at al levels who might have need of the data. Each sheet had a dimensioned diagram and major data such as builder and year, tractive effort, and all types of mechanical appliance data nd well as reference to drawings pertinent to the locomotive. As changes occurred, the sheets were updated, and the official kept their books current. (From C&OHS Collection, DS-07-023)

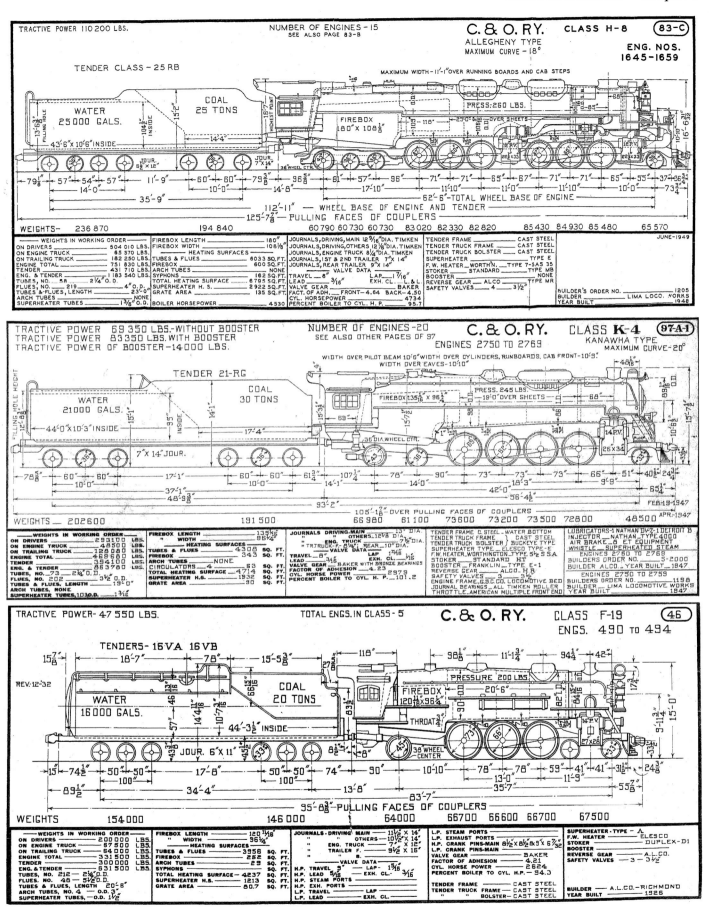

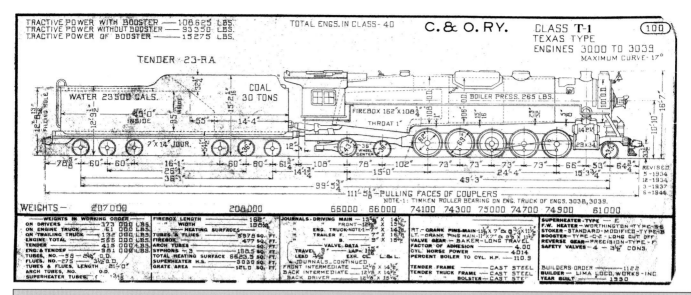

Additional Sources of Information for C&O Steam Locomotives

- *C&O Power*, Phil Shuster, Gene Huddleston & Alain Staufer, Medina, Ohio 1965, 350 pages. The standard and most complete reference for all C&O steam locomotives 1900-1956. Out of print but often available second hand.
- *Chesapeake & Ohio All Time Steam Roster, Midwest Railroader*, Fremont, Ohio, no date, 78 pages of roster data on C&O locomotives number-by-number with one line entries.
- *Chesapeake & Ohio Super Power* by Eugene L. Huddleston, C&O Historical Society, Clifton Forge, Va. 2005, hardbound 176 page treatment in great detail of all C&O locomotive of the Super Power variety 1930-1948 including Lima, Alco, and Baldwin (C&O Hist. Society Cat No. BK-04-383)
- *Allegheny, Lima's Finest* by Eugene L. Huddleston and Thomas W. Dixon, Jr., Hundman Publishing, Edmonds, Wash., 1984, 244 pages with detailed data, drawing and photos on C&O H-8 2-6-6-6 type.
- *Chesapeake & Ohio Greenbrier Type Steam Locomotives*, T. W. Dixon, Jr., C&O Historical Society, C. Forge, VA, 1994, 64 pages. (C&O Hist. Soc. Cat. No. BK-10-500)
- *Chesapeake & Ohio K-2, K-3, and K-3a 2-8-2's* by Bob Hundman and Tom Dixon, Pacific Fast Mail, Edmonds, Wash. , 978 (32 pages of photos, drawings and data on C&O 2-8-2s.)
- *Chesapeake & Ohio H-7 Series* by Thomas W. Dixon, Jr., NJ International, Annapolis, Md. ca. 1980, 48 pages with drawing.
- *Old Dominion Steam*, by Thomas W. Dixon, Jr., J&D Studios, Hampton, Va. 1988, 64 page book about C&O steam in Virginia.
- *The Van Sweringen Berkshires*, by Eugene L. Huddleston, NJ International, Hicksville, NY 1985. 18 pages about C&O, Erie, NKP and PM 2-8-4s and their relationship.
- *Pere Marquette Power*, Thomas W. Dixon, Jr. and Arthur B. Million, C&O Historical Society, Clifton Forge, Va. 1984, 244 pages, complete roster data and detailed history and photos for all PM locomotives including numbers of those taken into C&O roster in 1947. (Available from C&O Historical Society, Cat. No. BK-07-454H)
- *The Texas in Ohio C&O T-1 Texas Type 2-10-4 Steam Locomotive*, T. W. Dixon, C&O Historical Society, Clifton Forge, Va., 24 pages, (Available from C&O Historical Society, Cat. No. BK-03-355)
- *World's Greatest Steam Locomotives* by Eugene L. Huddleston.,TLC Publishing (VA) (June 2001) 144 pages
- *Lima Super Power Steam Locomotives* by Dixon and Kohls, TLC Publishing; 1 edition (December 15, 2010) 144 pages

C&O Historical Society Reprints:
- C&O Steam Locomotive Diagrams, updated to 1936 (Cat. No. DS-09-184)
- C&O Steam Locomotive Diagrams, updated to 1948 (Cat. No. DS-07-023)
- C&O Locomotive Information, AMC, For 1943 (DS-03-263)
- C&O Locomotive Information, AMC, For 1948 (DS-03-264)
- C&O Manual for Locomotive Firemen, 1947 (DS-08-109)
- C&O Steam Locomotive Mileage Since Repairs, 1954 (DS-09-304)
- C&O Steam Locomotive Tender Capacities and Assignments (DS-09-301)
- C&O K-4 Class 2-8-4 Kanawha Type Locomotive Builder Photo Album (DS-09-306)
- C&O Class J-3 4-8-4 Greenbrier Locomotive 600-604, 605-606, Photos (DS-09-327)
- C&O Class J-3A Greenbrier Type Locomotive, 610-614, Photos (DS-09-328)
- T-1 Class 2-10-4 605 606, Photos (DS-09-336)
- F-19 Class 4-6-2 Pacifics 490-494 (DS-09-337)
- L-1 Class 4-6-4 Streamlined Hudsons 490-494 Photos (DS-09338)
- G-9 Class 2-8-0 Consolidations 1010-1059 (DS-09-339)
- H-6 2-6-6-2 Compound Articulated Steam Locomotives 1300-1309 Photos (DS-09-323)
- H-4 2-6-6-2 Articulated Steam Locomotives 1325-1474 Photos (DS-09-324)
- K-2 Class 2-8-2 Mikado Type Steam Locomotives 1160-1209 (DS-09-325)
- M-1 Class Steam-Turbine-Electric Locomotive 500-502 Photos (DS-09-330)

The Chesapeake & Ohio Railway - A Concise History and Fact Book

CHAPTER EIGHT
Diesel Locomotives

This photograph shows three car-body type diesels at the Clifton Forge yard in 1952. The units on either side are EMD F7s (in two different paint schemes), and the unit in the center is an EMD E8 passenger engine. (C&O Ry. Photograph, C&OHS Collection, CSPR CL48)

In the diesel era C&O began buying locomotives from all the major builders except Lima, the preferred builder in the steam era. Of course Lima never made an appreciable impression in the overall diesel market and soon merged with Baldwin. After buying several Alco and Baldwin products as well as General Motors-Electro-Motive Division (EMD) engines, C&O settled more or less on EMD as its preferred supplier. Many people believe that this was based in part on the fact that GM was one of C&O's biggest customers, receiving huge quantities of parts and raw materials to its Midwestern plants (especially in Michigan on the former Pere Marquette lines), and sending out finished automobile products. Another reason may have been that the huge EMD provided a ready parts and maintenance base that the smaller builders couldn't match.

EMD E8 units took over all C&O passenger runs (except those handled by the previously purchased E7s on the former PM lines in Michigan), while an additional group of seven sets of ABA FP7s were purchased for use on some branch lines, extra passenger movements, and to fill in if needed for E8s that were out of service. But essentially the FP7s were used in freight service far more regularly than passenger. A few GP7s and GP9s were equipped with steam generators for passenger switching and for some special needs.

Although Alco S-2 model switchers were common in C&O yards, a few of their bigger road switchers were used by C&O, but the big orders were first for EMD F7 road freight units, which were initially used in areas not serving the coal fields. In Michigan, the EMD E7s had been handily power-

ing the new *Pere Marquette* streamliners since 1946, and the unusual BL2s came just after the 1947 merger.

Logically enough, the EMD GP7 general purpose 1,500 horsepower road switcher units came next, and they were quickly followed by the GP9 1,750 horsepower diesels. It was the latter two models that dieselized the larger part of the C&O through the fall of 1956, as steam gradually and then rapidly gave way.

Indeed, by early 1954 over 75% of C&O operations were dieselized. Then a sudden boom for export coal arose, and the C&O had to return many steam locomotives to ac-

C&O dieselized its passenger service in very short order with 40 EMD E8 passenger diesels painted the distinctive yellow/blue/silver (gray) color to match the new lightweight cars received in 1950. Here, No. 4008 poses with a long consist, the archetype of a streamliner. (C&O Ry. Photograph, C&OHS Collection, CSPR CL202)

F7s were often used on fast manifest freight trains. Here an ABA set is moving a heavy manifest east at Russell, Kentucky. The C&O never repeated its initial orders for the car-body road diesels, but opted for the hood-type "road switcher" GP7 and GP9 units that could be used equally well in road or switching duties. (C&O Ry. Photograph, C&OHS Collection, CSPR 10393.58)

Deep in the New River Gorge of West Virginia, four GP9s take a coal train east. The old combined dept/tower was erected in the early 1890's and still served as a train-order station in this 1957 photograph. (Gene Huddleston, C&OHS Collection, COHS 1033)

tive service that had been stored serviceable in the previous couple of years. These included the more modern classes, of course, the older locomotives having already gone to scrap. Notably at this time C&O also leased several of the Richmond, Fredericksburg & Potomac's 4-8-4s, as well as reactivating its own J-3a class 4-8-4s, not for passenger service, but for fast freight and even coal drags. H-8s were also revived, and the old and new 2-6-6-2s still held their own in the coal fields branches handling many of the mine runs. The steamers were generally used in the coal fields and main line west of Hinton and east of Russell. The very last of steam were 2-6-6-2s running out of Peach Creek yard at Logan, W. Va., with the last trip being made on September 26, 1956. With enough diesels on hand to cover all traffic requirements and the diesel builders capable of supplying needs quickly, C&O finally sent the last of its big steam to scrap, saving a few which were given to parks and towns across the system, and storing a few more at its Russell yard for use in future donations. It was these few at Russell that were finally pulled out and cosmetically restored to become important part of the B&O Railroad Museum collection in Baltimore after the C&O/B&O affiliation.

On the bell-weather Alleghany grade run between Hinton and Clifton Forge which had been the operation against which so much of C&O steam had been built, strings of GP7s and GP9s became the regular power, replacing the giant H-8 2-6-6-6 steamers. But the "Geep" units were rated fairly small in horsepower in comparison with the H-8s so they were used in multiple. Initially three units were used on the head end with an H-8 pusher, but as more Geeps arrived they were used three or four on the head and one pusher, then finally the standard became five units on the front with no pusher. This was the common practice on this important line until the arrival of what came to be called "second generation" diesels. In the western lines the EMD F7s were widely used on fast freight and on coal trains in and out of the giant terminal at Russell, which was their maintenance base, but they also wandered over the system fairly regularly as well.

In the early 1960s, several important forces began to further shape the C&O's diesel fleet. First, the C&O and B&O "affiliation" resulted in many of C&O's units being leased or sold to B&O even before the ICC approved the control case (the two companies had separate books and financially operated as separate entities). Most of C&O's

Of all C&O diesels bought to replace steam, the archetype was the GP7 and GP9 from EMD. Here a pair of GP9s takes a train of coal out of Clifton Forge down the James River Subdivision, replacing a Mikado that would have been used for this in the steam era. (C&O Ry. Photograph, C&OHS Collection, CSPR 4144)

F7 units, usually in ABA configuration (the "B" unit having no cab) were used in several directions from their Russell, Kentucky maintenance base. Here a set has a westbound coal train on the Cincinnati Division near Greenup, with the Ohio River in the background. (C&OHS Collection, COHS 20856)

The GP30s from EMD were the first of the C&O's Second Generation, higher horsepower units, arriving in 1962. (C&O Ry. Photograph, C&OHS Collection, CSPR 4868)

Four SD18s, No. 1804 at the head ready to leave Handley, W. Va. terminal to take a coal train to Hinton at 11 am on an overcast June day in 1964. Alco RSD-5 at right. Photograph by Gene Huddleston. (C&OHS Collection, COHS 20272)

F7s went to B&O, as did some of its switchers. It would not be until the late 1960s that the motive power fleets of both roads would be completely merged operationally.

The second important force affecting the C&O diesel fleet was the arrival of the "second generation" diesel. This is the name given to new locomotives, generally of higher horsepower and more efficiency, being fielded by the major builders. Although Alco continued to build units into the second generation era, it was decidedly an "also ran" in the diesel market, with its second place status being taken over by General Electric's locomotive division.

C&O was ready for new diesels at this time because most of its units were well used and approaching a decade in age, many had been transferred to B&O, and there was also an interest in modernizing the fleet to accommodate new business that was expected as a result of the B&O control. Therefore, C&O got its early second generation units in

1962-64 in the form of EMD GP30 units of 2,250 horsepower, General Electric U25Bs of 2,500 horsepower, EMD SD18s of 1,800 horsepower, as well as SD35s of 2,500 hp rating, and GP35s of 2,500 hp.

Most of these units went to work in merchandise freight and on lines other than the coal fields. In the coal fields, the tried and true versatile GP9s and GP7s still held sway both on the mainline coal trains and on the branches with the mine runs, until the late 1960s when second generation units began gradually supplanting them.

During the remainder of the 1960s, C&O stuck with EMD and GE, buying their latest models progressively over the years. By the late 1960s these newer units had infiltrated the coal fields and were more and more seen on coal trains and even on the branches.

C&O SD-35 locomotive 7460 at Pikeville, Kentucky, on October 3, 1973. pulling westbound empties in its yellow nose and "Big C&O" lettering paint scheme. (C&OHS Collection, COHS 21807)

This Chessie System, C&O SD-50 No.8555 was only a few weeks old when photographed pushing a coal train up Cranberry Grade near Amblersburg, W.Va. on the B&O, in March 1984. Jim Moseley photograph. (C&OHS Collection, COHS 21807)

GP9 No. 5912 in broadside at C&O's Grand Rapids, Michigan engine terminal about 1955. (C&O Ry. Photograph, C&OHS Collection, CSPR 10228.96)

In 1972 Chessie System was created as a holding company for C&O, B&O, and Western Maryland, under which the pace of merging operations accelerated. By then remaining passenger trains had been taken over by Amtrak and with them the last of the E-units on both C&O and B&O. F-units on the B&O were soon all retired, as well a most of the earlier classes of the non-EMD builders. The old GP7s and GP9s, however, continued in service on branches, as switchers, and even on mainline trains, but they soon were wiped away as newer and newer units arrive, balanced more-or-less

between EMD and GE builders. Under Chessie System all units had the same paint scheme, with a large C&O, B&O, or WM lettering under which designated which component company owned them.

The last units C&O lettering were the SD50s from EMD, received in 1984. Soon thereafter the CSX merger was consummated and all units were eventually repainted into the various schemes that CSX has had over the past two decades. Most C&O units now (2012) have been retired.

When CSX took over it tried a number of paint schemes. One of the best is this one with blue, gray, and yellow. Most recently the design has been simplified and the yellow has been changed to a more golden hue. (C&OHS Collection, COHS 35097)

The Chesapeake & Ohio Railway - A Concise History and Fact Book

AMERICAN LOCOMOTIVE COMPANY
NEW YORK

Class, 404-DL-238   1000 B. H. P. Diesel Locomotive   Road Number, 5005
BUILT FOR THE CHESAPEAKE & OHIO.

WEIGHT IN POUNDS WORKING ORDER		1-1000 H. P. DIESEL ENG. Turbo-Charged (Buchi System)			MOTORS				GAUGE OF TRACK
					Type	Number	Gear Ratio	Suspension	
Total	Driving Wheels	Cylinders	Diam.	Stroke					
238125	238125	6	12½″	13″	GE. 731-D	4	75/16	Spring Nose	4′-8½″

CAPACITY			WHEEL BASE	
SWITCHING SERVICE			Truck	Total
Tractive Effort—Pounds	Speed—M. P. H.			
*59500	Starting	@ 25% Adhesion	8′-0″	30′-6″
34000	8.0	Continuous	WHEEL DIAM.	AXLES
*Based on weight including ½ variable supplies	60	Max. Speed	Driving	Driving
				Journal / Center
			40″	7″ x 14″ / 8¼″

Alco S-2 Switcher 5005 was one of the first diesels to arrive for use on the old C&O (some diesels had been in use on the Pere Marquette and the PM District (after 1947 merger,) but none on the old lines, until April 1949. This unit came in June 1949. (Alco Photo, C&OHS Collection, COHS 35197)

Alco RSD-7 units such as 6805 seen here at Handley, W. Va. in April 1956, right after its delivery to the C&O, were originally intended to replace H-4 and H-6 2-76-6-2s one-for-one. They were mainly used in the Logan Coal Fields up until their transfer to B&O in 1964. (Gene Huddleston photo, C&OHS Collection, COHS 1298)

The U-25 B General Electric units arrived in mid-1963 as C&O was adding to its fleet with new second generation diesels. They were used on the Alleghany grade at first but then transferred to lines west and north of Russell and in Michigan before returning to the Alleghany line in about 1969. They were all retired by 1979. (C&O Ry. Photo, C&OHS Collection, CSPR 5061)

C&O acquired some Alco RSD-5s. No. 5592 is seen here at Peach Creek yard, working on the Logan coal field lines. Although C&O bought a number of Alco and some Baldwin units, it was largely EMD-oriented until GE units became an important pat of the second generation fleet. The RSD-5s such as this were almost all gone by 1962, just ten years after their arrival. (C&OHS Collection, COHS 35204)

Among the few Baldwin units on the C&O roster were the DRS6 -6-15 model, acquired in 1949. Along with AS-616s they were used in and around Cincinnati, especially on transfer runs between Stevens Yard and Cheviot Yard. The three in this class were retired in 1963, 1967 and 1969. (Baldwin Photo, C&OHS Collection, COHS 29082)

Another odd diesel that C&O got in its early dieselization days was the "Cow and Two Calves" TR-3s of 1949. Used mainly as yard units but occasionally in other service, they were finally retired in the 1970s. (C&O Ry. Photo, C&OHS Collection, CSPR 2500)

(C&O Ry. Photographs, C&OHS Collection, CSPR 10228.10 (top right) and CSPR 10228.12 (top left)

Some C&O GP7s had dynamic brakes and some did not. These photos show No. 5767 in 1955, one which did not. They were kept most often in Michigan in later years but initially were used system-wide. (C&O Ry. Photo, C&OHS Collection)

(C&O Ry. Photographs, C&OHS Collection, CSPR 10228.9 (bottom right) and CSPR 10228.11 (bottom left)

The Chesapeake & Ohio Railway - A Concise History and Fact Book

(C&O Ry. Photographs, C&OHS Collection, CSPR 10228.96 (top right) and CSPR 10228.99 (top left)

This set of photos taken in 1955 shows GP9 No. 5912 and 5915, units which had the dynamic brakes. They are painted in the initial scheme used on GP7s and 9s, which included stripes, Progress logos and Roman lettering similar to the steam era. (C&O Ry. Photos, C&OHS Collection)

(C&O Ry. Photographs, C&OHS Collection, CSPR 10228.97 (bottom right) and CSPR 10228.98 (bottom left)

C&O E8 Details and Modifications
by Tod Hanger

- Vertical grab irons added below number boards about 1952.
- Bottom stripe of locomotive painted aluminum until 1954, gray after that.
- Grab irons added above windshields on cab roof and on sides of the locomotive above the logo. 1954-55
- Change in lettering contour on a few letters and spacing between words noted in March 11, 1954 drawing.
- Stripes discontinued from wrap around to back of locomotive. 1954
- Change in contour of painting design on nose in 1955.
- Top of nose repainted blue to eliminate glare, 1954.
- Radio antenna added to roof, centered above windshield, with coaxial cable in surface mounted conduit beginning just behind top of the headlight and running up center bar of windshield to base of antenna in 1957.
- Pyle-National Gyralite Model 20755 oscillating light (triangular bulb arrangement) replaced single red/white oscillating light.
- Coupler cover removed and m.u. connections added, along with air and signal line piping to pilot, added in 1957.
- Grab irons added in an angle arrangement up the side of the nose for access to windshield area, 1959.

Figure 1. This photo is annotated to show changes made to the E8s fleet over its life. No. 4019 is resting between runs at Charlottesville, Va., July 19, 1970. (T. W. Dixon, Jr. Photo, C&OHS Collection, COHS 31293)

1. Blue paint on nose to reduce glare - circa 1954
2. Gyralite circa 1955
3. Trainline air hose added 1957
4. Coupler cover removed 1957
5. Grab rails added 1952

6. Bottom stripe changed from Aluminum to Gray paint - 1954
7. M.U. connector added -1957
8. Radio antenna and conduit - 1957
9. Winterization hatches
10. Ladder rest added 1954-55

The information on this page and the next is taken from the Winter 2011 issue of the C&O Historical Magazine. This is typical of the information contained in the magazine. To subscribe, contact The Chesapeake & Ohio Historical Society.

Figure 2. E8 4027 at the end of its life on No 42, the Virginia section of The George Washington, *at Newport News, Va., February 7, 1971. T. W. Dixon, Jr. photo, (C&OHS Collection, COHS 31294)*

1. Ladder rest and grab irons above windshield added 1954-55
2. Grab irons added to right side and on top of nose 1959.

Rear view of E8 4008 shows how the yellow stripe bent around the rear end of the locomotive. This was eliminated in 1954 and as units were repainted the rear was made solid blue. Note the backup light, visible only in a photo such as this.
(C&O Ry. Photo, C&OHS Collection, CSPR 10228.60)

Figure 4. These two photos taken of two units in exactly the same spot at the Charlottesville terminal in 1962 show the change in spacing of the road name on the side. No. 4021 was taken on Aug. 22, 1962 and has the wide spacing while 4003 was taken on August 20, 1962 with the narrowed spacing. R. D. Patton Photos (C&OHS Collection, COHS 31295 (top) and COHS 31296 (bottom).

Alco RSD-7 No. 6805 is seen here at St. Albans, W. Va., beside a still-active 2-6-6-2 in April 1956. The RSD-7s were bought with the idea that they would be a one-for-one replacement for a 2-6-6-2. (Gene Huddleston Photo, C&OHS Collection, COHS 1299)

The All Time Diesel Locomotive Roster of the Chesapeake & Ohio Railway

The diesel locomotive roster, reproduced on pages 112 through 116, was originally compiled for and was published in the book *Chesapeake & Ohio Diesel Locomotives,* by Carl W. Shaver and David Gilliland, published by C&O Historical Society in 1994. It includes all the C&O diesels that were purchased up to 1986. Paint schemes would have been C&O (various styles) and Chessie System. The book uses this roster as an index and goes on to dedicate a separate section to each entry with photo, mechanical data, history, and dispositions. It is expected that a reprint of this book will be available from the Society in 2013.

This roster covers all locomotives owned by the Chesapeake & Ohio Railway Company and its predecessors, from 1939 until the 1986 merger with the Baltimore & Ohio Railroad Company.

Arrangement of the locomotives in this roster is in numerical order, using the "Road Numbers" column (first on the left). A locomotive will appear in this column once for each C&O number it has carried. Columns showing previous and subsequent numbers appear at the left and right sides of the roster, respectively.

PREVIOUS ROAD NUMBERS	ROAD NUMBERS	BUILDER	MODEL	HORSEPOWER	BUILDER'S NOS.	DATE	SUBSEQUENT C&O ROAD NUMBERS
(FSUD 1, 2)	—	GM-EMD	NW5	1000	4148, 4149	1, 2,47	—
(M&NE 1)	1	GE	44-ton	380	28501	8/46	8303
(M&NE 2, 3)	2, 3	GM-EMD	NW2	1000	5555, 5556	4/48	5297, 5298
(PM 10)	10	GM-EMC	SW1	600	902	7/39	
(PM 11)	11	GM-EMD	SW1	600	1712	4/42	8401
(PM 20, 21)	20, 21	GE	70-ton	600	28506, 28508	1/47	—
(PM 22)	22	GE	70-ton	600	28510	1/47	—
(PM 51, 52)	51, 52	GM-EMD	NW2	1000	1715, 1716	10, 11/42	5275, 5276
(PM 53, 54)	53, 54	GM-EMD	NW2	1000	1717, 1718	2, 3/43	5277, 5278
(PM 55)	55	GM-EMD	NW2	1000	3463	4/45	5280
(PM 56)	56	GM-EMD	NW2	1000	3464	11/45	5281
(PM 57)	57	GM-EMD	NW2	1000	3465	4/46	5282
(PM 58)	58	GM-EMD	NW2	1000	3466	4/46	9565
(PM 59-64)	59 - 64	GM-EMD	NW2	1000	3467 - 3472	4, 5/46	5284-5289
—	80 - 82	GM-EMD	BL2	1500	4724 - 4726	6/48	—
—	83	GM-EMD	BL2	1500	4727	7/48	1839
—	84, 85	GM-EMD	BL2	1500	4728, 4729	7/48	—
—	95 -98	GM-EMD	E7A	2000	6262 - 6265	7/48	
(PM 101, 102)	101, 102	GM-EMD	E7A	2000	2911, 2912	6/46	—, 4522
(PM 103 - 106)	103 - 106	GM-EMD	E7A	2000	4552 - 4555	4/47	4510 - 4513
(PM 107, 108)	107, 108	GM-EMD	E7A	2000	4722 - 4723	7/47	4514, 4515
6211	140T	C&O	slug	—	—	8/85	—
6227	141T	C&O	slug	—	—	9/85	—
6062	142T	C&O	slug	—	—	10/85	—
5946	143T	C&O	slug	—	—	11/85	—
6215	144T	C&O	slug	—	—	12/85	—
6136	145T	C&O	slug	—	—	1/86	—
6143	146T	C&O	slug	—	—	2/86	—
6013	147T	C&O	slug	—	—	3/86	—
6036	148T	C&O	slug	—	—	4/86	—
6186	149T	C&O	slug	—	—	5/86	—

The Chesapeake & Ohio Railway - A Concise History and Fact Book

PREVIOUS ROAD NUMBERS	ROAD NUMBERS	BUILDER	MODEL	HORSEPOWER	BUILDER'S NOS.	DATE	SUBSEQUENT C&O ROAD NUMBERS
6168	150T	C&O	slug	—	—	6/86	—
4512, 4515	1414, 1417	GM-EMD	E7A	2000	4554, 4723	4, 7/47	—
4520, 4521	1418, 1419	GM-EMD	E7A	2000	6262, 6263	7/48	—
4523	1422	GM-EMD	E7A	2000	6265	7/48	—
4522	1425	GM-EMD	E7A	2000	2912	6/46	—
4003, 4016	1468, 1469	GM-EMD	E8A	2250	14762, 14775	8, 12/51	—
4025, 4026	1470, 1471	GM-EMD	E8A	2250	14784, 14785	1/52	—
4027, 4028	1472, 1473	GM-EMD	E8A	2250	18081, 18082	5/53	—
(CSS 1502)	1502 (1st)	GM-EMD	GP7	1500	10134	6/50	5705
(CSS 1503)	1503 (1st)	GM-EMD	GP7	1500	15253	10/51	5747
(CSS 1504)	1504 (1st)	GM-EMD	GP7	1500	15270	11/51	5764
(CSS 1505)	1505 (1st)	GM-EMD	GP7	1500	17038	10/52	5817
(CSS 1506)	1506 (1st)	GM-EMD	GP7	1500	15284	12/51	5778
(CSS 1507)	1507 (1st)	GM-EMD	GP7	1500	17286	10/52	5839
(CSS 1508)	1508 (1st)	GM-EMD	GP7	1500	17280	10/52	5833
—	1500 - 1524	GM-EMD	GP15T	1500	817054-1 to -24	10-11/82	—
—	1800 - 1818	GM-EMD	SD18	1800	27598 - 27616	1 - 3/63	7300 - 7318
83	1839	GM-EMD	BL2	1500	4727	7/48	—
—	1840	GM-EMD	BL2	1500	6275	10/48	—
—	1841 - 1847	GM-EMD	BL2	1500	6276 - 6282	1 - 3/49	—
—	1850 - 1856	GM-EMD	NW2	1000	6268 - 6274	11, 12/48	9558 - 9564
5574	2000	Alco	RSD5	1600	79431	4/52	—
5575, 5576	2001, 2002	Alco	RSD5	1600	79702, 79703	4/52	—
5587, 5589	2003, 2004	Alco	RSD5	1600	79952, 79954	6/52	—
5591, 5592	2005, 2006	Alco	RSD5	1600	80190, 80191	6, 7/52	—
6700 - 6709	2007 - 2016	Alco	RSD12	1800	81943 - 81952	4, 5/56	—
—	2100 - 2103	Alco Prod.	C630	3000	3486-01 to -04	10/67	—
5530	2200	Baldwin	DRS-6-6-15	1500	74701	11/49	—
5534 - 5536	2202 - 2204	B L H	AS-616	1600	74918 - 74920	11/50	—
5538 - 5542	2205 - 2209	B L H	AS-616	1600	74922 - 74926	12/50	—
5546	2211	B L H	AS-616	1600	74951	1/51	—
5547 - 5549	2212 - 2214	B L H	AS-616	1600	74966 - 74968	1/51	—
5551 - 5558	2215 - 2222	B L H	AS-616	1600	75171 - 75178	7 - 9/51	—
5559, 5560	2223, 2224	B L H	AS-616	1600	75345, 75346	2/52	—
5562, 5563	2225, 2226	B L H	AS-616	1600	75348, 75349	2/52	—
5565 - 5569	2227 - 2231	B L H	AS-616	1600	75351 - 75355	2, 3/52	—
5528, 5529	2232, 2233	B L H	AS-616	1600	75391, 75392	7/53	—
—	2300 - 2329	GE	U23B	2250	37228 - 37257	9, 10/69	—
—	2500, 2501	GE	U25B	2500	34566, 34567	8/63	8100, 8101
—	2502, 2503	GE	U25B	2500	34569, 34570	8/63	8102, 8103
—	2504	GE	U25B	2500	34568	8/63	8104
—	2505	GE	U25B	2500	34724	8/63	8105
—	2506, 2507	GE	U25B	2500	34725, 34726	9/63	8106, 8107
—	2508 - 2529	GE	U25B	2500	34731 - 34752	10 - 12/63	8108 - 8129
—	2530 - 2537	GE	U25B	2500	34753 - 34760	1/64	8130 - 8137
—	3000, 3001	GM-EMD	GP30	2250	27798, 27799	8, 10/62	—
—	3002 - 3015	GM-EMD	GP30	2250	27584 - 27597	12/62, 1/63	—
—	3016, 3017	GM-EMD	GP30	2250	28410, 28411	8/63	—
—	3018 - 3047	GM-EMD	GP30	2250	28494 - 28523	8 - 10/63	—
—	3045 (2nd)	GM-EMD	GP35	2500	30987	9/65	3583
—	3047 (2nd)	GM-EMD	GP35	2500	30988	9/65	3584
—	3300 - 3303	GE	U30C	3000	36300 - 36303	6/67	—
—	3304 - 3312	GE	U30C	3000	36767 - 36775	5 - 7/68	—
—	3520 - 3539	GM-EMD	GP35	2500	29110 - 29129	5, 6/64	—
—	3537 (2nd)	GM-EMD	GP35	2500	29989	9/65	—
—	3560 - 3575	GM-EMD	GP35	2500	29392 - 29407	9 - 11/64	—
—	3563 (2nd)	GM-EMD	GP35	2500	30990	9/65	—
—	3574 (2nd)	GM-EMD	GP35	2500	30991	9/65	—
—	3582	GM-EMD	GP35	2500	31439	12/65	—
3045 (2nd)	3583	GM-EMD	GP35	2500	30987	9/65	—
3047 (2nd)	3584	GM-EMD	GP35	2500	30988	9/65	—
—	3780 - 3794	GM-EMD	GP40	3000	39246 - 39260	12/71	—
—	3850 - 3899	GM-EMD	GP38	2000	33681 - 33730	11, 12/67	—
—	3900 - 3919	GM-EMD	GP39	2300	34785 - 34804	6, 7/69	—
—	4000 - 4002	GM-EMD	E8A	2250	14759 - 14761	8/51	—
—	4003	GM-EMD	E8A	2250	14762	8/51	1468
—	4004 - 4015	GM-EMD	E8A	2250	14763 - 14774	8 - 12/51	—
—	4016	GM-EMD	E8A	2250	14775	12/51	1469
—	4017 - 4024	GM-EMD	E8A	2250	14776 - 14783	12/51 - 1/52	—
—	4025, 4026	GM-EMD	E8A	2250	14784, 14785	1/52	1470, 1471
—	4027, 4028	GM-EMD	E8A	2250	18081, 18082	5/53	1472, 1473
—	4029, 4030	GM-EMD	E8A	2250	18083, 18084	5/53	—
—	4065 - 4089	GM-EMD	GP40	3000	38545 - 38569	6 - 8/71	—
—	4090 - 4099	GM-EMD	GP40	3000	39236 - 39245	12/71	—
—	4165 - 4184	GM-EMD	GP40-2	3000	7394-01 to -20	11/72	—
—	4262 - 4281	GM-EMD	GP40-2	3000	776085-01 to -20	1/78	—
—	4282 - 4286	GM-EMD	GP40-2	3000	777091-01 to -05	2, 3/78	—
—	4372 - 4391	GM-EMD	GP40-2	3000	786288-01 to -20	1/80	—
—	4392 - 4421	GM-EMD	GP40-2	3000	787289-01 to -30	2, 3/80	—
103, 104	4510, 4511	GM-EMD	E7A	2000	4552, 4553	4/47	—
105, 106	4512, 4513	GM-EMD	E7A	2000	4554, 4555	4/47	1414, —
107, 108	4514, 4515	GM-EMD	E7A	2000	4722, 4723	7/47	—, 1417

PREVIOUS ROAD NUMBERS	ROAD NUMBERS	BUILDER	MODEL	HORSEPOWER	BUILDER'S NOS.	DATE	SUBSEQUENT C&O ROAD NUMBERS
95, 96	4520, 4521	GM-EMD	E7A	2000	6262, 6263	7/48	1418, 1419
102	4522	GM-EMD	E7A	2000	2912	6/46	1425
98	4523	GM-EMD	E7A	2000	6265	7/48	1422
—	4820 - 4829	GM-EMD	GP38	2000	36666 - 36675	7/70	—
—	5000	Alco	S2	1000	76770	4/49	9160
—	5001	Alco	S2	1000	76771	4/49	
—	5002 - 5004	Alco	S2	1000	76781 -76783	6/49	
—	5005, 5006	Alco	S2	1000	77130, 77131	9/49	9161, 9162
—	5007 - 5010	Alco	S2	1000	77132 - 77135	9/ or 10/49	
—	5011, 5012	Alco	S2	1000	77136, 77137	9/ or 10/49	9163, 9164
—	5013, 5014	Alco	S2	1000	77138, 77139	9/ or 10/49	
—	5015	Alco	S2	1000	77140	10/49	9165
—	5016 - 5021	Alco	S2	1000	77141 - 77146	10/49	
—	5022,	Alco	S2	1000	77147	10/49	9168
—	5023, 5024	Alco	S2	1000	77148, 77149	10/49	
—	5025	Alco	S2	1000	77150	10/49	9169
—	5026	Alco	S2	1000	77165	10/49	
—	5027 - 5032	Alco	S2	1000	77796 - 77801	10/ or 11/49	
—	5033	Alco	S2	1000	77802	10/ or 11/49	9172
—	5034, 5035	Alco	S2	1000	77803, 77804	10/ or 11/49	
—	5036	Alco	S2	1000	77805	10/ or 11/49	9173
—	5037 - 5044	Alco	S2	1000	77806 - 77813	10, 11/49	
—	5045, 5046	Alco	S2	1000	77827, 77828	12/49	9174, 9175
—	5047 - 5050	Alco	S2	1000	77941 - 77944	12/49, 1/50	
—	5051	Alco	S2	1000	77945	1/50	9179
—	5052 - 5057	Alco	S2	1000	76897-76902	1/50	
—	5060 - 5065	GM-EMD	NW2	1000	10381 - 10386	9/49	—
—	5066 - 5079	GM-EMD	NW2	1000	10367 - 10380	6, 8/49	—
—	5080 - 5089	GM-END	SW9	1200	11713 - 11722	4/52	—
—	5090, 5091	GM-EMD	SW9	1200	17262, 17263	1/53	—
—	5092, 5093	GM-EMD	SW9	1200	19298, 19299	12/53	—
—	5100 - 5104	Alco	S4	1000	80622 - 80626	7, 8/53	—
(B&O 9024)	5100 (2nd)	Alco	S2	1000	70253	9/43	—
—	5105 - 5113	Alco	S4	1000	80629 - 80637	8, 9/53	
—	5114, 5115	Alco	RS1	1000	80851, 80852	9/53	
—	5200 - 5213	GM-EMD	NW2	1000	10259 - 10272	8 - 10/49	—
—	5214 - 5235	GM-EMD	SW7	1200	10273 - 10294	1, 2/50	
—	5236 - 5239	GM-EMD	SW7	1200	10295 - 10298	3/50	
—	5240 - 5244	GMD	SW9	1200	A149 - A153	1, 2/51	
—	5245 - 5261	GM-EMD	SW9	1200	15504 - 15520	10, 11/51	
—	5262 - 5265	GM-EMD	SW9	1200	15521 - 15524	11/51	
51, 52	5275, 5276	GM-EMD	NW2	1000	1715, 1716	10, 11/42	—
53, 54	5277, 5278	GM-EMD	NW2	1000	1717, 1718	2, 3/43	—
55	5280	GM-EMD	NW2	1000	3463	4/45	—
56	5281	GM-EMD	NW2	1000	3464	11/45	—
57	5282	GM-EMD	NW2	1000	3465	4/46	—
59 - 64	5284 - 5289	GM-EMD	NW2	1000	3467 -3472	4, 5/46	—
2, 3	5297, 5298	GM-EMD	NW2	1000	5555, 5556	4/48	—
—	5500, 5501	Alco	RS2	1500	76826, 78627	5/49	—
—	5528, 5529	BLH	AS-616	1600	75391, 75392	7/53	2232, 2233
—	5530	Baldwin	DRS-6-6-15	1500	74701	11/49	2200
—	5531, 5532	Baldwin	DRS-6-6-15	1500	74702, 74703	11/49	—
—	5533	BLH	AS-616	1600	74917	11/50	—
—	5534 - 5536	BLH	AS-616	1600	74918 - 74920	11/50	2202 - 2204
—	5537	BLH	AS-616	1600	74921	12/50	—
—	5538 - 5542	BLH	AS-616	1600	74922 - 74926	12/50	2205 - 2209
—	5543	BLH	AS-616	1600	74927	12/50	
—	5544, 5545	BLH	AS-616	1600	74928, 74929	1/51	—
—	5546	BLH	AS-616	1600	74951	1/51	2211
—	5547 - 5549	BLH	AS-616	1600	74966 - 74968	1/51	2212 - 2214
—	5550	BLH	AS-616	1600	74969	1/51	
—	5551 - 5558	BLH	AS-616	1600	75171 - 75178	7 - 9/51	2215 - 2222
—	5559, 5560	BLH	AS-616	1600	75345, 75346	2/52	2223, 2224
—	5561	BLH	AS-616	1600	75347	2/52	
—	5562, 5563	BLH	AS-616	1600	75348, 75349	2/52	2225, 2226
—	5564	BLH	AS-616	1600	75350	2/52	
—	5565 - 5569	BLH	AS-616	1600	75351 - 75355	2, 3/52	2227 - 2231
—	5570 - 5573	Alco	RSD5	1600	79437 - 79430	3, 4/52	
—	5574	Alco	RSD5	1600	79431	4/52	2000
—	5575, 5576	Alco	RSD5	1600	79702, 79703	4/52	2001, 2002
—	5577 - 5579	Alco	RSD5	1600	79704 - 79706	4/52	—
—	5580 - 5586	Alco	RSD5	1600	79945 - 79951	5/52	
—	5587 - 5588	Alco	RSD5	1600	79952, 79953	6/52	2003, —
—	5589	Alco	RSD5	1600	79954	6/52	2004
—	5590	Alco	RSD5	1600	80189	6/52	
—	5591, 5592	Alco	RSD5	1600	80190, 80191	6/52	2005, 2006
—	5593 - 5595	Alco	RSD5	1600	80192 - 80194	6, 7/52	—
—	5600, 5601	Alco	RS3	1600	81160, 81161	4/55	—
—	5700 - 5709	GM-EMD	GP7	1500	10129 - 10138	4, 6/50	
—	5710 - 5714	GM-EMD	GP7	1500	10532 - 10536	3, 4/50	—
—	5715 - 5719	GM-EMD	GP7	1500	10139 - 10143	6/50	—
—	5720 - 5735	GMD	GP7	1500	A154 - A169	3 - 6/51	—
—	5736 - 5738	GMD	GP7	1500	A239 - A241	6/51	
—	5739 - 5797	GM-EMD	GP7	1500	15245 - 15303	10/51 - 1/52	

PREVIOUS ROAD NUMBERS	ROAD NUMBERS	BUILDER	MODEL	HORSEPOWER	BUILDER'S NOS.	DATE	SUBSEQUENT C&O ROAD NUMBERS
—	**5800 - 5811**	GM-EMD	GP7	1500	16692 - 16703	5, 6/52	—
5900	**5809 (2nd)**	GM-EMD	GP7	1500	18064	4/53	5875 (2nd)
—	**5812 - 5828**	GM-EMD	GP7	1500	17033 - 17049	10, 11/52	—
—	**5829, 5830**	GM-EMD	GP7	1500	17287, 17288	12/52	—
—	**5831 - 5839**	GM-EMD	GP7	1500	17278 - 17286	10/52	
—	**5840 - 5855**	GM-EMD	GP7	1500	17289 - 17304	1, 2/53	—
—	**5856 - 5859**	GM-EMD	GP7	1500	18077 - 18080	3/53	—
—	**5860, 5861**	GM-EMD	GP7	1500	18060, 18061	3/53	—
—	**5862 - 5885**	GM-EMD	GP7	1500	18036 - 18059	4/53	—
5809 (2nd)	**5875 (2nd)**	GM-EMD	GP7	1500	18064	4/53	—
—	**5886 - 5897**	GM-EMD	GP7	1500	18065 - 18076	4/53	—
—	**5898, 5899**	GM-EMD	GP7	1500	18062, 18063	4/53	—
—	**5900**	GM-EMD	GP7	1500	18064	4/53	5809 (2nd)
—	**5901 - 5919**	GM-EMD	GP9	1750	20183 - 20201	12/54	—
—	**5920 - 5928**	GM-EMD	GP9	1750	21193 - 21201	12/55	
—	**5929 - 5937**	GM-EMD	GP9	1750	20646 - 20654	8/55	
—	**5938 - 5945**	GM-EMD	GP9	1750	20847 - 20854	8 - 9/55	
—	**5946**	GM-EMD	GP9	1750	20855	9/55	
—	**5947 - 5977**	GM-EMD	GP9	1750	20856 - 20886	9 - 10/55	
—	**5978 - 5997**	GM-EMD	GP9	1750	21026 - 21045	10, 11/55	
—	**5998 - 6008**	GM-EMD	GP9	1750	21182 - 21192	12/55	—
—	**6000A (1st)**	GM-EMD	TR4A	1200	11945	6/50	6600A
—	**6000B (2nd)**	GM-EMD	TR4B	1200	11946	6/50	6600B
—	**6001A (1st)**	GM-EMD	TR4A	1200	11947	6/50	6601A
—	**6001B (1st)**	GM-EMD	TR4B	1200	11948	6/50	6601B
—	**6009 - 6012**	GM-EMD	GP9	1750	21487 - 21490	3/56	—
—	**6013**	GM-EMD	GP9	1750	21491	3/56	—
—	**6014 - 6033**	GM-EMD	GP9	1750	21492 - 21511	3/56	—
—	**6034 - 6035**	GM-EMD	GP9	1750	21524 - 21525	4/56	—
—	**6036**	GM-EMD	GP9	1750	21526	4/56	—
—	**6037 - 6048**	GM-EMD	GP9	1750	21527 - 21538	4/56	—
—	**6049 - 6061**	GM-EMD	GP9	1750	21686 - 21698	6/56	—
—	**6062**	GM-EMD	GP9	1750	21699	6/56	—
—	**6063 - 6088**	GM-EMD	GP9	1750	21700 - 21725	6/56	—
—	**6089 - 6099**	GM-EMD	GP9	1750	22090 - 22100	6, 7/56	—
—	**6100 - 6108**	GM-EMD	GP9	1750	22101 - 22109	7/56	—
—	**6109 - 6134**	GM-EMD	GP9	1750	22017 - 22042	9/56	
—	**6135**	GM-EMD	GP9	1750	22043	9/56	—
—	**6136**	GM-EMD	GP9	1750	22044	9/56	—
—	**6137 - 6142**	GM-EMD	GP9	1750	22045 - 22050	9/56	—
—	**6143**	GM-EMD	GP9	1750	22051	9/56	—
—	**6144 - 6158**	GM-EMD	GP9	1750	22052 - 22066	11/56	—
—	**6159 - 6166**	GM-EMD	GP9	1750	22540 - 22547	9/56	—
—	**6167**	GM-EMD	GP9	1750	22550	11/56	—
—	**6168**	GM-EMD	GP9	1750	22551	11/56	—
—	**6169 - 6185**	GM-EMD	GP9	1750	22552 - 22568	11/56	—
—	**6186**	GM-EMD	GP9	1750	22569	11/56	—
—	**6187 - 6208**	GM-EMD	GP9	1750	22570 - 22591	11-12/56	—
—	**6209 - 6210**	GM-EMD	GP9	1750	23368 - 23369	6/57	—
—	**6211**	GM-EMD	GP9	1750	23370	6/57	—
—	**6212 - 6214**	GM-EMD	GP9	1750	23371 - 23373	6/57	—
—	**6215**	GM-EMD	GP9	1750	23374	6/57	—
—	**6216 - 6226**	GM-EMD	GP9	1750	23375 - 23385	6-7/57	—
—	**6227**	GM-EMD	GP9	1750	23386	7/57	—
—	**6228 - 6238**	GM-EMD	GP9	1750	23387 - 23397	7/57	—
—	**6239 - 6263**	GM-EMD	GP9	1750	23501 - 23525	8/57	—
—	**6500A, 6501A**	GM-EMD	TR3A	1000	10253, 10256	7, 10/49	9552, 9555
—	**6500B, 6501B**	GM-EMD	TR3B	1000	10255, 10258	7, 10/49	9554, 9557
—	**6500C, 6501C**	GM-EMD	TR3C	1000	10254, 10257	7, 10/49	9556, 9553
6000A, 6001A	**6600A, 6601A**	GM-EMD	TR4A	1200	11945, 11947	6/50	9622, 9624
6000B, 6001B	**6600B, 6601B**	GM-EMD	TR4B	1200	11946, 11948	6/50	9623, 9625
—	**6700 - 6709**	Alco	RSD12	1800	81943 - 81952	4, 5/56	2007 - 2016
—	**6800 - 6811**	Alco	RSD7	2400	81901 - 81912	2-4/56	—
—	**7000 - 7015**	GM-EMD	F7A	1500	9728 - 9743	9/50	—
—	**7016 - 7031**	GM-EMD	F7A	1500	11842 - 11857	9/50	—
—	**7032 - 7085**	GM-EMD	F7A	1500	15969 - 16022	1 - 5/52	—
—	**7086 - 7093**	GM-EMD	F7A	1500	17264 - 17271	10, 11/52	—
8014, 8015	**7094, 7095**	GM-EMD	FP7A	1500	17490, 17491	12/52	—
1800 - 1818	**7300 - 7318**	GM-EMD	SD18	1800	27598 - 27616	1 - 3/63	—
—	**7420 - 7431**	GM-EMD	SD35	2500	29428 - 29439	9 - 11/64	—
—	**7425 (2nd)**	GM-EMD	SD35	2500	30741	8/65	—
—	**7428 (2nd)**	GM-EMD	SD35	2500	30740	8/65	—
—	**7450 - 7469**	GM-EMD	SD40	3000	31929 - 31948	7, 8/66	7550 - 7569
—	**7475 - 7481**	GM-EMD	SD40	3000	33154 - 33160	5/67	7575 - 7581
—	**7500 - 7515 (1st)**	GM-EMD	F7B	1500	11858 - 11873	9/50	—
—	**7516 - 7542 (1st)**	GM-EMD	F7B	1500	16023 - 16049	1-5/52	
—	**7543 - 7546**	GM-EMD	F7B	1500	17272 - 17275	10, 11/52	—
—	**7501 - 7506 (2nd)**	GM-EMD	SD40	3000	34779 - 34784	4/69	—
—	**7507 - 7516 (2nd)**	GM-EMD	SD40	3000	36696 - 36705	6/70	—
—	**7517 - 7526 (2nd)**	GM-EMD	SD40	3000	36746 - 36755	7/70	—
—	**7527 - 7536 (2nd)**	GM-EMD	SD40	3000	37204 - 37213	2, 3/71	—

PREVIOUS ROAD NUMBERS	ROAD NUMBERS	BUILDER	MODEL	HORSEPOWER	BUILDER'S NOS.	DATE	SUBSEQUENT C&O ROAD NUMBERS
7540 - 7469	7550 - 7569	GM-EMD	SD40	3000	31929 - 31948	7, 8/66	—
7475 - 7481	7575 - 7581	GM-EMD	SD40	3000	33154 - 33160	5/67	—
—	8000 - 8013	GM-EMD	FP7A	1500	16050 - 16063	2 - 4/52	—
—	8014, 8015	GM-EMD	FP7A	1500	17490, 17491	12/52	7094, 7095
2500, 2501	8100, 8101	GE	U25B	2500	34566, 34567	8/63	—
2502, 2503	8102, 8103	GE	U25B	2500	34569, 34570	8/63	—
2504	8104	GE	U25B	2500	34568	8/63	—
2505	8105	GE	U25B	2500	34724	8/63	—
2506, 2507	8106, 8107	GE	U25B	2500	34725, 34726	9/63	—
2508 - 2529	8108 - 8129	GE	U25B	2500	34731 - 34752	10 - 12/63	—
2530 - 2537	8130 - 8137	GE	U25B	2500	34753 - 34760	1/64	—
—	8200 - 8209	GE	U30B	3000	38218 - 38227	12/70, 1/72	—
—	8210 - 8222	GE	U30B	3000	38475 - 38487	11, 12/72	—
(GE 302, 301)	8223, 8224	GE	U30B	3000	35881, 35880	5/66	—
—	8225 - 8234	GE	U30B	3000	40068 - 40077	12/74	—
—	8235 - 8244	GE	B30-7	3000	41897 - 41906	5, 6/78	—
—	8245 - 8254	GE	B30-7	3000	42138 - 42147	2/79	—
—	8255 - 8264	GE	B30-7	3000	42279 - 42288	6, 7/79	—
—	8265 - 8278	GE	B30-7	3000	42770 - 42783	1/80	—
—	8279 - 8298	GE	B30-7	3000	43256 - 43275	3 - 5/81	—
1	8303	GE	44-ton	380	28501	8/46	—
11	8401	GM-EMD	SW1	600	1714	4/42	—
(BOCT 8419)	8419	GM-EMD	SW1	600	1604	5/42	—
—	8501 - 8506	GM-EMD	F7B	1500	16064 - 16070	2 - 4/52	—
—	8553 - 8575	GM-EMD	SD50	3500	837057-1 to -23	1 - 2/84	—
—	8624 - 8643	GM-EMD	SD50	3600	857095-1 to -20	11 - 12/85	—
5000	9160	Alco	S2	1000	76770	4/49	—
5005, 5006	9161, 9162	Alco	S2	1000	77130, 77131	9/49	—
5011, 5012	9163, 9164	Alco	S2	1000	77136, 77137	9/ or 10/49	—
(B&O 9099)	9164 (2nd)	Alco	S2	1000	81972	6/56	—
5015	9165	Alco	S2	1000	77140	10/49	—
5022, 5025	9168, 9169	Alco	S2	1000	77147, 77150	10/49	—
5033, 5036	9172, 9173	Alco	S2	1000	77802, 77805	10/ or 11/49	—
5045, 5046	9174, 9175	Alco	S2	1000	77827, 77828	11/49	—
5051	9179	Alco	S2	1000	77945	1/50	—
6500A	9552	GM-EMD	TR3A	1000	10253	7/49	—
6501C	9553	GM-EMD	TR3C	1000	10257	10/49	—
6500B	9554	GM-EMD	TR3B	1000	10255	7/49	—
6501A	9555	GM-EMD	TR3A	1000	10256	10/49	—
6500C	9556	GM-EMD	TR3C	1000	10254	7/49	—
6501B	9557	GM-EMD	TR3B	1000	10258	10/49	—
1850 - 1856	9558 - 9564	GM-EMD	NW2	1000	6268 - 6274	11, 12/48	—
58	9565	GM-EMD	NW2	1000	3466	4/46	—
6600A	9622	GM-EMD	TR4A	1200	11945	6/50	—
6600B	9623	GM-EMD	TR4B	1200	11946	6/50	—
6601A	9624	GM-EMD	TR4A	1200	11947	6/50	—
6601B	9625	GM-EMD	TR4B	1200	11948	6/50	—

Additional Sources of Information for C&O Diesel Locomotives

- *Chesapeake & Ohio Diesel Locomotives*, by Carl Shaver and David Gilliland, C&O Historical Society, Clifton Forge, Va., 1994, 136 pages. - This is the first and best reference for C&O diesels, start to finish. It has great details on every single class and type, with dispositions that we know up to that time. Scores of photographs and a great deal of background mechanical data make this a complete work. Other parts of the book give status of Chessie System and CSX diesels that came from C&O up to 1994. Long out of print, it is expected that the Society will issue a print-on-demand reprint (not an update) in 2013. Consult C&OHS at 800-453-COHS or chessieshop.com.

- *Chessie System Diesel Locomotives*, by Jerry Doyle, TLC Publishing, Lynchburg, Va., 1999, Full color, 112 pages, hardbound. Full history with good color photographs of all diesels purchased new for C&O during the Chessie System Era.

- *Chesapeake & Ohio Diesel Locomotives in Color 1949-1971*, by Jerry Doyle, C&O Historical Society, Clifton Forge, Va., 2006 - Hardbound, 122 pages, full color photographs. A treatment of C&O diesels in detail chronologically order-by-order, up to 1971. Excellent data and photographs. (Available from C&O Hist. Soc. Catalog No. BK-03-364)

- *Chesapeake & Ohio Railway Color Pictorial, Vol. 1*, by Harry Stegmaier, Four Ways West Publishing, La Mirada, Calif. 1998, Hardbound, 112 pages. Many full color photographs with considerable background historical data on C&O diesels, and some steam. Excellent photographs. Treats only first generation diesels.

- *CSX Diesel Locomotives*, by Patrick E. Stakem, TLC Publishing, Lynchburg, Va. 1999, 112 pages hardbound, full color photographs. Good detailed data on CSX diesels of C&O and other heritage.

- Articles appearing throughout the years 1969-present in the *C&O Historical Magazine*. Available on CD fully searchable by keyword. Order from C&O Historical Society (Catalog No. AV-08-102)

- These reprints of C&O materials are available from C&O Historical Society (800-453-2647 or chessieshop.com):

- C&O Early Diesel Diagram Set (Catalog No. DS-07-056)

- C&O Chesapeake District Diesel Locomotive Book (diagrams and much data) (Catalog No. DS-07-055)

- Chessie System Diesel Locomotive Classification Diagrams (Catalog No. DS-07-057)

- *Chesapeake & Ohio F7 and FP7 Diesel Locomotives*, by Karen Parker, 16 pages, C&OHS, Clifton Forge, 2004. Complete details on F7 and FP7s.

CHAPTER NINE

Depots, Towers, and Other Structures

The colonial-style station at White Sulphur Springs served the fabulous C&O-owned Greenbrier resort hotel. The tracks behind were for parking regular Pullman cars to this point as well as special movements, and private and business cars. (C&O Ry. Photograph, C&OHS Collection, CSPR 11846.33)

Any railroad requires a great number of structures to support its operations, passengers, employees, freight, equipment, locomotives, and maintenance work. These range from tiny watchmen's shanties and privies to huge shop complexes, and were distributed over the entire system in quantity required by the local, decentralized nature of the business. Today's railroads need few structures as all their business is conducted on a mass scale with just a few major customers and the trains go from point to point as solid units.

The most common and best known of all railway structures is the station or depot (the two words are interchangeable). On the C&O, depots come in a wide variety of styles, often based on when or where they were constructed. Some were built to common standards adopted and in use over a period of years, while others were unique in design or were copied from other structures off-line. Most of the depots and other buildings of the C&O were designed by its own engineers and draftsmen, with only a handful designed by outside architects.

C&O stations are of three types: a combination station, a passenger station, and a freight station. In the combination station, all of the company's business was conducted in one structure including waiting room and ticket office for

Of all C&O station designs the one that appeared in the most places was in vogue from about 1890 to about 1908. Buildings similar to this one at Alderson, W. Va. appeared in scores of locations, some large, some smaller, some tiny. This is a 1935 view of the large version at Alderson. William Monypeny photograph. (C&OHS Collection, COHS 3027)

117

C&O built hundreds of these fancy little waiting stations at flag stops where no agent or other C&O structure as present. This photograph is at Chickahominy, Virginia, June 1948. (J. I. Kelly Photograph, C&OH Collection, COHS 26248)

passengers, and an office and room to accommodate storage, receipt, and dispatch of mail, express, and less-than-carload freight. In locations where business required it, the functions were divided into two buildings, one accommodating passengers and baggage (and mail and express usually), and a second warehouse type building with the freight office that accommodated the receipt, storage, and dispatch of in- and out-bound freight. In some large cities passenger station functions were shared with other railroads in a "union station."

The structures of the Virginia Central and early C&O were simple clapboard or board-and-batten rectangular buildings often roughly built, which provided basic shelter for passengers, baggage, and freight while awaiting transportation. A few were built of brick by the late 1850s. By the time C&O was building its westward extension across West Virginia a standard was adopted for small-town combination station that comprised a rectangular building of about 30x90 feet in size, with frame structure and board-and-batten siding. At one end it had a porch that led to a passenger waiting room and ticket/freight office where the agent did the company's business. There was a squared-off bay window in the office area that allowed the agent and/or operator to see arriving and departing trains. To the rear of the office was a freight warehouse for transfer of incoming and outbound freight that had a couple of large doors leading to both the track and street sides. Many of these combination stations were built along the line as it pushed west, and some survived into the 1960s, used for other purposes by then, of course.

When the C&O built its line down the Virginia Peninsula from Richmond to Newport News in 1881, a number of stations were erected along this new line, and they all had a particular design. These stations had a two-story end that housed the waiting room and offices on the first floor and

living quarters for the agent on the second floor. Attached to this was the one-story freight handling area with its large doors. There is, as of this writing (2012), one surviving example, in private hands, at Lee Hall, Virginia (though it has been modified much).

In 1889, when C&O built its line from Huntington down the Kentucky side of the Ohio River to Cincinnati, another design was used for the new stations here, which consisted of a simple rectangular building set up like the early 1870s stations, but with some decorative boards used around the eaves and gables, but still having a very plain rectangular/bay window structure. In 1890 C&O absorbed the Richmond & Alleghany Railroad's line from Richmond to Clifton Forge via Lynchburg. The stations on this line had been designed by the R&A's chief engineer, Walter G. Berg. The R&A's small town design was a plain rectangular structure like the C&O's except it had a hipped instead of a gabled roof that had a considerable eaves overhang on all sides. These stations were taken over and used by C&O until modern times.

In 1890 as C&O was improving its physical plant under the new management of M. E. Ingalls and George W. Stevens, a standard station design was adopted that was built in

Beginning in the late 1880s, C&O built many of these octagonal signal towers (known as "cabin" on the C&O). This is a view of AD Cabin at Alderson, W. Va. with all three of its operators posing in about 1895. (C&OHS Collection, COHS 510)

The Chesapeake & Ohio Railway - A Concise History and Fact Book

In 1910, when C&O merged the Chicago, Cincinnati & Louisville and thus acquired its Chicago Division across Indiana, it inherited the CC&L stations, which were a fairly simple design with square bay window, gabled roof with little overhang. When the Hocking Valley Railway came to C&O in 1930, its stations were of a variety of designs, but the majority had a clipped gable roof that set them easily apart, while several others had a rounded or octagonal end for the waiting room area. The Pere Marquette Railway's hundreds of stations came to C&O in the 1947 merger. PM had a wide variety of structures as it was composite of many smaller companies that had merged in 1900, and it built a wide variety of styles itself in the 1900-1920 era.

In towns with separate freight stations, the structures were seldom to any particular standard and were built to accommodate local conditions. They were usually frame board-and-batten buildings with gabled or hipped roofs and no bay window. They usually had an office for freight agent, clerk(s), and laborers at one end and the warehouse extending from it with any number of large freight doors on both the railroad and street sides. The side facing the track almost always had an elevated platform that was at box car door level for easy loading and unloading. These stations almost always had their own "house track" siding next to this platform and separate from the main line. In some cases older combination stations were converted to freight use when separate passenger structures were erected. In larger locations the freight station was often of brick construction. In some locations it had a two-story office area if a large amount of freight was being handled, to accommodate the clerks needed.

At locations where no agent was assigned, C&O often erected a small shelter station which was just a tiny (usually 10x10 feet) waiting room enclosed on three or four sides, into which passengers waiting for a train could rest away from the weather. These are often called "flag stop stations."

This unusual photograph shows two different versions of a standard C&O cabin. The wooden version at left replaced the octagonal cabin about 1900, and then as this photo shows, was replaced in some instances in the 1920s and 1930s with a red brick tower. However, many of the wooden towers lasted into the 1960s. (C&OHS Collection, CSPR 26249)

so many places that it is probably the most recognizable of C&O depots. It was a rectangular building that had an angled bay-window, and a gabled roof with decorative verge boards hung in the gables, board-and-batten sides with an angled tongue-in-grove wainscoting up to about 2 feet. It came in whatever size was needed to accommodate business, with the number of waiting rooms and freight doors added as needed for a particular location. These stations were built by C&O division carpenter forces and replaced many of the 1870s-era stations along the mainline. This design was used for many of the new stations along the many branch lines being built at the time.

This design was modified in 1908 to eliminate the decorative verge boards, and depots of this style were built in a number of places, especially along branches. At the same time, another design was instituted which had a squared of-fice/waiting room area with a hipped roof, and a long freight area with a gabled roof attached at one end. These were built in wood and brick at a number of locations. Finally, about 1914, a new standard was adopted which was a rectangular building, wider that the older buildings, with a hipped roof and no overhang on the eaves at all. It had either a squared-off bay window or no bay window. Not a lot of these were built because by this time new stations weren't needed.

Beginning about 1908, C&O replaced a number of older stations with this very plain hipped roof and no-bay-window design. This is Alleghany, Virginia in 1935. (William Monypeny photograph, C&OHS Collection, COHS 3021)

The other most common C&O structure was the signal tower. These two-story buildings were called "cabins" on the C&O, whereas most other American railroads styled them as "towers." They were identified by a one- or two-letter telegraphic call sign so the tower at Alleghany was known as "A Cabin," the one at Avis yard in Hinton as "HX Cabin," and so on. The Virginia Central is not believed to have had separate towers, but accommodated its signal operations in stations. By the 1880s C&O was using separate towers to house operators to give trains instructions as they passed over the road. These early towers had a square base and an octagonal second floor with windows on most sides, for easy viability. By the 1890s the early towers had been redesigned with a standard octagonal top that was larger. Some of these were attached to the top of standard combination stations in a rather unique and interesting building that has become somewhat of a C&O icon.

By 1900 C&O wanted its operators to have more space as they now often had responsibility to throw many switches in their area using large levers. Therefore C&O adopted a rectangular standard, the upper floor of which had large windows on three sides. More of these were built than any other style, and one is known to have survived, next to the passenger station at Staunton, Virginia.

C&O had many ancillary structures that were often seen next to or near stations and towers, including section laborers bunkhouses (rectangular board-and-batten with no decorations), coal houses to house coal for station stoves, and section foremen's dwellings (3-6 room houses with porch, always facing the railway.) Another very common structure was the section tool house, a simple gabled structure with the end facing the track, into which velocipedes, handcars, and later motor cars used by the Maintenance-of-Way (MofW) forces could be pushed and stored. They were located every few miles along the line.

Water tanks were needed to supply steam locomotives at frequent intervals and appeared as wooden tanks elevated above the tracks with an attached steam-powered pump house (unless supplied by a spring or stream at a higher level). Later, water tanks were of steel, sanding on steel legs, while others were of the standpipe design with a cylinder tank placed on a concrete slab with attached pumping or water delivery mechanism. These quickly disappeared after the end of steam, in the mid-1950s.

At terminals and yards a coaling station was built to fuel steam locomotives. In early times this facility was a trestle built above the engine tender height onto which coal cars were shoved, and the coal was then dumped trough chutes into the tenders. Later, wooden towers were erected on legs above engine terminal tracks, the coal was placed in the wooden hopper by conveyor or skip-bucket, and then dumped into engine tenders as needed. In the 1920s most of these were rapidly replaced by similar concrete structures and many of these survived the steam era because they were hard to demolish, and a few even survive to this day (2012), forlorn silent reminders of another time, when steam ruled the rails.

Each terminal had its yard and an engine house. This could be of the familiar roundhouse design, with many stalls accessed by a turntable, and on the C&O all roundhouses were of brick construction. At smaller terminals engine houses were rectangular board-and-batten wooden frame structures with one or more tracks running straight through them. They could accommodate locomotives based on the number of tracks running through and the length of the structure. The last of these to survive was at Thurmond, W. Va., but it was burned in the 1990s.

Major shop facilities on the C&O were at Huntington, West Virginia, Clifton Forge, Virginia, and Russell, Kentucky. The major rebuilding and overhaul of steam and later diesel locomotives was accomplished at Huntington, with Clifton Forge and Russell capable of lesser repairs and rebuilds. On the old Hocking Valley lines the major car shop was at Logan, Ohio, and locomotive shop at Mound Street in Columbus. On the Chicago line Peru, Indiana, had a large shop complex, and on the Pere Marquette, Grand Rapids was the major Pere Marquette Shop, with Saginaw as a secondary facility.

These facilities all had scores of large brick and concrete buildings capable of housing dozens of large steam locomotives at one time in various stages of repair, and occupied large tracts of land with many yard tracks around them. Car shops were often near the locomotive facilities. On the C&O, freight cars were repaired, rebuilt and often built from scratch at the huge facility at the west end of Russell yard, called Raceland Car Shops. Some cars are still maintained and rebuilt there. Steam locomotives required constant attention, maintenance, refurbishment, and rebuilding, whereas diesels are much simpler, requiring far less maintenance (think of them as huge representations of automotive technology). So today shops are smaller and fewer.

C&O also had massive yards and the coal dumping, merchandise transfer, and ore handling piers on its ocean terminal at Newport New, Virginia, and its Great Lakes terminal at Toledo, Ohio (Presque Isle). C&O's largest yard was at Russell, Kentucky, where coal and merchandise freight was received classified and dispatched westbound. The second yard used for coal gathering and classification was

for eastbound traffic at Clifton Forge, Virginia. In between, C&O maintained smaller yards for operational needs on the mainline and for marshalling coal from mines and distributing cars to mines along several branch lines in West Virginia and Kentucky.

Other small structures were needed in yards such as yard offices for the management of the yard, engine terminal offices, shelters for switchmen, towers for hump yards, and sometimes a large office building for the division superintendent and his staff.

Signal structures consisted generally of steel masts, towers, or bridges, on which signals were mounted high above the track so they could be seen at a distance by crews of oncoming trains. In earlier times these consisted of semaphore arms, and beginning in the 1920s lighted signals in targets (faces) of one-two-or-three lights were mounted. These were controlled by operators in towers, automatically, or later by a dispatcher at terminals when centralized traffic control was introduced. On the C&O, many types of signal platforms were used, but the one that is most often associated with the railway is the cantilevered signal tower, in which a steel trussed tower has an arm extending over the track, on which the signal heads are mounted. Sometimes a single steel mast consisting of a 5-inch or so pipe was placed

beside the roadway, with the signal head(s) on it. Finally, some complete bridges were built across a group of tracks, usually in regions where three or more tracks were present. C&O signals were always placed on the right or engineer's side of the governed track. Present signal practice does not follow this pattern. All the old C&O types are being rapidly replaced at this writing (2012) and will be gone in a matter of a year or two.

C&O's one great venture into "Moderne" building design was the depot at Prince, W. Va., built in 1946. It is the station for Beckley and the surrounding coal area, it is still in use today by Amtrak. (C&OHS Collection, CSPR 973)

C&O station at Huntington, W.Va. trackside view circa 1925 with passenger train present, headed by C&O F-15 Pacific, No. 454. This large station, built in 1913, housed Huntington Division offices in the upper floors. Today (2012) it is still CSX headquarters in the City. (C&OHS Collection, COHS 545)

Seebert, West Virginia, on the Greenbrier Branch, is a typical C&O standard station of the 1890-1908 era, when so many were built. This design is probably the iconic station for C&O historians and fans as most lasted into recent decades. This is how it looked new in about 1910 (built in about 1902). Note the paddle train order signals on the bay window. (C&OHS Collection, COHS 35237)

In 1908 C&O simplified the standard station eliminating the fancy Victorian style verge boards in the gables, producing stations that looked like this one at Man, W. Va. on the Logan Branch, shown here is later days in 1972. T. W. Dixon, Jr. Photo. (C&OHS Collection, COHS 35241)

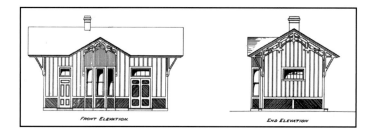

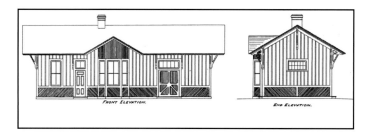

These three drawings show the evolution of the C&O standard combination station from 1890 to 1908 to 1920. (C&OHS Collection, details from C&O standard drawings). Top S-24, middle S-20, and bottom S-233.

Finally, the C&O's last standard small-town combination station design was this very simple version with little eaves overhang and squared-off bay window. This example is at Toano, Virginia, on the Peninsula Subdivision, shown in June 1951 as a passenger train with a J-2 passes. (J. I. Kelley Photo, C&OHS Collection, COHS 263)

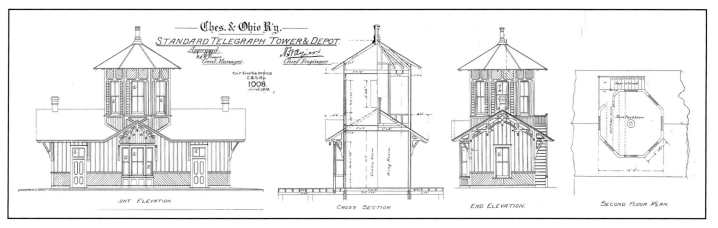

Another non-standard station that has become an icon of the C&O is the depot/tower combination structure of which were a little over a dozen. This photo is of the one at Stockyards, West Virginia (later renamed Pence Springs), in about 1891. The drawing 1008 shows the structure's C&O standard. (C&OHS Collection, DRW 1008).

In the 1900-1915 era C&O erected a number of stations following a design such as this one at Lightfoot, Va. (Peninsula SD), which had a square bay, but extended eaves and decorative boards at the top of the walls. It was an adaptation of a Pennsylvania RR design. (C&OHS Collection, COHS 35245)

Non-standard stations abounded as well. This one was at Providence Forge, Virginia (Peninsula SD), and had a two story area, the top of which was living quarters for the agent, with a single story freight area (seen here in later years in 1973). T. W. Dixon, Jr. photo., C&OHS Collection, COHS 71955)

When C&O acquired the Richmond & Alleghany in 1890, it inherited a number of depots, which were used to the end. This one at Howardsville, Va., is a good example of an R&A style station with hipped roof, large eaves overhang, and squared bay widow. W. H. Odell photograph (C&OHS Collection, COHS 35937)

Another style of which a number of stations were built is well illustrated by the station at South Portsmouth, Kentucky (Cincinnati Division). These structures had a hipped roof with one or more dormers (depending on size), and squared bay. They were built both in brick (as this one) or frame styles. (C&OHS Collection, COHS 35262)

C&O built a number of stations to fit the Colonial theme it used in its 1920s-1950s advertising. This one was built to fit in with Colonial Williamsburg, Va. (on the Peninsula SD), and is of red brick. Others of differing but generally neo-Georgian style, were built at a number of other locations. (Bruce Fales photo, courtesy of Jay Williams Collection).

Charlottesville, Virginia, home of Thomas Jefferson, was another great place for a C&O station in the Virginia Colonial (neoclassical) style. This is the street side of the large station here. C&O Ry. Photo. C&OHS Collection, COHS 20190)

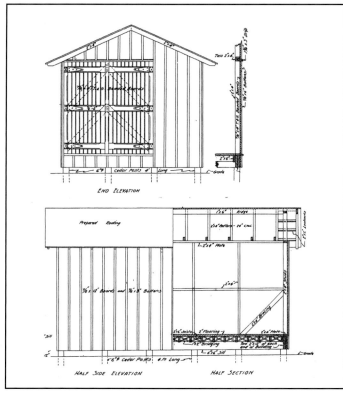

The standard section tool house was at hundreds of locations across the system. The photo (top) and drawing are from the C&OHS Collection, COHS 2561 and Detail of C&O drawing S-5, R1.

Another small structure is illustrated by this "portable" telegraph office. When no longer needed at a location, it was put on a flatcar and moved. Its diamensions were 9x14 feet. C&O Ry. Photograph, C&OHS Collection, CSPR 10025.198)

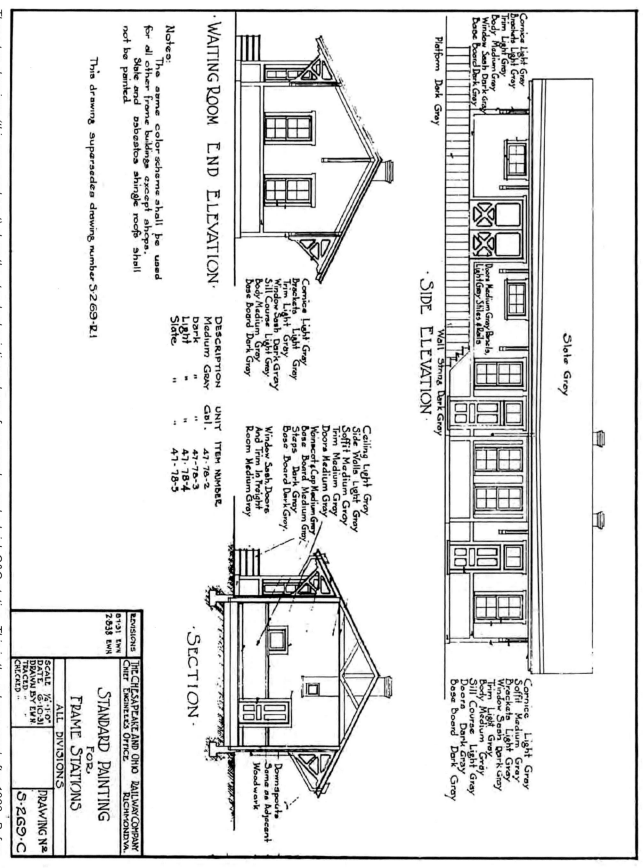

Slate Gray

· SIDE ELEVATION ·

Cornice Light Gray
Brackets Light Gray
Trim Light Gray
Window Sash Dark Gray
Body Medium Gray
Base Board Dark Gray

Platform Dark Gray

Wall String Dark Gray

Doors Medium Gray, Rails,
Light Gray, Stiles & Rails

Cornice Light Gray
Soffit Medium Gray
Brackets Light Gray
Window Sash Dark Gray
Trim Light Gray
Body Medium Gray
Sill Course Light Gray
Doors Dark Gray
Base Board Dark Gray

· WAITING ROOM END ELEVATION ·

Cornice Light Gray
Brackets Light Gray
Trim Light Gray
Window Sash Dark Gray
Sill Course Light Gray
Body Medium Gray
Base Board Dark Gray

DESCRIPTION		UNIT	ITEM NUMBER
Medium Gray	Dark	Gal.	47-78-2
	Light	"	47-78-3
	Slate	"	47-78-4
		"	47-78-5

Ceiling Light Gray
Side Walls Light Gray
Soffit Medium Gray
Trim Medium Gray
Doors Medium Gray
Wainscot & Cap Medium Gray
Base Board Medium Gray
Steps Dark Gray
Base Board Dark Gray

Window Sash, Doors
And Trim In Freight
Room Medium Gray

· SECTION ·

Downspouts
Same as Adjacent
Woodwork

Notes:
The same color scheme shall be used
for all other frame buildings except shops.
Slate and asbestos shingle roofs shall
not be painted.

This drawing supersedes drawing number S-269-R.1

REVISIONS
8-1-31 EWN
2-838 EWN

THE CHESAPEAKE AND OHIO RAILWAY COMPANY
CHIEF ENGINEER'S OFFICE. RICHMOND VA.

STANDARD PAINTING
FOR
FRAME STATIONS
ALL DIVISIONS

SCALE ½"=1'-0"
DATE G-10-31
DRAWN BY EWN
TRACED
CHECKED

DRAWING Nº
S-269-C

These two drawings (this page and next) show the standard painting scheme for a wooden and a brick C&O station. This is the scheme used after 1923. Before this the "Colonial Buff" yellow scheme was used. The medium gray with trim in darker gray was standard on most wooden buildings on the C&O as well a stations. (C&O Drawings S-269-C and 269-D, from C&O Historical Society Collection, from reprint, Cat. No. DS-02-223)

The Chesapeake & Ohio Railway - A Concise History and Fact Book

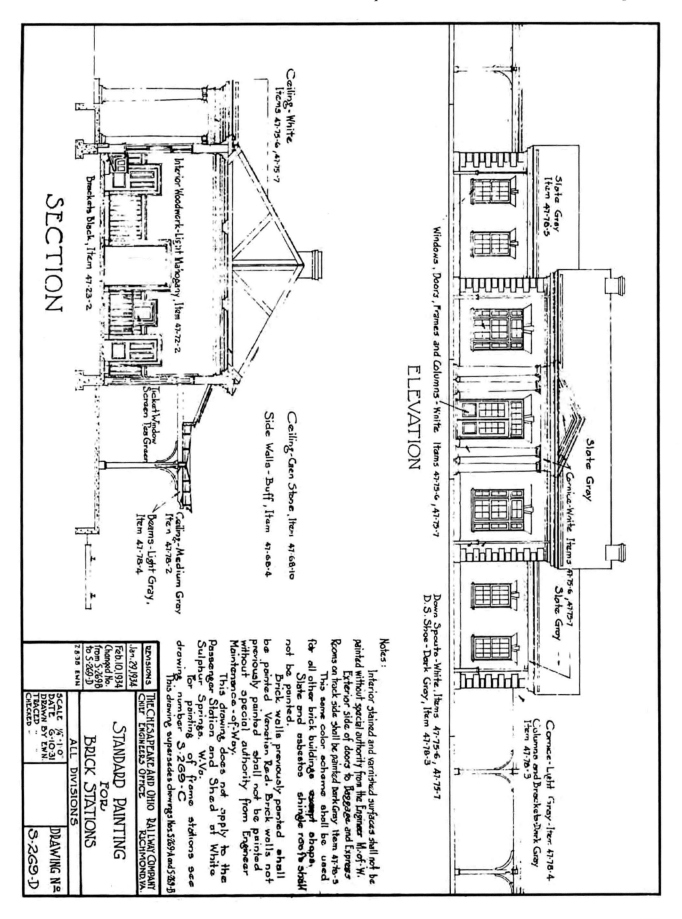

SECTION

Ceiling-White
Items 47-75-6 , 47-75-7

Interior Woodwork-Light Mahogany, Item 47-72-2

Brackets Black, Item 47-23-2

Ticket Window
Screen Pea Green

Ceiling-Green Shoe, Item 47-68-10

Side Walls - Buff , Item 47-68-4

Ceiling-Medium Gray
Item 47-78-2

Beams-Light Gray,
Item 47-78-4

ELEVATION

Windows, Doors , Frames and Columns-White. Items 47-75-6 , 47-75-7

Slate Gray
Item 47-76-5

Slate Gray

Cornice-White Items
47-75-6 , 47-75-7
Slate Gray

Down Spouts-White. Items 47-75-6 , 47-75-7
D.S. Shoe-Dark Gray, Item 47-78-3

Cornice-Light Gray-Item 47-78-4
Columns and Brackets-Dark Gray
Item 47-78-4

Notes:

Interior stained and varnished surfaces shall not be painted without special authority from the Engineer M. of W.

Exterior side of doors to Baggage and Express Rooms on track side shall be painted DarkGray, Item 47-76-5

This same color scheme shall be used for all other brick buildings except shape, Slate and asbestos shingle roofs shall not be painted.

Brick walls previously painted shall be painted Venetian Red. Brick walls not previously painted shall not be painted without special authority from Engineer Maintenance-of-Way.

This drawing does not apply to the Passenger Station and Shed at White Sulphur Springs, W.Va.

For painting of frame stations see drawing number S-269-C

This drawing supersedes drawings Nos.S-269-A and S-269-B

REVISIONS	
Jan. 29,1934	
Feb.10,1934 Changed No. from S-269B to S-269-D	
2-8-38 E.N.N	

THE CHESAPEAKE AND OHIO RAILWAY COMPANY CHIEF ENGINEERS OFFICE — RICHMOND,VA.	
STANDARD PAINTING FOR BRICK STATIONS	
ALL DIVISIONS	

SCALE ½"=1'-0"	DRAWING No.
DATE G-10-31	
DRAWN BY E.N.N.	S-269-D
TRACED	
CHECKED	

A standard wooden water tank is seen in this June 1948 view at South Anna, Va. (J. I. Kelly photo, C&OHS Collection, COHS 127)

Two steel water tanks are seen here at Thurmond, W. Va., one of the standpipe variety and one on the hemispherical bottom style on legs. (C&OHS Collection COHS 13142)

Passing under a two track cantilever signal tower is C&O Train No.141 with 12 cars at speed at Ft. Lee, Va. just east of Richmond, Aug. 19, 1941. Taken by J.I. Kelly from the D.W. Johnson collection. (C&OHS Collection COHS 35791)

In a few places a full bridge was used because of the number of tracks to be signaled. This one is at Russell and is seen here in 1959. (C&O Ry. Photo. C&OHS Collection, CSPR 10787.T5)

128   *The Chesapeake & Ohio Railway - A Concise History and Fact Book*

Initially C&O coaling stations were towers of timber construction such as this one at English Lake, Indiana. Starting about 1917 they were almost all replaced with concrete style such as are shown on this page. This particular one lasted to the end of steam, as did the one at Sproul, W. Va. (C&OHS Collection, COHS 71955)

The largest of the cylindrical coaling towers were like this 800-ton capacity facility at Hinton, W. Va. Identical structures to this were also at Stevens Yard in Kentucky and Richmond's Fulton Yard. As can be seen, 4 locomotives can be serviced at once. The hoist and sand house are at left.
(C&O Ry. Photo, C&OHS Collection, CSPR 215)

Although there were exceptions, most concrete C&O coaling stations were built by three companies: Fairbanks-Morse, Roberts & Schaefer, and Ogle. C&O coaling towers were of the cylindrical or rectangular styles with a few exceptions. This 300-ton cylindrical one is at West Hamlin, W. Va., on the Logan Branch. At least 5 other structures of this exact design were used on C&O lines. K-3a No. 2338 is passing by with some box cars and empty hoppers in 1952. Gene Huddleston Photo, (C&OHS Collection, COHS 1778)

C&O coal dock at Newport News, Va., 1930's or 40's Note old original coal trestle in background From the collection of Wayne W. Link. (C&OHS Collection, COHS 70449)

COALING STATIONS

LOCATION	Storage Capacity in Tons	REMARKS
Norfolk..............Va	100	Platform
Phoebus..............Va	From Cars	Direct Coaling Machine
Newport News..........Va	300	Elevator
Fulton..............Va	800	Elevator
Gordonsville..........Va	120	Platform
Orange..............Va	From Cars	Direct Coaling Machine
Potomac Yards.........Va	....	R. F. & P. R. R.
Charlottesville........Va	300	Elevator
Waynesboro............Va		N. & W. R. R.
Staunton.............Va	125	Elevator
Clifton Forge..........Va	800	Elevator
Clifton Forge M. L........	50	Elevator
Strathmore...........Va	500	Elevator
Gladstone............Va	300	Elevator
Lynchburg............Va	100	Elevator
Balcony Falls.........Va	300	Elevator
Eagle Mountain........Va	50	Platform
Covington............Va	75	Elevator
Ronceverte..........W Va	75	Elevator
Marlinton..........W Va	200	Coal Trestle
Hinton............W Va	800	Elevator
Hinton M. L........W Va	50	Elevator
Rainelle..........W Va	From Cars	Direct Coaling Machine
Quinnimont.........W Va	From Cars	Crane
Raleigh...........W Va	300	Elevator
Thurmond..........W Va	500	Elevator
Ansted...........W Va	As desired	From Mine Chutes
Handley...........W Va	500	Elevator
Dry Branch........W Va	As desired	From Mine Chutes
Cane Fork.........W Va	50	Elevator
Whitesville.......W Va	500	Elevator
Charleston........W Va	From Cars	Direct Coaling Machine
St. Albans........W Va	500	Elevator
Sproul...........W Va	200	Elevator
Danville..........W Va	300	Elevator
West Hamlin.......W Va	300	Elevator
Peach Creek.......W Va	500	Elevator
Huntington........W Va	300	Elevator
Paintsville.........Ky	300	Elevator
Martin.............Ky	300	Elevator
Shelby.............Ky	300	Elevator
Jenkins............Ky	From Cars	Direct Coaling Machine
Ashland............Ky	From Cars	Direct Coaling Machine
Olive Hill.........Ky	From Cars	Direct Coaling Machine
Lexington..........Ky	300	Elevator
Louisville.........Ky	....	Big 4 R. R.
Russell............Ky	1000	Elevator
Limeville..........Ky	From Cars	By Hand
G. B. Cabin........O	500	Elevator
Parsons Yards......O	500	Elevator
Parsons Main Line..O	600	Elevator
Toledo Docks.......O	From Cars	Direct Coaling Machine
Walbridge.........O	500	Elevator

COALING STATIONS—Continued.

LOCATION	Storage Capacity in Tons	REMARKS
Fostoria............O	From Cars	By Hand
Marion.............O	From Cars	Direct Coaling Machine
Logan..............O	120	Crane
Nelsonville.........O	300	Elevator
Carey..............O	500	Elevator
Fostoria............O	From Cars	By Hand
Pomeroy............O	From Cars	Direct Coaling Machine
Wellston...........O		B. & O. R. R.
Garrison..........Ky	From Cars	By Hand
Concord...........Ky	500	Elevator
Maysville.........Ky	From Cars	By Hand
Stevens...........Ky	800	Elevator
Covington.........Ky	50	Elevator
Cincinnati.........O		Cincinnati Union Terminal
Cheviot............O	400	Elevator
Richmond.........Ind	From Cars	Direct Coaling Machine
Muncie...........Ind		N. K. P. R. R.
Peru.............Ind	500	Elevator
English Lake.....Ind	300	Elevator
Stony Island.....Ind		N. K. P. R. R.
New Buffalo......Mich	300	Elevator Electric
Benton Harbor....Mich	Pit	Electric Conveyor
Waverly..........Mich	From Cars	By Crane
Muskegon (North Yard)............Mich	Pit	Electric Conveyor
Traverse City (Boardman)..........Mich	100	Elevator Electric
Petoskey.........Mich	Pit	Electric Conveyor
Erie (Ottawa Yard)...Mich	300	Elevator Electric
Plymouth.........Mich	250	Elevator Electric
Flint (McGrew).....Mich	150	Elevator Electric
Saginaw..........Mich	500	Elevator Electric
Lake.............Mich	250	Elevator Electric
Baldwin..........Mich	250	Elevator-Oil
Ludington........Mich	500	Elevator Electric
Ludington........Mich	Pit	Electric Conveyor (For Coaling Ferries)
Bad Axe..........Mich	Pit	Electric Conveyor
Port Huron.......Mich	100	Elevator Electric
Grand Rapids (Wyoming)............Mich	500	Elevator Electric
Grand Ledge......Mich	From Cars	Electric Conveyor
Lansing (Ensel)...Mich	150	Elevator Electric
Detroit..........Mich	500	Elevator Electric
Alma.............Mich	From Cars	Electric Conveyor
Edmore...........Mich	Pit	Electric Conveyor
Sarnia...........Ont	Pit	Electric Conveyor
Chatham..........Ont	From Cars	Elevator Electric 2 Chutes Combine Coal and Cinders 5 ton Capacity
Blenheim.........Ont	100	Elevator Gas Engine
St. Thomas.......Ont	200	Elevator Electric

Additional Sources of Information for C&O Depots, Towers, and Other Structures

- *Chesapeake & Ohio Standard Structures*, by Thomas W. Dixon, Jr., C&O Hist. Soc., Clifton Forge, Va., 1991. Reprint available from C&O Hist. Society (Cat. No. BK-10-502). Reproduces standard drawings and photos of buildings from 1870s through 1920s. Includes Depots, towers (cabins), dwellings, water tanks, signals. A good overview of the most common C&O standards.
- *Chesapeake & Ohio Facilities in Color, Vol. 1 - Midwest*, by Eugene L. Huddleston, Morning Sun Books, Scotch Plains, NJ, 2008, 128 pages, hardbound. Many great photos of C&O depots, towers and other facilities in Michigan, Indiana and Ohio
- *Chesapeake & Ohio in Hinton, West Virginia*, C&O Historical Society, Clifton Forge, Va. 2011, (Cat. No. BK-08-470), 96 pages of the C&O in Hinton. Includes photos and drawings of roundhouse, coaling station, depot, and many other structures at Hinton.
- *The Chesapeake & Ohio Railway at Gladstone, Virginia*, by Christopher W. Wiley, C&O Historical Society, Clifton Forge, Va. 2000. 28 page booklet on history of Gladstone, with photos and drawings of depot, roundhouse, coaling station, etc. (Available from C&O Historical Society, Cat. No. BK-00-255)
- *The Chesapeake & Ohio Railway at Hawks Nest, West Virginia*, by Thomas W. Dixon, Jr., C&O Hist. Soc., Clifton Forge, Va. 2000, 26 pages on C&O's Hawks Nest branch. Includes drawings of depots, tower, etc. (Available from C&O Historical Society, Cat. No. BK-00-228)
- *Chesapeake & Ohio Alleghany Subdivision* by Thomas W. Dixon, Jr., 144 pages, C&O Hist. Society, Clifton Forge, Va. 1985; reprint available from Society (Cat. No. K-10-501). History of C&O mainline Clifton Forge, Va. to Hinton, W. Va. Includes much on structures including towers, depots, etc.
- *Riding That New River Train*, by Eugene L. Huddleston, C&O Hist. Soc., Clifton Forge, Va., 1989, 136 pages, with history of the mainline Hinton to Handley, W. Va. Includes photos and material on structures. Reprint available from C&O Society (Cat. No. BK-10-499)

C&O Historical Society Reprints:

- *C&O Depot Painting Standards* (Cat. No. DS-02-223) - A few drawings that C&O standard brick and frame station paint schemes before 1923 and after the change in 1923.
- *Drawing Set for Small Buildings* (Cat. No. DS-08-099) - Numerous small structures of all types shown in original C&O drawings. Plans, sections, elevations
- *Hinton-Thurmond Historic American Buildings Survey & Historic American Engineering Record Drawings* (Cat. No. DS-8-083) This is a set that show depots, engine houses and other structures for these two important terminals. Excellent resources with dimensioned drawings.
- *C&O Wooden Water Tank Standard Drawings* - Standards for two major C&O wooden water tanks, 50,000 and 100,000 gallons. (Cat. No. DS-02-221)
- *Pere Marquette Roundhouses and Engine Terminal Drawings*, 1941 (Cat. No. DS-0-201). Plans of all major PM roundhouses.
- *Drawing Set for Small Miscellaneous Structures & Standards* (Cat. No. DS-08-137). Many interesting small building drawings from C&O files.
- *C&O Maintenance-of-Way Standard Drawings, Vol. 1* (DS-07-034)- Structures, small buildings, switches, track arrangements, signs, etc.
- *List of Structures, Bridges, Culverts, Grade Crossings & Tunnels* (Ca. 1945) (Cat. No. DS-08-228)
- *C&O Historical Magazine, Misc./Issues 1969-Present*. Structures are often dealt with in the magazine, including detailed photos, plans, drawings, maps. Purchase entire run of magazines on CD from C&O Historical Society (Cat. No. AV-08-102).

CHAPTER TEN

The Hocking Valley and the Pere Marquette

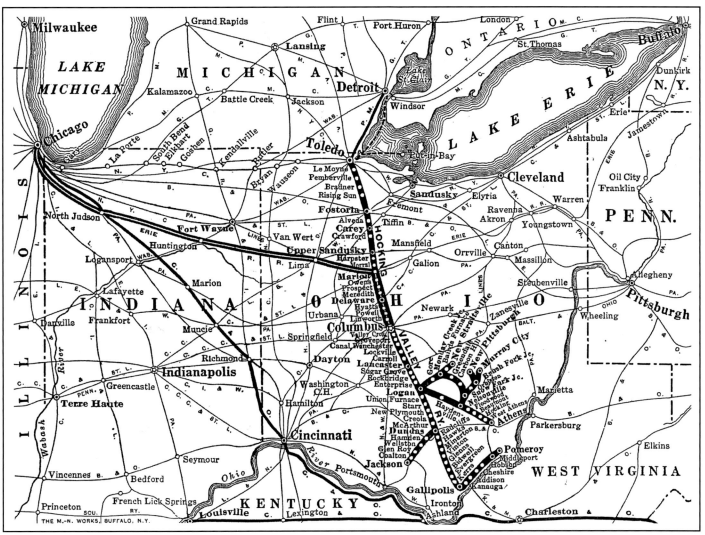

This map shows the HV system at its height in the late 1920s. It can be seen how it became the straight backbone of C&O's westbound coal through Ohio. (C&OHS Collection)

Although the C&O was made up of many smaller lines that were eventually merged, most of this consolidation occurred in the very distant past (distant, that is, as far as railroading history goes), but there were two mergers that occurred, in 1930 and 1947 respectively, of fairly large railways that bring histories of their own. These lines still have some interest among railroad historians and modelers. They are the Hocking Valley Railway of Ohio and the Pere Marquette Railway of Michigan and Ontario.

The Hocking Valley Railway

When the Hocking Valley Railway was merged into the C&O on May 1, 1930, it was operating 320.61 miles of owned trackage. 21.21 miles of leased track, and 6.75 miles of joint trackage. It had 157.53 miles of second track, 149.43 miles of sidings, and 260.16 miles of yard track. It's total revenue for 1929 was $20,888,859.68. HV was originat-

ing in the coal fields southeast of Columbus somewhat over 300,000 tons of bituminous annually, much reduced from its high days at the turn of the 20th Century to 1920. The Hocking had 143 steam locomotives, about 6,000 revenue freight cars and a few old wooden passenger cars. Most importantly, it was carrying over 20 million tons of coal delivered to it by C&O at Columbus bound for Toledo for Great Lakes shipping, as well as Fostoria and Marion for interline shipment.

Coal had been extracted from the Hocking Hills of southeastern Ohio as early as 1825. As with C&O, HV was preceded by a canal in the pre-railroad days. Finally in 1864 the Mineral Railroad Company was organized to carry coal to Columbus from Athens, about 72 miles. Before it began construction the name was changed to Columbus & Hocking Valley Railroad which was opened to Athens in 1870

The HV's Nelsonville yard was the center of its coal business. This postcard view show the yard in its heyday about 1910. (C&OHS Collection COHS 867)

with a major coal fields branch completed in 1871. The line was delivering so much coal to Columbus that other lines couldn't handle the traffic, so a new line called the Columbus & Toledo was built, finishing its 124-mile line in 1877 on an almost straight north-south line between the two cities, and at that time the two roads were put under joint management. Other small lines were put in operation at this time including the Ohio & West Virginia, and in 1881 were consolidated under one company called the Columbus, Hocking Valley & Toledo Railway. With its coal revenue as a major pat of its traffic, the line continued to prosper. It also soon had a good business in iron, steel, and industrial products as industry began to develop in the region, but by 1897 due to labor

issues and other problems the company was in receivership. A reorganized company called simply the Hocking Valley Railway Company took over the property in 1899.

In 1910 the C&O purchased the majority of the capital stock of the HV, and C&O's president George W. Stevens became the HV's president as well. The reason for acquiring control of the HV was to give C&O a better control of its outlet to the Great Lakes and other connections to Midwestern points for its burgeoning coal business. C&O also bought control of the Kanawha & Michigan Railroad, and by that means could ship its coal via the K&M at Gauley Bridge W. Va., thence to the K&M connection with the HV. Previ-

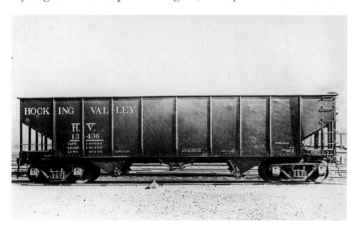

A "modern HV Steel hopper car built in 1920 was similar to its owner C&O's fleet. (C&OHS Collection COHS 35792)

In the early years the CHV&T had a fancy logo as displayed on this box car new at American Car & Foundry's Huntington, W. Va. Plant in 1899 just before the CHV&T became the HV. (C&OHS Collection COHS 35793)

HV had some of the last and most modern 4-4-0s. Obsolete on most lines, the HV had a basically local passenger train fleet often no more than 2-4 cars, so the old American type was good enough. No. 81 was built by Brooks in 1905. (C&OHS Collection COHS 35794)

ous to this time C&O had been forced to give its coal to the competitor Norfolk & Western at Kenova, W. Va. However, in 1914 C&O was forced by court action to divest the K&M, leaving it with a gap between C&O lines and the HV. In that year C&O organized a subsidiary called the Chesapeake & Northern which completed a line from the C&O's mainline Cincinnati Division at Limeville, Kentucky (about 18 miles west of Russell) across the giant Limeville (Sciotoville) Bridge to a connection with the N&W mainline at Waverly, Ohio, where it gained trackage rights on N&W into Columbus so its trains could reach the HV. While all this was happening, HV's own coal fields were in decline. C&O coal was growing by leaps and bounds, so C&O finally completed the last link to the HV at Valley Crossing, near Parsons yard in Columbus. Therefore, from 1927 onward C&O had its own direct line to HV. In 1929 HV began development of what would become C&O's huge Presque Isle coal and ore terminal and docks on the Maumee River across from Toledo. At that time C&O gained permission to fully merge the HV lines into its own, which occurred May 1, 1930. The HV then became the Hocking Division of C&O. Hocking Valley shopped its locomotives at its Mound Street yards in Columbus and it built and maintained its freight cars at its Logan, Ohio shops. In the late 1920s the Logan shops built not only HV but also a large number of C&O wooden cabooses. The HV had a small passengers service that included local trains serving the lines southeast of Columbus, and several trains with through cars operating between Columbus and Toledo, and sending through passengers on to Detroit via the Pere Marquette Railway.

When the HV was merged into C&O in 1930 President Harahan of the C&O said that he would be happy to sell the lines southeast of Columbus for a dollar to anyone who would assume the debt, reflecting the decline in the coal business in that region.

This classy HV mail, baggage, and express car was of composite (steel under-frame, wooden body), built by Pullman in 1906. (C&OHS Collection COHS 35795)

One of HV's high-stepping 4-6-0s is seen here on a 4-car train north of Columbus in the 1920s. (C&OHS Collection COHS 3579)

For the heavy coal trains that C&O delivered to it, HV had 2-6-6-2 Mallets such as 201 shown here at Columbus in about 1902. (C&OHS Collection COHS 7279)

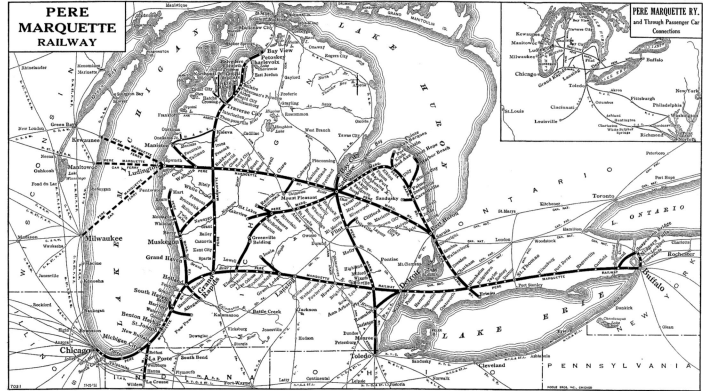

This map shows the PM system in the 1940s at its height. Note the trackage rights line (on NYC) across Ontario to Buffalo on the east and the car ferry routes on the western end of the system. (C&OHS Collection)

The Pere Marquette Railway

The Pere Marquette Railway Company was merged into C&O on June 6, 1947. At this time, the PM consisted of 1,949 miles of road and it had 283 locomotives, 113 passenger cars, and 14,335 freight cars. The PM was created in 1900 when three Michigan carriers were consolidated: the Chicago & West Michigan, Flint & Pere Marquette, and Detroit, Grand Rapids & Western. The consolidated road consisted of 1,700 miles of line, with most of it in Michigan. It also operated a cross-Lake Michigan car ferry service. The PM traces its ancestry to 51 smaller companies that were eventually consolidated into these three major companies that created it in 1900.

In the early days PM predecessors had relied heavily on the lumber and forest products business, but by 1900 this traffic was in decline in Michigan. Many of PM's branches were no longer profitable because of these changing traffic patterns, and over the next decades it became known as the "Poor Marquette" because of its financial weakness.

The old F&PM line came out of Toledo and angled northwest to Flint, thence to Saginaw, and onto the Great Lakes port city of Pere Marquette (later renamed Ludington, by which name it is still known). It also had lines in the "thumb" area of Michigan. The Detroit, Grand Rapids & Western had a series of lines in a triangle Grand Rapids-Saginaw-Plymouth-Detroit. In 1903 PM acquired the Lake Erie & Detroit River Railroad which owned over 200 miles

of line in Ontario and had trackage rights over the Canadian Southern and Michigan Central (NYC) across Ontario to Buffalo, New York.

On Lake Michigan, PM operated a fleet of ferries that carried railroad cars across the lake to Wisconsin ports where connections were made with western railroads. This would become a very important link in the 1920s-1960s, with C&O ordering the newest and last reciprocating steamships (called "boats" on the Great Lakes) for the service in 1951. The new boats were delivered in 1952 (Spartan) and 1953 (Badger). At one time in the late 1940s, PM was operating a fleet of seven Car Ferries.

A PM 4-6-2 Pacific takes a passenger train out of Fort Street Union Depot with the Detroit skyline in the background in 1946. Robert G. Lewis photo. (C&OHS Collection, COHS 32041)

Following the Second World War, PM traffic increased as the automobile trade flowered, and C&O decided that it would merge the line to better realize savings and improve operational control. As this occurred, the PM president, Robert J. Bowman, became the C&O's president, but as the two lines merged they still remained fairly autonomous in operations, with the PM being called first "The Pere Marquette District" (while the rest of the C&O was "The Chesapeake District"), and then later "The Northern Region."

The cross-Lake Michigan car ferries were given much attention in the 1945-1960 era, when some of the older "boats," were refurbished and lengthened, the PM's modern ferries *City of Saginaw* (1932) and *City of Midland* (1941) were supplemented by C&O-ordered *Spartan* and *Badger* (1952-53). By avoiding the congestion of the Chicago terminals, cars bound for the northwest could be sent via C&O from Northeast through Buffalo or Detroit to Ludington, thence across the Lake, saving much time. This worked very well until the early 1970s. The service was closed and the boats sold, but a private company has revived it and now operates one of the boats (Badger), but only carrying people and automobiles. The PM line to Ludington has been abandoned and the rails are gone.

The northern ex-PM lines performed well for the C&O until the 1970s when auto business began to suffer, and gradually the maze of lines became as much a liability for C&O as a benefit. Unless they directly served active factories, many ex-PM lines were abandoned. The fabulous *Pere Marquettes* passenger trains of 1946-1950 soon lost their original equipment and received the same Pullman-Standard lightweight cars used on the rest of C&O, and that business steadily eroded as new roads were built and the Interstate System matured. Only a small part of the once large PM system is left on the CSX map.

The backbone of PM's fleet of fast freight train power after 1937 was the fabulous 2-8-4 Berkshire type, of which PM purchased 50 between 1937 and 1944. No. 1203 is handling a manifest near Plymouth, Mich., in 1947. (C&O Ry. Photo, C&OHS Collection, CSPR 810.25)

After a receivership in 1917, PM was acquired by the Van Sweringen railroad magnates of Cleveland in 1924. As part of this complicated holding company operation, the ICC allowed C&O control of PM in 1929. The entry into the Vans Sweringen railroad group allowed PM to get preference for interchange traffic with C&O and other of the Vans' lines and improved its financial picture immensely. By this time the automobile industry had ensconced itself in Michigan, located in some of the very cities that PM served and was growing. Therefore, the business in raw materials and parts going into the factories and finished automobiles coming out became the mainstay of PM traffic for the rest of its life.

Influenced by joint Van Sweringen policies, PM got big Super Power steam in 1937 with its fabulous 2-8-4 Berkshire types, which helped its fast freight business and were very important in keeping WWII traffic flowing to and from the auto factories as they were converted to war production. Ever larger car ferries were purchased for the trip from Ludington to the Wisconsin ports of Manitowoc, Milwaukee, and Kewaunee.

In 1946 C&O used the PM as a test area for the postwar streamliner with which C&O Chairman Robert R. Young was so in love, and in August 1946, put into service two sets of fast, modern, all-coach, diesel powered trains between Detroit and Grand Rapids called The Pere Marquettes. They were a great success, and gave Young the ammunition he needed to press forward his plans for C&O and his ideas on how to change American railroading.

The first diesels came to PM. EMD E7s were purchased beginning in 1946 for the Pere Marquettes passenger trains. Here No. 108, still in full PM paint is ready to leave Grand Rapids for Chicago with the newly established Pere Marquettes west of Grand Rapids. It is using the equipment purchased originally for the never-run Chessie. (C&OHS Collection, COHS 1760)

The most modern and longest lived of the PM's car ferries was CITY OF MIDLAND, *purchased in 1941 and transferred to C&O, which op-* *erated it to 1983. Here the boat is leaving Ludington with the big red PM funnel mark. (C&O Ry. Photo, C&OHS Collection, CSPR 2424)*

Pere Marquette/C&O Lake Michigan Car Ferries

The PM and then C&O operated several car ferry operations in Michigan, one across the Detroit River between Detroit and Windsor, Ontario, and another across the same water between Port Huron and Sarnia, Ontario, and across Lake Erie between Erieau, Ontario, and Conneaut, Ohio. But the biggest marine business on the old PM was the cross-Lake Michigan railroad car ferry service that F&PM started in 1897. Before then F&PM had operated break-bulk streamers across the lake, but the emergence of bigger boats allowed whole railroad cars to be carried across. By 1903 PM had seven boats in service crisscrossing the lake many times per day. The modern fleet began with PM 21 and 22 in 1924, *City of Saginaw* 31 in 1930, *City of Flint 32* in 1930, and these were followed by *City of Midland 41* in 1941. After C&O took control of PM, it went on a major campaign to upgrade and improve the service, and more importantly, to advertise it widely to customers who wanted to avoid the Chicago terminal mess. In 1952-53 C&O received the two ultra-modern ferries *Spartan* and *Badger*, both measuring 410 by 60 feet, and powered by the last reciprocating steam power plant built for Lake Michigan navigation, the huge Skinner triple expansion "Uniflow" engines, consuming good old West Virginia C&O-originated coal. The two boats (large ships by any measure except for Great Lakes terminology) cost C&O a then huge $5 million each. They had a speed of 20 mph and combined with the other five PM boats made a fleet of seven serving the three Wisconsin ports of Kewaunee, Milwaukee, and Manitowoc. They could carry 32 railroad cars, 14 automobiles, and numerous passengers, who were accommodated with a full service dining room, deck chairs, lounges, and all the accoutrements that one would expect on a passenger ship. For those wanting privacy for the average crossing time of four hours, a limited number of state rooms were also available on many of the PM boats.

At Manitowoc the ferries used the Soo Line's dock as well as the Chicago & North Western's dock in the same city. The Green Bay & Western Railroad maintained a large two-ship ferry station in Kewaunee, which C&O used. C&O had its own piers and small yard in Milwaukee, and even stationed one of its own switchers there to handle the railroad car traffic. Connection here was via the Chicago, Milwaukee, St. Paul & Pacific (The Milwaukee Road). The C&O ferries were designated as an extension across the lake of U. S. Highway Rt. 10. The transportation of people and their automobiles was an important revenue enhancer for the boats, with over $1 million in revenue per year (almost all of it in the summer vacation months). When there was not a full load of railroad cars, autos were carried on the railroad car deck in addition to the auto deck. Passengers could also book passage if they didn't have an auto. C&O heavily promoted this service, even as PM had done before with brochures, highway maps, and billboards. It even issued a widely acclaimed movie about the service in 1960 called "The Golden Link."

As the shape of railroading changed, however, the need for the cross-lake traffic decreased, and though the three newest ships (*City of Midland, Spartan,* and *Badger*) remained in service until July 1983, they had become a liability and the service was sold to others. The new operators couldn't make a go of it, and the railroad line to Ludington was abandoned by CSX. One of the ferries (Badger) remains today, operated by the Michigan-Wisconsin Transportation Company, during summer months strictly for passengers and their autos.

The Chesapeake & Ohio Railway - A Concise History and Fact Book

Automobiles cram the auto deck of CITY OF MIDLAND and a
few overflow into the freight car deck in this 1956 view. (C&O Ry.
Photo, C&OHS Collection, CSPR 3805)

Farm tractors are being loaded onto Badger in this night photo
from the 1950s. (C&O Ry. Photo, C&OHS Collection, CSPR 2840)

Spartan's freight car deck is being loaded in this 1953 photo. Crews had to load the boats carefully to maintain balance, with a few cars on
each side at a time. (C&O Ry. Photo, C&OHS Collection, CSPR 3199)

Spartan at speed crossing Lake Michigan "with a bone in her teeth" (the bow wave) in a dramatic publicity photo. In 1966. (C&O Ry. Photo, C&OHS Collection, CSPR 5291)

Additional Sources of Information for Hocking Valley and Pere Marquette

There are few published sources of information on the Hocking Valley, but more son ton the PM; data about them appear in small entries in many publications.

The best source of data is the *C&O Historical Magazine*, 1969-Present. Many article have appeared about various aspects of these two predecessor railroads, especially the Pere Marquette. Entire run of magazine is available on fully searchable CD from C&O Historical Society Catalog No. AV-08-102)

Hocking Valley:
- *The Hocking Valley Railway* by Edward W. Miller, Ohio University Press, Athens, Ohio, 2007, hardbound, 348 pages. - Best complete history of the HV including all aspects.
- *HV Passenger Car Diagram Book* (C&O Historical Society Reprint, DS-08-131)

Pere Marquette:
- *Pere Marquette Power,* by Arthur B. Million and Thomas W. Dixon, Jr., C&O Historical Society, Clifton Forge, Va., 1984, 244 pages, fully illustrated. Detailed, complete history of all PM steam and diesel power. Reprint available from C&O Historical Society (Cat. No. BK-07-454H)
- *The Pere Marquette in 1945* - C&O Historical Society, Clifton Forge, Va., 1990-91. 76 pages of data on all PM operations, and data first published by the PM itself in 1945. The Society's update includes photos in additional to reprint of original text. Packed with data.
- Historical Society (Cat. No. BK-08-466)
- *Pere Marquette Passenger Car Pictorial*, by Arthur B. Million, Pere Marquette Historical Society, Inc., Grand Haven, Mich., 2002, 300 pages, hardbound, fully illustrated. Detailed history of PM's passenger car fleet.
- *Chesapeake & Ohio's Pere Marquettes - America's First Postwar Streamliner 1946-1971*, by Thomas W. Dixon, Jr., TLC Publishing, Lynchburg, Va. 2004, softbound, 96 pages, fully illustrated,. Complete detailed history of the trains operating Detroit-Grand Rapids-Chicago that made such an impression when first introduced. (Available from C&O Historical Society, BK-03-348)

C&O Historical Society Reprints:
- PM District Track Charts, Updated to 1947. (Cat. No DS-08-177)
- C&O Northern Region Bridge Book, 1955 (DS-07-041)
- PM District Diesel Diagram Book, 1952 (DS-02-220)
- PM Crane Diagram Book, 1946 (DS-07-040)
- A Brief Corporate History of The Pere Marquette Railway Company 1873-1913 (Typescript issued by PM in 1913) (DS-04-028)
- PM Locomotive Diagram Book, 1946 (DS-07-044)
- PM Freight Car Diagram Book, 1942 (DS-07-042)
- PM Maintenance-of-Way Standards Book (DS-09-180)
- PM fast Freight Schedules, 1940. (DS-08-136)
- C&O Northern Region Manifest Freight Schedules (1965) (DS-08-127)
- C&O Northern Region Station List (DS-08-067)
- PM Lightweight Passenger Car Diagrams (DS-07-054)

CHAPTER ELEVEN
Corporate History

C&O, Chessie System, and CSX President Hays Watkins, Jr. with Terminal Tower background taken when he became C&O President in 1971. Used for the Railway Age *cover July 1971. (C&OHS Collection, CSPR 5291)*

The C&O is generally traced in a direct line from the Louisa Railroad of central Virginia, to is successor, the Virginia Central, to the new C&O of 1868, through its 1878 reorganization, and down to its effective merger with B&O and WM in the late 1960s and early 1970s under Chessie System and into today's CSX.

Through these years many other lines were merged into the C&O and each of these had many predecessors as well, so that in the end C&O was made up of at least 190 different predecessor companies, each of which had some hand in the development of the company we knew in the mid-20th Century. The corporate histories of these companies and their work is complicated and not of great importance to us today, except to know that the C&O wasn't created out of whole cloth, that it didn't burst on the scene full blown, nor even with an exact vision of what it was or what it wanted to be. The circumstances of history and of the territory and era in which it operated all worked to create the system as it was finally fashioned.

In the paragraphs below some of the people who led the C&O are discussed, and all its presidents are listed. There is not room for a listing of its predecessors, but a few are important.

First, the acquisition of the Richmond & Alleghany Railway in 1890 did two things. It gave C&O the low-grade line from the coal fields to the sea that it needed to make it the great coal hauler of the 20th Century. Secondly, because of R&A's pedigree was a direct successor of the old James River & Kanawha Canal. George Washington was honorary president of the canal when it was incorporated, and so C&O was able to claim that it was "George Washington's Railroad," and always listed him

as its first president. However, it really was Washington's vision of opening the interior of America to good transportation along the route that C&O later followed that is his real inheritance for C&O.

For a general tracing of the C&O's development see Chapter One of this book.

Men of the C&O

As with any organization, the C&O was composed of people, and among those many had an important effect on the development of the line over its many years of existence. Their work has descended to us today in the form of the remaining elements of the line now submerged into CSX. Their vision, hard work, foresight, and sometimes dogged determination in the face of great odds, ensured that C&O was an important element in the development and creation of the modern technological civilization which we enjoy, in the development of its region, in the winning of two great wars, and in the development of thousands of towns and communities.

Among all these people a few stand out because they supervised the C&O at particular turning pints in its history:

The first was Collis P. Huntington, who took a small Virginia-based railroad and turned into a major east-west trunk line. Following him was the team of Melville E. Ingalls, who completely rebuilt the C&O and supervised its creation as a great coal hauler and its expansion to Cincinnati. George W. Stevens worked under Ingalls as general manager and did much of this work. Then he was president from 1900 until his death while hard at work in 1920, during which time he really built the modern C&O as we know it. Following him C&O fell into the hands of the great financial geniuses, O. P. and M. J. Van Sweringen of Cleveland, who used C&O's money to create a huge railroad empire. Once this fell apart during the 1930s, it was picked up by perhaps the most interesting personality to run the C&O since Huntington, Robert R. Young, known as the "Populist of Wall Street." He took C&O through WWII and then embarked it on a program of forward-looking development and improvement under the slogan of "C&O for Progress." Much of what he preached fell of deaf ears in the decade 1945-1955, but he was later proved right in much of what he said.

Young placed Walter J. Tuohy at the head of C&O as president in 1949, and it was Tuohy who led the line through the hard years of the 1950s-60s, when railroading faltered in the face of airline, barge, and motor-truck/highway competition.

The last great personage in C&O's history was Hays T. Watkins. A self-made man from rural Kentucky, he became president after ascending through the finance department, and in 1972 created the Chessie System holding company, and finally in 1981 engineered the creation of CSX Corporation, which is today's embodiment of the C&O (and many other lines).

There were many people who supported these men, and others who merit attention, but these people stand out as the great movers in C&O history. In what passes for railroad history today, the people are often forgotten. These people should be remembered as the creators of the C&O and its successor.

Presidents of the C&O:

Frederick Harris - 1836-1840 (Louisa RR)
Charles Y. Kimbrough 1840-1845 (Louisa RR)
Edmund Fontaine 1845-1850 (Louisa RR)
            1850-1865 (Virginia Central RR)
Williams C. Wickham - 1865-1866 (Virginia Central RR)
Edmund Fontaine 1866-1868 (Virginia Central RR)
Williams C. Wickham 1868-1869 (Virginia Central RR)
Collis P. Huntington - 1869-1888 (C&O RR, then C&O Ry.)
Melville E. Ingalls - 1888-1900
George W. Stevens - 1900-1920
William J. Harahan - 1920-1929
John J. Bernet - 1929-1935
William J. Harahan - 1935-1937
George D. Brooke - 1937-1942
Carl E. Newton - 1942-1946
Robert J. Bowman - 1946-1949
Walter J. Tuohy - 1949-1966
Gregory S. Devine - 1966-1971
Hays T. Watkins - 1971-1986 (C&O and Chessie System)
Hays T. Watkins - 1986-1991 (CSX)

Collis P. Huntington - Builder of the C&O

Following the devastation of the War Between the States, the Southern railroads, including Virginia Central, had no capital and were having trouble attracting it. The Virginia Central was lucky to catch the eye of C. P. Huntington. He became President of the new C&O in 1869, built it through to his namesake city on the banks of the Ohio, and guided it

Collis P. Huntington
C&O President 1869-1888
(C&OHS Collection, COHS 12233.15)

until 1889 as president, except for the time of its receivership.

Huntington was a self-made 19th century man. Born poor in Connecticut in 1822, he first tried his hand as a traveling salesman until he had money to open a hardware store in Oneonta, New York. He went west with the gold rush in 1849 and set up shop in San Francisco, becoming a partner in the hardware business with Frank Hopkins. He developed a political skill and when he became aware of the transcontinental railroad plans in 1860, joined with Hopkins as well as Charles Crocker, and Leland Sanford to incorporate the Central Pacific. The story of their construction of the CP is well known as it connected with the Union Pacific at Promontory Point, Utah, on May 10, 1869.

Meanwhile, Huntington had purchased a number of small railroads and in 1865 consolidated them into the Southern Pacific. It was this SP that he then built across the southwest to New Orleans. Huntington wanted to control a true coast-to-coast railroad, and when the Virginia Central people approached him, he decided that their new C&O route would fit the eastern part of his plan, so he built the C&O, connecting it with other of his lines in the 1880s. By 1886 he was, in fact, controlling a vast network of lines from the Pacific coast to Newport News, but he tended to neglect the C&O's development. In 1886 he incorporated what would become today's giant Newport News Shipbuilding and Dry Dock Company, builder of America's super aircraft carriers today.

He gained control of other lines in the South, and between 1886 and 1888 incorporated the C&O as the

Williams C. Wickham
Va. Central President 1865-66 and
1868-69 (COHS 7511)

Melville E. Ingalls
C&O President 1888-1900
(C&OHS Collection, COHS 12233.25)

W.J. Harahan
C&O President 1920-29 & 1935-37
(C&OHS Collection, COHS 34818)

George W. Brooke
C&O President 1937-1942
(C&OHS Collection, COHS 30103)

eastern part of his new Newport News & Mississippi Valley Company. But then C&O experienced a financial crash and was reorganized without receivership. It left the NN&MV Company, and Huntington lost control.

Huntington left an indelible mark on the C&O. Without him whether or when it would have been built across West Virginia is question. His namesake city became the largest in West Virginia, his shipbuilding company is the largest in America today, his vision for Newport News was realized and more. He was the right man at the right time for C&O.

George W. Stevens - Creator of the Modern C&O

George W. Stevens was in charge of the C&O for thirty years, from 1890-1900 as General Superintendent under president M. E. Ingalls, and 1900-1920 as president himself. It was during his tenure that the C&O was expanded, its coal branches built, its business multiplied by many fold, its income ballooned, and its physical plant, locomotives, and cars were brought up to the best standards.

George W. Stevens
C&O President 1900-1920
(C&OHS Collection, COHS 680)

How much effect Stevens actually had on all this and how much of it was simply because of the many circumstances that obtained, it is hard to say, but that he was a good manager there is no question, and since he managed the change, it went well and the C&O grew massively.

Stevens created the C&O's safety program, established the safety bulletin which later became the company's award-winning magazine, and developed a veterans association to help instill espirit d' corps among the employees, featuring an annual gathering first on his birthday each year at his home near Glasgow, Virginia (Virginia Manor). The Vets association later became huge and by the 1950s was using the West Virginia State fairgrounds for is annual meeting.

Stevens was a wise selector of subordinates, and built up a cadre of experienced railroaders that operated the C&O very well. He died sat White Sulphur Springs while dictating a letter to his secretary.

The Van Sweringens - Wider Visions for the C&O

Before this, the Vans, as O.P. and M.J. were called, were successful real estate developers, creating the planned community of Shaker Heights outside Cleveland. To get people from Shaker Heights to downtown Cleveland they incorporated a rapid transit system. Then to get the final

O. P. and M. J. Van Sweringen (C&OHS Collection, CSPR 10595)

few miles into the city center, they bought control of the New York, Chicago & St. Louis Railroad (always known as the Nickel Plate Road). So just to get access for their transit system they took control of a 1,700-mile railroad extending in several states.

Once they got into railroad financing, the Vans' energy and acumen began working and they assembled, over the period from 1916 to 1930, a huge variety of railroads, mainly in the Middle-American region, but also stretching into the far West. They got around the ICC restrictions by keeping each railroad as a separate independently operating company, but they controlled them by controlling a pyramid of holding companies that owned them. This was the first time this type of financing had been tried on a large scale.

Eventually, the Vans were able to control the NKP, then C&O (1922), Pere Marquette, Hocking Valley, Erie, and several other connecting lines and interests in many others, but for these five roads (eventually four after 1930) they were able to gain a portion of consolidated control and operation. This manifested itself clearly in 1930 when the companies set up the Advisory Mechanical Committee and the Advisory Committee on Way and Structures. These committees and their staffs sat at Cleveland in the Van's landmark Terminal Tower building and developed locomotive, car, structure, and Maintenance-of-Way standards. The committees also jointly selected most new designs for equipment. The locomotive part of the AMC was particularly active and designed some of the best steam locomotives of the modern era. For example, the 2-8-4 type was developed from an excellent Erie design and eventually all the roads under the AMC had scores of these wonderfully efficient high-powered locomotives. C&O was, in fact, the last of the Vans' lines to acquire the "Van Sweringen Berkshires" as the family of 2-8-4s was called, though on C&O they were called "Kanawhas." The AMC was active in the design and creation of all of the C&O's great Super Power locomotives after 1930, right up to 1948, even though the Vans were a distant memory by that time.

Terminal Tower at Cleveland Ohio, where the Van Sweringen brothers ran their immense railroad empire.
(C&OHS Collection, CSPR 3873)

The Depression era saw the Vans' grip on their house-of-cards holding company maze began to slip as revenues to support it declined and individual companies went into bankruptcy. By 1935 both the brothers were dead and their empire in shambles. But, because of the connections established during their time, C&O first merged the HV (1930), and then after WWII decided to also merge the NKP and PM. The PM merger was allowed in 1947, but the NKP's minority stockholders created so much of regulatory opposition that C&O let the line go, simply distributing the NKP stock it owned to its stockholders as an extra C&O dividend. Eventually, 15 years later, the NKP was merged into C&O competitor Norfolk & Western.

The Advisory Mechanical Committee and its locomotives has remained a much studied but little understood episode in railroading and in the history of steam locomotive design in the United States.

C&O has always been involved in combinations of railroads that looked to operate in a context lager than just this one mid-sized railway. First it was built and operated by C. P. Huntington in the 1870s and 1880s as part of his effort to control railroads that actually linked both coasts of the United States. In the years 1886-1888 he actually achieved this, but then lost control. In the 1890s C&O was under the control of the Vanderbilts and Morgans, who controlled numerous railroads. They were replaced by a syndicate headed by the Pennsylvania Railroad which came to control the C&O and the N&W. Right after the turn of the 20th Century C&O was also part of a group of

companies controlled by Edwin Hawley. It was during this time that C&O bought interests in the Hocking Valley and Kanawha & Michigan (the later it had to divest because of court cases). The in the 1922-1930s era C&O was the keystone in the Van Sweringen group. Finally, after gathering in the HV and PM, C&O was on its own until the modern merger movement begin with C&O's control of B&O in the early 1960s. Western Maryland was added, and then finally these three merged with five other major southeastern lines to form today's CSX. Thus C&O has a long history of being a part of a bigger picture in railroading, sometimes for the better and sometimes for the worse.

During the 1930s C&O remained financially sound despite falling revenues and the fact that fully half of American railroads were in receivership in this era. Because coal was the basis for industrial work, steel-making, heating, electrical generation, etc., C&O's income remained strong, based on coal, even as its other income declined. By the early 1930s, C&O initiated a major improvements campaign that saw the enlargement of many clearance-restricting tunnels and the boring of new ones so that its entire mainline from Clifton Forge, Virginia, to Russell, Kentucky, was double tracked.

Because of its 1930s work C&O was perfectly positioned to handle the unprecedented World War II traffic. C&O also was well positioned geographically to serve the nation during the war. It served what became the government run "Hampton Roads Port of Embarkation" through its large yard and piers on the Newport News side of that huge harbor. It handled thousands of troop trains to and from this location, and millions of tons of war materiel in an expedited and efficient way that earned it much praise.

Robert R. Young - "Gadfly of the Rails", "Populist of Wall Street" - "C&O For Progress"

CEO Robert R. Young circa 1955.
(C&OHS Collection, CSPR 10133.19)

In 1937 Robert R. Young, a Wallstreet investor and financier, bought up many of the devalued Van Sweringen companies and thereby gained control of the C&O and its allied lines

By 1942 Young managed to became Board Chairman of the C&O and immediately after the war began to use C&O to implement his forward-looking, progressive ideas about how railroading needed to change to meet the coming postwar competition from highway trucks and good roads, commercial airlines, private automobiles, buses, and barges. In 1948 he adopted the "C&O

For Progress" logo and slogan to illustrate how he and C&O would lead American railroading into the modern era. Young continued as an iconoclast, using C&O as his base until he decided he wanted to control the New York Central, and in 1954 left to take over that huge but failing railroad. He would die by his own hand in 1958.

Men of the Modern C&O - Walter J. Tuohy and Hays T. Watkins

Walter J. Tuohy
C&O President 1948-1966
(C&OHS Collection, CSPR 10133.8)

Walter J. Tuohy became president of the C&O in 1949, just as Robert R. Young was using the C&O as the laboratory for his new "progressive" ideas for railroading. Born in 1901, Tuohy began is career as a clerk on the Illinois Central Railroad in 1917 and through the 1920s and 1930s was an executive in a number of coal companies and operations. In 1943 he became a vice president of the C&O with responsibility for coal traffic, and in 1949, on the retirement of Robert Bowman, he became president. He would serve a C&O's CEO until his death, in his office, in 1966.

Tuohy was a polar opposite of his boss, Robert Young. A quiet, conscientious, intelligent, and kindly man, he was a good manager and organizer and could get the best results from his subordinates. Under his leadership most of what Young had wanted was implemented on the C&O. The company was in a great position for the future, when in 1958, Tuohy began negotiations to acquire control of the B&O. The capstone of his career was the B&O control and creation of the "Affiliated" C&O/B&O Railroads. This would lead to the creation of Chessie System and then to CSX.

Hays T. Watkins
C&O President 1971-1986
Chessie System, CSX President 1971-1986
(C&OHS Collection, CSPR 5157)

Hays T. Watkins came to the C&O in 1949 in the financial staff, rising to the position of treasurer in 1963, then vice-president, finance, finally becoming president in 1971, later chairman and president of Chessie System and then of CSX in 1982. He retired as Chairman/CEO in 1991.

Born in 1926, Watkins attended school in his native Kentucky, including Bowling Green Business University. His rise within the C&O's Cleveland offices was quick due to his obvious intelligence, and his managerial, and leadership talent. He was instrumental in the B&O take-over and engineering the affiliation of these two roads. He had a reputation as an unusually thoughtful and intelligent executive during his tenure as head of C&O and later C&O/B&O finances, and was the obvious choice to succeed Gregory S. DeVine, who held the CEO's office after the death of Walter Tuohy in 1966 until 1971. At the age of 45 Watkins was one of the youngest railroad chief executives ever.

His belief that railroads had to make their service more reliable and customer-friendly, and that management had to be sensitive to profits as well as traffic volume.

Watkins directed the creation of the Chessie System holding company for C&O, B&O, and WM, and approved the bright new image for its equipment. He argued forcefully that deregulation was the only hope for the survival of railroading in the modern environment, and when the Staggers Railroad Deregulation Act of 1980 was passed, he and Chessie System led the way in making the most of the new environment. In that same year he brought Chessie System into partnership with Seaboard System, and the two eventually merged into today's CSX. It was clear by the mid-1980s that Watkins, more than any other railroad CEO had moved his company through the difficult days of deregulation and into a new railway era. The effect of Watkins' work in this period can hardly be overestimated. He is a true successor to the great men of the C&O, as well as the last.

Mergers

C&O and B&O engineers shaking hands to symbolize the new union.
(C&O Ry. Photo, C&OHS Coll. CSPR 11094.78

C&O was no stranger to mergers, having absorbed Hocking Valley in 1930 and Pere Marquette in 1947, and it tried and failed to absorb NKP in 1947, after which there was little further discussion as to future mergers, at least in public, for a decade. By 1958 the picture of eastern railroading was not good. Baltimore & Ohio, New York Central, and Pennsylvania were all having major problems, and were looking for merger partners. Cash-rich, prosperous C&O was a great target. Robert Young had unsuccessfully tried to absorb NYC in the 1940s-50s, and eventually left C&O when he couldn't, to take over NYC until his 1958 death.

In 1958 C&O made its move and began secret talks with B&O. It was felt that B&O would compliment C&O. With little duplication of service the merger could be effectively end-to-end. It would open northeastern markets to C&O, and the coal business fit right in with C&O's experience.

These talks became public in 1960 when C&O offered to exchange 1¾ shares of C&O stock for each B&O share, a very attractive deal. NYC wanted to be included and began buying B&O stock. However, C&O continued buying B&O stock until it gained control and eventually reached 80 percent ownership. By this time NYC had given up and sold its B&O stock to C&O as well. A conference was held at White Sulphur Springs in which C&O, B&O, and PRR decided on PRR and NYC merging even though no NYC representative was present.

In June 1961 ICC hearings on C&O-B&O began, and a huge amount of testimony ensued. It soon became evident in the hearings that B&O was in bad shape and that a union with C&O would be good for it, its shippers and its labor. ICC allowed an "affiliation" of the two companies in January 1963. Between 1961 and 1963 C&O had been helping B&O by leasing it 14,334 hopper cars, 1,275 box cars, 664 specialty cars, 124 locomotives and 339 units of maintenance equipment.

In June 1964 C&O also asked for control of Western Maryland, in which B&O already owned 63% of stock.

Although ICC allowed C&O and B&O (and WM) to merge most of their activities, the companies remained separate, and they had to maintain separate sales staffs, supposedly still competing for business at localities jointly served. The two began to operate under the title C&O/B&O Railroads.

In 1965, out of the blue, Walter Tuohy of C&O announced talks with Norfolk & Western (which was in the process of merging Wabash and NKP into its structure). The next several years were the spent in negotiating this possible union. The ICC recommended merger in March 1969.

Discussions on how to effect the merger continued until finally in March 1971 it was announced that the plan was abandoned. The collapse of the Penn-Central and failure of the C&O and N&W to come to agreeable terms caused the breakdown. Had the merger occurred the C&O would have been folded into N&W just as Wabash and NKP.

In 1971 Hays T. Watkins succeeded Gregory Devine as C&O President (Devine had taken over on Tuohy's death in 1966), and created a holding company named Chessie System to hold the assets of the C&O, B&O, and WM. Chessie System made a grand publicity splash with its bright yellow paint, but the companies remained in tact with locomotives and cars still lettered C&O, B&O, and WM. However, they were now in fact a totally integrated railroad.

This condition continued until 1981 when Chessie System agreed with Seaboard System (itself a merged company consisting of the Atlantic Coast Line, Seaboard Air Line, Louisville & Nashville, Clinchfield, and some smaller lines) to merge their railroads. The merger occurred gradually, first at top levels, then by 1985 there was a new joint paint scheme for the new company: CSX. It was supposed to stand for C: Chessie System, S: Seaboard System, X-multiplied, implying that the two together equaled more efficiency and business. Such was the muddled publicity thinking of the time.

In 1986 the merger of all the subordinate companies occurred with CSX Corporation holding new companies, including a railroad called CSX Transportation.

Eventually this complicated structure ended and the company was completely integrated as CSX Transportation, which at this writing (2012) remains the same, the only change being absorption of a number of ex-New York Central lines upon the sale of Conrail.

Additional Sources of Information for C&O Corporate History

Very little is available in the rail fan press about the presidents and other executives of the C&O. This information must generally be gleaned from other sources. Corporate history generally receives little attention in the rail fan press.

The C&O Historical Magazine, 1969-Present, offers numerous good articles that give background on may of C&O's presidents and officials. It is available from C&O Historical Society (Cat. No. AV-08-102)

• *Chesapeake & Ohio Railway - Corporate History - Interstate Commerce Commission Valuation, 1916.* - Approx. 250 pages, softbound, available from C&O Historical Society (Catalog No. DS-09-187). Details in great specificity all the predecessors of the C&O up to the 1916 date of valuation by the ICC. Includes large corporate history flow chart that shows how each company flowed into the over scheme of things. - From an old typescript.

• *Chessie's Road,* by Charles W. Turner, updated by Thomas W. Dixon, Jr. and Eugene L. Huddleston (Richmond 1956, Clifton Forge 1986 and 1993), publishing in final expanded form by C&O Historical Society, Clifton Forge, Va. 323 pages. Reprint available from C&O Historical Society (Catalog No. BK-10-539) – The first part of this book, which is the 1956 book, gives a good corporate history of the C&O.

• *Robert R. Young, The Populist of Wall Street,* by Joseph Borkin, Harper & Row, NY, 1969. 236 pages, hardbound. The fascinating story of Young and his career in financing and railroading.

• *Just Call Me Hays,* by Hays T. Watkins, CSX Corporation, 2001, hardbound, 328 pages. Autobiographical account of Hays Watkins career with C&O, Chessie System and CSX. Some really great insights into the people and events of the 1950s-1980s.

• *Collis Potter Huntington,* by Cerinda W. Evans, The Mariner's Museum, Newport News, Va. 1954 - two volumes, hardbound, 774 pages.

• *The Great Persuader [C. P. Huntington],* by David Lavender, Doubleday & Co., Garden City, BY 1970, hardbound, 444 pages.

• *The Van Sweringens of Cleveland - Biography of an Empire,* by Ian S. Haberman, Western Reserve Historical Society, Cleveland, 1979, hardbound, 202 pages.

• *Invisible Giants - The Empires of Cleveland's Van Sweringen Brothers,* by Herbert H. Harwood, Jr., Indiana University Press, Bloomington, Ind., 2003, hardbound, 342 pages.

• *The Van Sweringen Railroad Empire* by Thomas W. Dixon, Jr., C&OHS, 2005. (Order from C&O Historical Society, Cat. No. BK-06-437)

CHAPTER TWELVE
Coal and the C&O

H-4 2-6-6-2 No. 1331 brings a mine run shifter into Peach Creek with loads from the mines, in about 1950. Peach Creek (near Logan, W. Va.) was the marshalling yard for the many branches of the Logan Coal District.
(Gene Huddleston Photo, C&OHS Collection, COHS 1124)

The one thing that made the C&O world-renowned is the coal that it hauled in such quantity for so many years, coal that still flows like a black river from the same region and over the same railroad routes to this day. This said, it should be noted that although coal was the one most important product that C&O hauled, actual income from all other products it hauled, when taken together, was a substantial part of the railway's revenue, at least from the 1930s forward, and especially so after the Pere Marquette merger in 1947.

Strangely enough, Collis P. Huntington, who completed the C&O through West Virginia in the 1870s, didn't see that coal was going to be the dominant product that C&O carried. He was focused entirely on C&O as the eastern link in his transcontinental plans. He was knowledgeable about coal deposits along the route and apparently believed that the coal in West Virginia, in conjunction with the iron ore deposits in western Virginia, would result in good traffic as C&O carried the ore to the coal area or the coal to the ore region. This traffic did develop and was an important part of early C&O business, but throughout the 1870s coal was just another of the many products that C&O was carrying, and, in fact, agricultural products generally led the way in C&O's traffic.

With the opening of the line from Richmond to Newport News in 1881, C&O had a good outlet where coal was loaded on coastal shipping and carried to the Northeast far more cheaply that it could be taken there by rail, thus making C&O coal competitive with Pennsylvania coals.

Then, in 1889, C&O cemented its eastward route for coal by acquiring the Richmond & Alleghany's descending water line along the James River from Clifton Forge via Lynchburg to Richmond. This descending grade made hauling heavy coal trains east easy. Before this C&O faced heavy grades via Charlottesville.

In 1873, the first year of its completion to the West Virginia coal area, C&O shipped 22,813 tons of coal, all from Kanawha mines. By 1880 it was shipping 333,829 tons eastward and 110,328 tons westward to connections. Then the line was completed down the Virginia Peninsula from Richmond to Newport News, giving access to coastal shipping, and C&O coal gained markets in the Northeastern states. By 1887, the total C&O coal trade was 1,007,367 tons, and it was becoming evident that coal was the C&O's future. Most of the increase from this era came from the New River coal fields, mainly from mines right beside the C&O main line. As early as 1876 C&O established a coal agency that bought coal from the mine owners at the mine, shipped it and then resold it to end user customers. This gave a big boost to the mine owners by providing them with a ready market and encouraged the development of the business at this early stage.

Stowe, W. Va., on the Buffalo Subdivision in the Logan Coal District was the site of this medium-sized mine called Guyan Eagle No. 4. It is sending out neatly trimmed loads of large lump coal in this June 1954 view of the tipple.
(C&O Ry. Photo, C&OHS Collection, CSPR 10057.CC06)

This is the C. H. Mead mine at Mead, W. Va. Located on the Stone Coal Branch, which was a mine that was served jointly by the C&O and the Virginian Railways, seen here in 1954 with cars of both railways present.
(C&O Ry. Photo, C&OHS Collection, CSPR 10057.D09)

This arrangement lasted until the mid-1880s, after which time the mine operators and cooperative retail agencies were on their own for selling the coal. However, C&O helped in many ways over the years.

When C&O acquired the R&A line down the James River from Clifton Forge through Lynchburg to Richmond in 1889-90, it had the perfect route for the eastbound coal. The Cincinnati Division from Huntington to Cincinnati was opened in late 1888, providing a better connection for westbound coal. In 1895, trackage agreements with the Louisville & Nashville opened the Louisville market. In the early 1890s the first branches reaching back from the main line were built in the New River and Kanawha fields: Kenney's Creek, Hawks Nest, and Cabin Creek lines being the first, and by 1895 coal flow over the C&O was 2,981,000 tons. In 1883, C&O's yard at Newport News could handle 25 cars, but 10 years later it could accommodate 4,000 cars at once. By 1900, coal traffic reached over 5,000,000 tons.

During the period 1900-1920 under the presidency of George W. Stevens, scores of mine branches were built and the flow of coal was ever expanding, especially westbound traffic. C&O's major coal field regions were all in full operation by this time: New River, Coal River, Kanawha, and Big Sandy, the latter in eastern Kentucky, and by 1909 coal amounted to 13,635,215 tons, coming off of scores of branches and out of hundreds of mines.

After acquisition of the line across Indiana to Chicago, and the Hocking Valley to Columbus and Toledo, traffic continued to expand westbound, and eastward traffic grew as well. In 1920 C&O hauled 35,701,295 tons.

During the 1920s the business continued to be very good, as C&O coals were recognized as superb for steaming and for metallurgical purposes. C&O was making so much from this huge traffic that it was constantly able to upgrade and improve its locomotives, cars, and roadway, and as a re-

sult weathered the Great Depression well. Based on its past earnings and the fact that even during very bad economic times coal was still king, C&O managed not only to stay out of receivership during the Depression, but continued its large program of improvements, positioning it well for World War II. It hauled more coal than ever before, reaching 56,917,650 tons in 1944 from 280 mines. After the war, export coal became important in the eastbound trade, and the boom lasted, with ups and downs, through the 1950s and 1960s. By the 1970s, business was down on both fronts, though the amount of coal carried was still very large. Since then, the eastbound trade has been very dependent on world economic conditions and has vacillated wildly.

To handle the major portion of the coal business, C&O installed a giant yard and several piers for dumping coal at Newport News, and likewise at Presque Isle in Toledo for Great Lakes shipping. During the modern era transfer of coal at both locations has been largely turned over to private operators for whom C&O now simply hauls the coal, leaving others to market, store, and transfer it to ships and boats.

It can be said that everything the C&O did it did with coal in mind, from the size and power of its locomotives to the building of its cars, to the construction of its yards, its branches, and its right-of-way. Everything else that it carried, whether bananas or auto parts, was simply nice to have traffic possible, because of the great reason for the C&O to exist: coal!

In the 1930s, C&O started calling itself the "Coal Bin of America," and so it was, supplying the power that made much of the country go. By the 1940s it was the largest originator of bituminous coal in the world, and remained so for a long while. Today much of the CSX coal business still flows over the old routes of the C&O, both east and west. Today's traffic consists mainly of unit trains headed to electrical power generation plants or for export overseas.

The Republic Steel Corporation tipple at Republic, Kentucky is seen here in June 1954. The mine opening is at the top of the hill with a steep tram to the tipple. This is on C&O's Road Creek Subdivision off the coal rich Big Sandy Branch. (C&O Ry. Photo, C&OHS Collection, CSPR 10057.035)

Once assembled at the marshaling yards, long trains of loaded coal were sent to the mainline and thence to the large classification yards at Russell and Clifton Forge. Here an ABA set of F-units with FP7 8007 in the lead powers loads out of the Logan fields toward the mainline at Barboursville in May 1957. (Gene Huddleston Photo, C&OHS Collection, COHS 1178).

The marshalling yard at Danville, W. Va., on the Coal River Subdivision was typical of the assembly yards in the C&O coal districts. It has a 300-ton coaling station and 100,000-gallon water station. In this June 1950 scene a K-4 2-8-4 is to the right of the coal dock while a 2-6-6-2 simmers behind it. The K-4 was used to take a coal train to St. Albans and thence to either to Handley or Russell. The depot is in the mist to the left rear. (Gene Huddleston Photo, C&OHS Collection, COHS 1144)

This Handley, W. Va., photo illustrates a dual function as both a marshalling/collecting yard and as a mainline division-point yard. K-4 No. 2716 is bringing in a coal train, from a branceline marshalling yard on Coal River or Logan districts while H-4 1361 is backing westbound with a Paint Creek mine shifter run, in July 1955. (Gene Huddleston Photo, C&OHS Collection, COHS 1678)

The huge yard at Newport News held thousands of C&O hopper cars waiting to be dumped into ships carrying the coal to the Northeastern U. S. or overseas. This scene is in 1948. (C&O Ry. Photo, C&OHS Collection, CSPR 1439)

The Chesapeake & Ohio Railway - A Concise History and Fact Book

The large coal dumping piers and ore receiving piers at Presque Isle near Toledo was C&O's gateway for Great Lakes shipping. Note the smoke from switchers working the yards behind the piers. (C&O Ry. Photo, C&OHS Collection, CSPR 797)

Eastbound coal was classified at Clifton Forge, Va. Most was sent down the James river Line to Richmond and thence to Newport News for dumping into ships. Some was also sent over the Mountain Subdivision via Charlottesville, especially after the arrival of diesels. The coal came in from the Alleghany Subdivision to the west. This photo shows the yard in 1956 clogged with coal. (C&O Ry. Photo, C&OHS Collection, CSPR 10393.169)

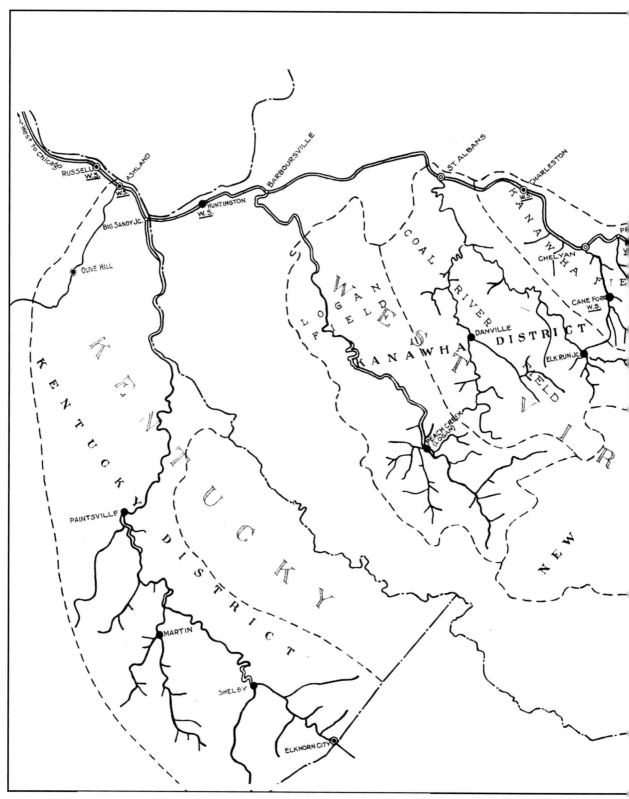

C&O Drawing No. 9941 shows the principal marshalling yards/assembly points in the coal fields region. One error the draftsman made was to mislabel the Powellton Branch as the Morris Creek Branch. The Morris Creek branch is actually the very short fine just east of Handley. (C&OHS Collection)

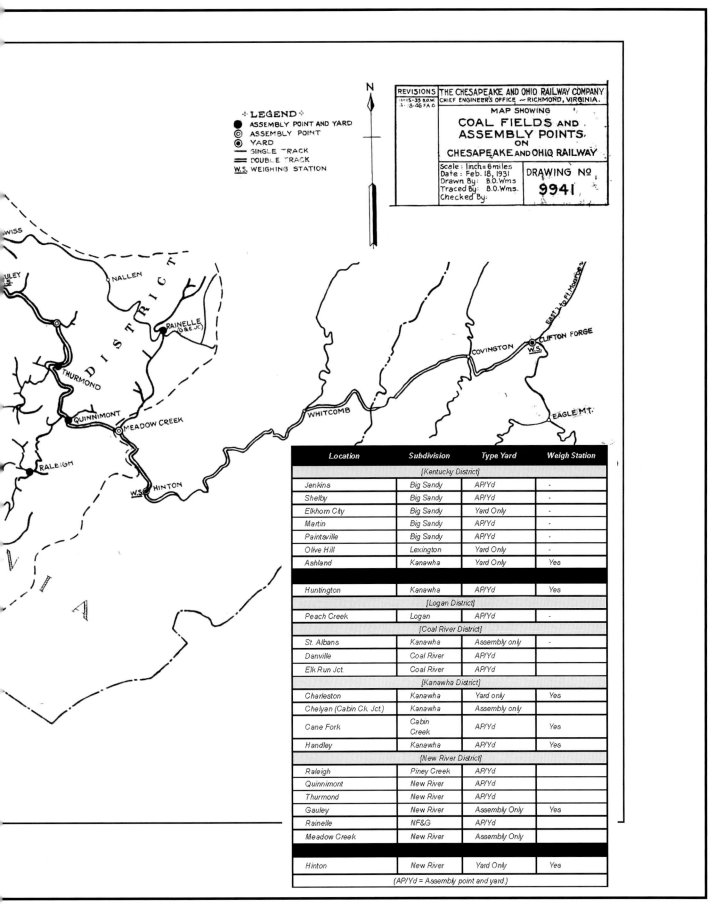

÷ LEGEND ÷
● ASSEMBLY POINT AND YARD
◎ ASSEMBLY POINT
◉ YARD
— SINGLE TRACK
═ DOUBLE TRACK
W.S. WEIGHING STATION

N

REVISIONS | THE CHESAPEAKE AND OHIO RAILWAY COMPANY
11-15-35 B.O.W. | CHIEF ENGINEER'S OFFICE ~ RICHMOND, VIRGINIA.
1- -8-46 F.A.O. |
MAP SHOWING
COAL FIELDS AND
ASSEMBLY POINTS
ON
CHESAPEAKE AND **OHIO RAILWAY**

Scale : 1inch=6 miles
Date : Feb. 18, 1931
Drawn By: B.O.Wms.   DRAWING N⁰
Traced By: B.O.Wms.   **9941**
Checked By:

Location	Subdivision	Type Yard	Weigh Station
[Kentucky District]			
Jenkins	Big Sandy	AP/Yd	-
Shelby	Big Sandy	AP/Yd	-
Elkhorn City	Big Sandy	Yard Only	-
Martin	Big Sandy	AP/Yd	-
Paintsville	Big Sandy	AP/Yd	-
Olive Hill	Lexington	Yard Only	-
Ashland	Kanawha	Yard Only	Yes
Huntington	Kanawha	AP/Yd	Yes
[Logan District]			
Peach Creek	Logan	AP/Yd	-
[Coal River District]			
St. Albans	Kanawha	Assembly only	-
Danville	Coal River	AP/Yd	
Elk Run Jct.	Coal River	AP/Yd	
[Kanawha District]			
Charleston	Kanawha	Yard only	Yes
Chelyan (Cabin Ck. Jct.)	Kanawha	Assembly only	
Cane Fork	Cabin Creek	AP/Yd	Yes
Handley	Kanawha	AP/Yd	Yes
[New River District]			
Raleigh	Piney Creek	AP/Yd	
Quinnimont	New River	AP/Yd	
Thurmond	New River	AP/Yd	
Gauley	New River	Assembly Only	Yes
Rainelle	NF&G	AP/Yd	
Meadow Creek	New River	Assembly Only	
Hinton	New River	Yard Only	Yes
(AP/Yd = Assembly point and yard.)			

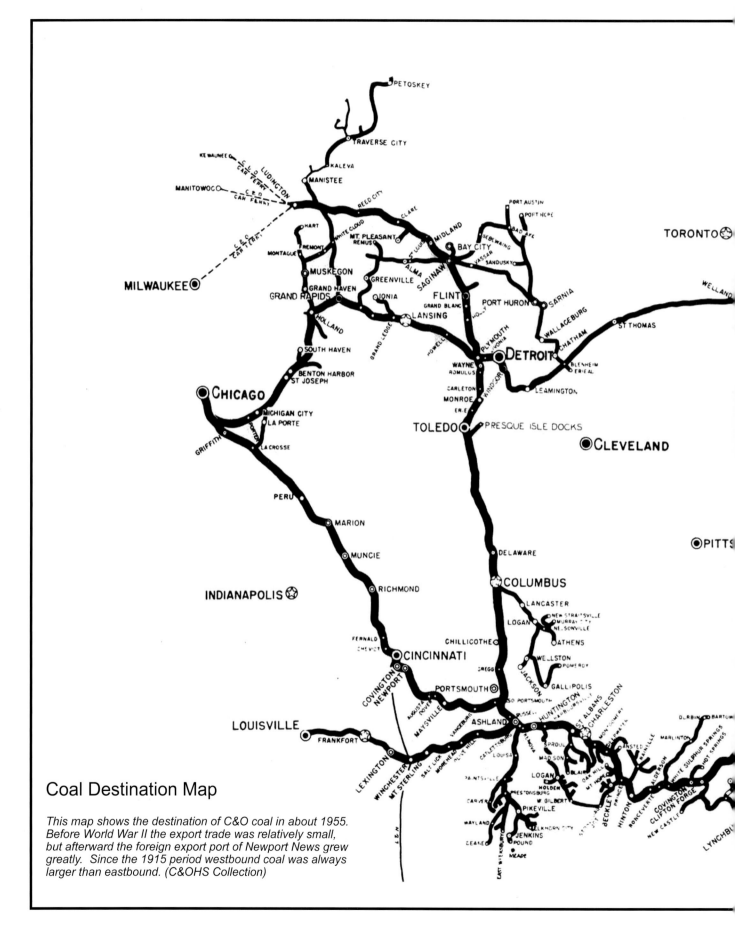

Coal Destination Map

This map shows the destination of C&O coal in about 1955. Before World War II the export trade was relatively small, but afterward the foreign export port of Newport News grew greatly. Since the 1915 period westbound coal was always larger than eastbound. (C&OHS Collection)

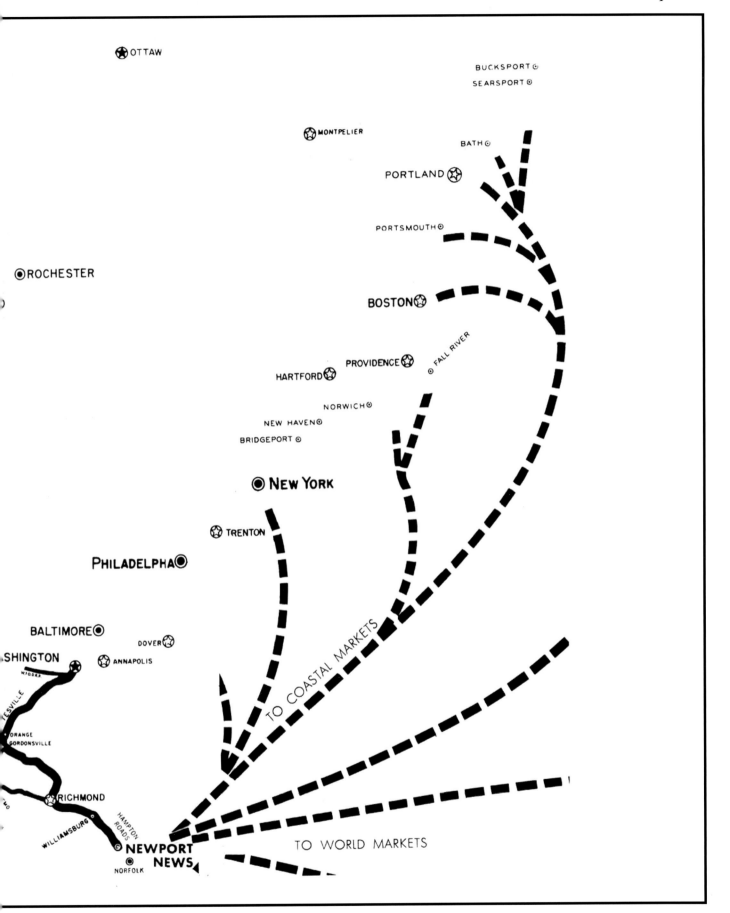

Additional Sources of Information for Coal and the C&O

Coal trains, mines, and operations are often treated in the articles in the C&O Historical Magazine 1969-Present. All back issues available on a searchable CD from C&O Historical Society (Available Catalog No. AV-08-102)

Four books that give hundreds of photos, maps, and background historical data on C&O coal operations are:

- *Chesapeake & Ohio in the Coal Fields*, by Thomas W. Dixon, Jr., C&O Historical Society, Clifton Forge, Va., 1995, 112 pages, hardbound.
- *Chesapeake & Ohio in the Coal Fields of West Virginia and Kentucky*, by Thomas W. Dixon, Jr., C&O Historical Society, Clifton Forge, Va., 2006, 112 pages, hardbound. BK-06-433
- *King Coal*, West Virginia Book Company, BK-7-061
- *Chesapeake & Ohio Freight Cars 1937-1965, Vol. 1 - Hoppers and Gondola Cars*, by Alfred Kresse, C&O Historical Society, Clifton Forge, Va., 1996, Hardbound, 204 pages. - Complete data on C&O's coal-carrying fleet of cars. (Buy from C&O Historical Society, Cat. No. BK-7-023)

Following C&O Historical Society Reprints (Available from the Society)

- Kaymoor Mine HABS/HAER Drawings Set (Cat. No. DS-8-107)
- C&O Coal Mine Directory, 1950 (Cat. No. DS-08-133)
- Chessie System Coal Mine Directory, 1981 (Cat. No. DS-03-238)
- Coal Mine Rating & Car Distribution, 1953 (Cat. No. DS-03-235)
- C&O Coal Mine Districts, Location Maps, Production Charts, 1944 (Cat. No. DS-02-224)
- C&O Track Plans and Scenes, Coal Mines (From C&O Drawings, plans, and plats) (Cat. No. DS-01-204)

CHAPTER THIRTEEN

Romance and Lore of the C&O

This is how C&O artists depicted John Henry in a 1950s rendering for use in publicity about him. In his romanticized view he is indeed the "Black Paul Bunyon." (C&O Ry. Photo, C&OHS Collection, CSPR 10175)

Why have so many people who do not have a direct connection with the territory served by the railway become interested in C&O and its operations and history over the years? Why is it so popular among model railroaders; among railfans and photographers; with ordinary folks not normally connected with a particular railroad interest?

The C&O definitely has a high profile among all these groups. This author believes that there are a number of things that attract people to the C&O. They are listed here, not necessarily in order of importance, because I think it is probably a convergence of these diverse aspects in the C&O that answers these questions.

One important factor in attracting people of all types to the C&O is its long use of its Chessie mascot or symbol in advertising. Chessie, the cuddly little kitten tucked under the covers of a C&O Pullman berth starting in 1933, became one of America's best known corporate symbols. She was indeed, as C&O called her 'America's Sleepheart' in the 1930s-1940s. She made such an impression on people that

they have passed her image down through several generations to the present time, especially in the region where C&O passenger services (and thus advertising) operated.

Another interesting aspect of C&O is the folklore that gathered around it. C&O crosses the Appalachian region where mountain folkways were prevalent, and where the people of the region were likely to have Romanticized the railway in many ways. After all, it was the region's lifeline to the rest of the world, and opened its wilderness to new ways. The editor of the *Border Watchman* newspaper in isolated rural Monroe County, West Virginia, in 1873 said of the first C&O train passing through his county: "Thanks be to God, our long night is over."   Of course people of all regions have Romanticized railroading. The image of the "brave engineer," the little red caboose, and scores of other ideals that associate with railroading became 19th and early 20th Century icons. This was particularly so in the C&O's mountain regions. It is interesting to note more folksong ballads have been composed featuring the C&O than any other railroad. Of course, almost all these feature tragic accidents and wrecks with all their drama and pathos.

The best known ballad relating to American railroading is probably John Henry, the "Black Paul Bunyon", and it originates with what was probably an actual person and actual event on the C&O during it's westward construction in 1870-73.

C&O also combined many elements that appeal to people: It had giant steam locomotives. They hauled heavy trains, and they struggled over steep mountain grades with a

Bronze statue of John Henry arriving at Talcott, W. Va. on a C&O train after having just passed through Great Bend Tunnel, the bore that legend says was the scene of John Henry's race with the steam drill. T. W. Dixon, Jr. photo. (C&OHS Collection, COHS 1061)

This ca. 1907 photo shows C&O's famous flyer, *The Fast Flying Virginian*, being made up at the Huntington depot. The man in the center with the white beard and coveralls is "Uncle" Billy Richardson the famous C&O engineer about whom a very famous song was written after he died at the throttle in 1910. (C&OHS Collection, COHS 6251)

backdrop of some of the most beautiful natural scenery in the eastern United States. The railway reached into narrow gorges, valleys, and gullies to tap the rich coal seams of West Virginia and Kentucky. Associated with this was the miner and his family ("The Coal Miner's Daughter"), the early labor movements, (the West Virginia mine wars) and the image of the mining frontier.

For the modeler, C&O offers many possibilities as big locomotives served all types of coal tipples and mines, small yards assembling coal loads, bigger yards classifying them, and even bigger terminals delivering them. C&O served a mining frontier, especially in its first 30 years, which gives it some of the aura that has long attached to the Colorado narrow gauge lines serving their mining frontier at about the same time.

The C&O has the aura connected with the American Frontier itself as the great historian Frederick Jackson Turner expressed it. When C&O was opening its wild new territory, Turner's American frontier was in Kansas and Colorado, yet C&O was accomplishing the same thing in the heart of the eastern U. S., in southern West Virginia and eastern Kentucky.

Despite its sparse population and remote area, and its mainline that was so curvy and steep, C&O nonetheless operated a high class passenger service that handled passengers from New York City and Washington, D. C., to Cincinnati, Chicago, Louisville, St. Louis, Columbus, and Detroit.

In this way it was truly the "Metropolitan Corridor" for its people, bringing the life of the nation to the smallest town on its line.

C&O was also in the hotel business, and not just the traditional railroad hotel of the 19th Century, placed at major stations to accommodate passengers when no commercial facilities were available, but rather, it became involved in the high class resort hotel business. First there was C&O President M. E. Ingalls' fascination with the Homestead Hotel at Hot Springs, Virginia. He bought the property, extended a 25-mile C&O line for the exclusive purpose of serving it, and rebuilt it, making it a preferred mountain spring resort retreat for high society in the great eastern cities. C&O's reputation was further enhanced when it bought the White Sulphur Springs, West Virginia, resort hotel in 1910 and built The Greenbrier, which truly became "America's Resort" (opened in 1913). With its wonderful past, White Sulphur Springs became and is today one of the nation's most historic and best known resorts. Golf came to America here, and Slammin' Sam Snead was the pro here for many years. President Martin Van Buren rode out for a stay at White Sulphur from Washington City on horseback in the 1820s. The hotel's guest register featured Henry Clay, Robert E. Lee, Woodrow Wilson, U. S. Grant, and almost every president since. President Dwight D. Eisenhower held a summit conference here in 1956. After his trip (which was made by C&O special train) decisions were made so that the hotel became the site

The Chesapeake & Ohio Railway - A Concise History and Fact Book

K-3 No. 1256 is seen here in the James River after its wreck in 1925. The song "Wreck of the 1256" resulted from this accident. (C&OHS Collection, COHS 6216)

for the relocation of the U. S. Congress in case of nuclear attack in the 1960s. The secret bunker became public knowledge in the 1990s and was decommissioned. Since then it has been a tourist attraction.

C&O molded much of its passenger service around the needs of the Greenbrier and the other "springs" resorts. This was especially the case in the last two decades of service.

Not only were Hot Springs and White Sulphur important resorts, but there were scores of others in western Virginia and eastern West Virginia, in the days when people of the humid hot cities went to the mountains for a month (usually August) of relaxation in the 1890s-1920s. C&O served many on its line and stages met the trains and carried people to many others nearby.

Because C&O operated through a remote area, the towns and communities that sprang up around it tended to become very C&O-centric, with a large percentage of their populations working for the railway, or connected with it in some way.

As the giant coal hauler of the mid-20th Century, C&O was known to everyone. This was natural because in that era everything was powered by coal, including home heating plants.

Another important fact is C&O's own publicity about itself. Its publicity operations were well ahead of their time, as they explored every aspect of the line to attract people as passengers, to attract business and industry it its region, and to make the C&O well known. In 1947, a year that it won many awards for it advertising, C&O was a household name, being the best known railroad name in the United States.

C&O was aware of its history, or rather the history of its region, and traded on it in every way possible, calling itself "George Washington's Railroad," probably one of the greatest strokes of public relations genius in railroading history, second only to C&O's other master stroke: Chessie.

It used every bit of its wonderful scenery to attract tourists, including the vistas of the Blue Ridge and Shenandoah, the grandeur of the New River Gorge (which it called "Grand Canyon of the East") the beauty of the Ohio River, and the bluegrass country of Kentucky. C&O had it all, or so it seemed to early tourist clientele.

B&O was the American railroad probably most aware of its history and the best at preserving it. C&O was equally aware of its history and used it to great effect, but was very poor in preserving it, tending to throw out the old and replace it with the most modern whenever possible. It could be argued that C&O had the money to do this, whereas B&O was often forced financially to keep using the old locomotives, cars, and stations until they became antiques worthy of preservation.

And last, perhaps, was C&O's mid-20th Century escapades in connection with its Chairman, Robert R. Young, who, from 1942 to 1954, pushed the C&O to the forefront

The Sportsman wrecked at Hawks Nest just a month after it was inaugurated in 1930. This scene shows the wreckage, near the station. The song "Wreck of the Sportsman" resulted from this accident. (C&OHS Collection, COHS 35799)

This circa 1900 illustration shows the Grand Hotel at White Sulphur Springs, W.Va. This was replaced, after the C&O acquired the property in 1910, with today's Greenbrier Hotel. (C&OHS Collection, COHS 31518)

of railroading by advocating advanced approaches to the industry in every facet from radical new passenger trains to continued use of coal in new types of locomotives. C&O originated the idea of using railroad-highway hybrid trailers and Trailer-on-Flatcar service. Called "The Gadfly of the Rails," Young made such a publicity splash in his time, that C&O was known everywhere. Mercurial to the last, he wanted a larger platform for his iconoclastic ideas and became chairman of the New York Central after a famous proxy fight, only to commit suicide a few years later.

For these reasons and many more, C&O encapsulates interesting, evocative, and attractive attributes that many other railroads have, but that C&O posses in particular quantity in a sort of microcosm.

Of course, C&O has receded into the past as a historical subject, with its remaining lines now just part of CSX, a massive new railroad system, but we can be assured that same lure will be present over those lines for a long time to come. C&O represented railroading in almost every aspect, and in every emblematic and archetypical way.

John Henry and the Folk Heroes of the C&O

When one thinks of American railroad folklore the three old folk ballads that most often come to mind are "Casey Jones" (of the Illinois Central), "John Henry" (of the C&O) and "The Wreck of Old 97" (of the Southern). Of these, it is John Henry that has appeared more often, in more locations, and in more versions, over a longer period of time than any other, including Casey and Old 97.

The story of John Henry centers around the C&O's westward construction across West Virginia in the 1870-73 period. The song always sets the John Henry story at Big Bend Tunnel at Talcott, W. Va., the longest bore on the C&O mainline, which was pushed through with considerable difficulty in the years 1870-1872. The legend and the song tell us that John Henry was an African-American ex-slave who may have come west with the railroad from central Virginia,

working as a driller. The driller was charged with driving a steel drill into the rock faces of the tunnel so that nitroglycerine charges could be placed to dislodge the rock. Supposedly, John Henry was so proficient at this work that when the new steam-powered drills arrived at the work, he challenged his foreman with a bet that he could do better at drilling that the new machine. And, so the legend goes, he did drill his holes faster and deeper within a limited time than the steam drill could, but that he died from exhaustion as a result. It is quite possible for such a thing to have happened because the new mechanical drills were still largely untested and very often had trouble with broken bits, clogged holes, etc.

From that incident, the laborers (also mostly African-American) on the line started singing about the exploits of this man of their race against the encroachment of the machine. The song was transmitted orally from one railroad to another and one labor-intensive industry to another, changing and being altered in hundreds of ways, so that John Henry ended up being depicted as a dock worker loading cotton in New Orleans, and as a farm worker in Jamaica. Anywhere the black man or the common worker was present in large numbers doing hard and rhythmic work, the songs took hold.

Because of this wide popularity of the legend, much research has been done. Four books have been written on John Henry by scholarly researchers. Of the two from the 1920s, when people were still living who worked on the tunnel at Talcott, one author tends to believe that John Henry lived and worked there and could have had his race with the machine, while the other gives it strictly to legend. A 1983 book traces the metamorphosis of the song and the legend and lists hundreds of versions of the ballad, and makes no real judgment as to the genesis of the legend.

However, a book published in 2007 on the subject by Prof. Scott Reynolds Nelson of the College of William and Mary, contends that John Henry was a convict, one of a group leased out by the state of Virginia to C&O contractor C. R. Mason for tunnel work, and that Henry worked at Lewis Tunnel near the top of Alleghany Mountain, located 42 miles east of the traditional Big Bend site. Prof. Nelson also believes that he was a New Jersey native who had come south after the war, and that he was small man, stranding only 5-feet 2-inches tall, not the ex-slave Paul Bunyon type of song and lore, and that he was killed at the tunnel and buried at Libby Prison in Richmond. Nelson contends, using recently discovered correspondence, that the steam drills were used only at Lewis, and not at Big Bend, and that if there was a contest, it would have occurred there. If this new work is to be believed, then the whole myth of Big Bend is exploded.

Beyond John Henry, there have been more folk songs composed centering around the C&O than any other American railroad. They all concern wrecks, and usually the brave engineer, who faces death courageously, trying to save his train and its passengers. The song that most closely

This photo, taken in the 1890s, shows African American workers drilling in the same way that John Henry did in 1872.
(C&OHS Collection, CSPR 9580)

follows this pattern is "Wreck on the C&O," supposedly composed and first sung by an engine wiper at the Hinton, W. Va. roundhouse. It tells of the young engineer George Alley, who took the C&O's new and already famous *Fast Flying Virginian* east from Hinton one day, struck a landslide and was killed. He stayed in the engine applying brakes and trying to stop rather than jumping when the slide was first seen, thus saving the train. Alley was the only fatality in the ensuing wreck. In the day of the early sound records, the song was recorded many times and became one of the most famous wreck ballads in the country.

The epitome of the "Brave Engineer," though, was "Uncle" Billy Richardson, a senior engineer on the run between Hinton and Huntington on the best C&O name trains, who was so famous in his time that when a train was called the agent would always announce to the waiting passengers "Richardson at the throttle!" One day in 1910, Billy, nearing his retirement age, leaned too far from the cab one night, try-

ing to see the road ahead, and was struck by a mail crane and killed. A song was composed about him and his tragic end that was recorded and became a popular seller in the 1920s.

Other songs include: "Wreck of the Sportsman", "Wreck of C&O No. 5", "The Guyandotte Bridge Disaster," "Wreck of the 1256", and "The Churchill Tunnel Disaster", as well as others.

In the 1890s another popular sheet music piece was "The Pretty Girl of Ronceverte," with scenes on the sheet music of C&O trains at that West Virginia station. Even in the late 1940s a pop-music song called simply "Chesapeake and Ohio" was recorded by Ella Fitzgerald.

These songs and connections with folkways of the region all served to elevate the C&O in the consciousness of the people in the region and far beyond. Who has not heard Johnny Cash's 1970s version of John Henry?

This 1950 photo shows the big tower of the Homestead Hotel at Hot Springs, Virginia, always an important C&O destination. C&O President (1889-1900) M. E. Ingalls purchased this property and rebuilt it in the 1890s. The Homestead and the Greenbrier were the mainstays of C&O's "Springs" passenger traffic and the center of much attention by the railway's passenger department.
(C&OHS Collection, CSPR 3147)

This 1954 aerial view shows the close relationship of C&O and the Greenbrier Hotel. The giant hotel building is in the background while the foreground is occupied by C&O's neat Colonial station. Note the area behind the station which was tracks which could accommodate a number of sleeping cars from special and regular movement.
(C&OHS Collection, CSPR 3738)

Additional Sources of Information for The Romance and Lore of the C&O

- *Scalded to Death by the Steam*, by Katie Letcher Lyle, Algonquin Books, Chapel Hill, NC, 1983. 212 pages.
  This book treats eight C&O wreck songs in great detail including illustrations, historical background, music scores, etc.

- *John Henry - Steel Drivin' Man*, by Scott Reynolds Nelson, Oxford University Press, Oxford & NY, 2006, hardbound, 214 pages.

- *John Henry, Tracking Down a Negro Legend*, N. C. University Press, Chapel Hill, N. C. 1929

- *John Henry, A Folk-Lore Study*, Louis W. Chappell, Reprinted 1968. Port Washington, N.Y.: Kennikat Press.

- *John Henry, a Bio-Bibliography*, Brett Williams, Greenwood Press, Westport, Ct. 1983

- *John Henry, An American Legend*, Ezra Jack Keats, Pantheon Press, NY 1965.

- *The Greenbrier, America's Resort*, by Robert Conte, Trans Allegheny Books (June 1989) Hardbound, 178 pages

- *The Valley Road , The Story of Virginia Hot Springs*, by Fay Ingalls, World Publishing, Cleveland, 1949, hardbound, 292 pages by the son of C&O President M. E. Ingalls.

- *The White Sulphur Springs*, by William A. MacCorkle, Charleston, W. Va., 1916.

- Article series on "C&O Folks Songs" by Ron Lane in *C&O Historical Newsletter*. Full series of *C&O Historical Newsletter and Magazine* 1969-present are available on a fully searchable CD from the Society (Catalog No. AV-08-102).

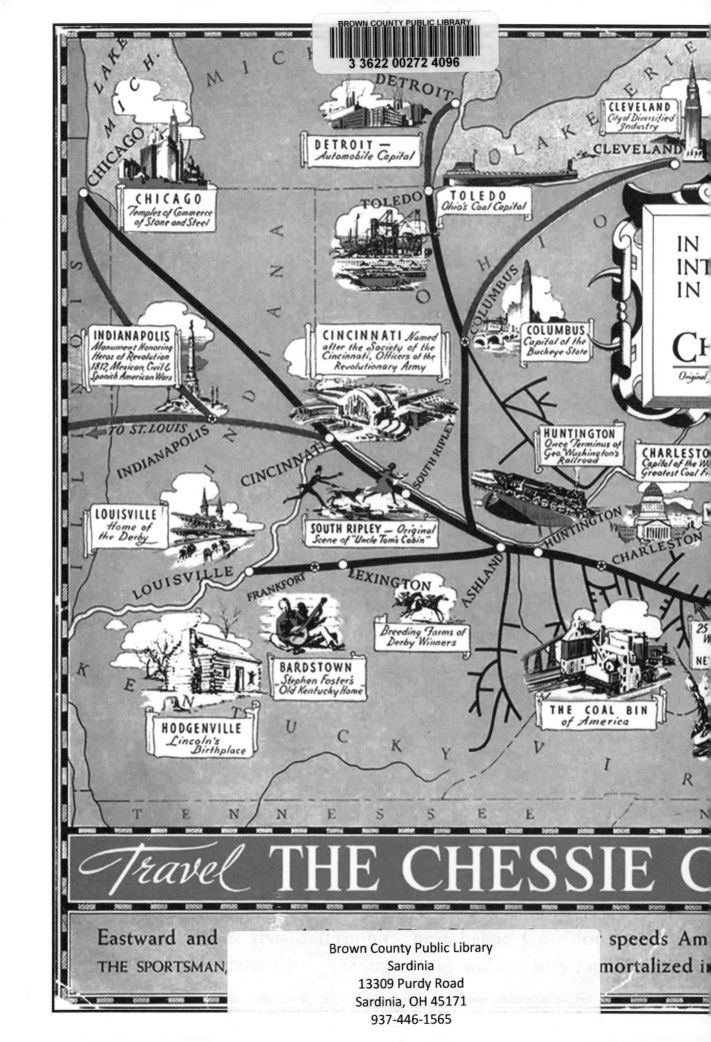

LAKE MICH.

DETROIT

CLEVELAND
City of Diversified Industry

DETROIT —
Automobile Capital

CLEVELAND

CHICAGO
Temples of Commerce
of Stone and Steel

TOLEDO

TOLEDO
Ohio's Coal Capital

LAKE ERIE

INDIANAPOLIS
Monument Honoring
Heros of Revolution
1812, Mexican, Civil &
Spanish American Wars

CINCINNATI Named
after the Society of the
Cincinnati, Officers of the
Revolutionary Army

COLUMBUS
Capital of the
Buckeye State

IN
INT
IN

Ch

Original

TO ST. LOUIS

INDIANAPOLIS

CINCINNATI

SOUTH RIPLEY

HUNTINGTON
Once Terminus of
Geo. Washington's
Railroad

CHARLESTO
Capital of the W
Greatest Coal Fi

LOUISVILLE
Home of
the Derby

SOUTH RIPLEY — Original
Scene of "Uncle Tom's Cabin"

HUNTINGTON

CHARLESTON

LOUISVILLE

FRANKFORT

LEXINGTON

ASHLAND

Breeding Farms of
Derby Winners

25
W

NE

BARDSTOWN
"Stephen Foster's
Old Kentucky Home"

HODGENVILLE
Lincoln's
Birthplace

THE COAL BIN
of America

KENTUCKY

VIR
R
N

TENNESSEE

Travel THE CHESSIE C

Eastward and speeds Am

THE SPORTSMAN, mortalized i